The Delicate Balance

The Delicate Balance

*Case Studies
in Counseling
and Care
Management
for Older Adults*

Edited by
Berit Ingersoll-Dayton, M.S.W., Ph.D.,
and
Ruth Campbell, M.S.W.

*HEALTH
PROFESSION.
PRESS*

Baltimore • London • Winnipeg • Sydney

Health Professions Press, Inc.
Post Office Box 10624
Baltimore, Maryland 21285-0624

www.healthpropress.com

Typeset by PRO-IMAGE Corporation, York, Pennsylvania.
Printed in the United States of America by Versa Press, Inc., East Peoria, Illinois.

The cases in this book are based on the authors' actual experiences. In all instances, names and identifying details have been changed to protect confidentiality.

Library of Congress Cataloging-in-Publication Data
The delicate balance : case studies in counseling and care management for older adults/ edited by Berit Ingersoll-Dayton and Ruth Campbell.
    p. cm.
  Includes bibliographical references and index.
  ISBN 1-878812-64-5
  1. Psychotherapy for the aged.   2. Aged—Counseling of.   3. Social work with the aged.
  I. Ingersoll-Dayton, Berit.   II. Campbell, Ruth, 1944–.
RC480.54.D45   2001
618.97′68914—dc21   2001024105

British Library Cataloguing in Publication Data are available from the British Library.

Contents

Preface

HEALTH CARE PROFESSIONALS WHO WORK WITH OLDER ADULTS MUST DEVELOP CREATIVE WAYS TO HELP THEM. When providing services to older people, practitioners often become intimately involved in the lives of their clients. Some gerontology professionals develop long-term relationships with their clients that become increasingly complex over time. This book was designed for social workers, psychologists, physicians, nurses, care managers, recreational therapists, occupational therapists, physical therapists, activity directors, nursing assistants, and foster care providers who want to learn more about the relationships that develop between therapists and their older clients. It is intended especially for practitioners and students who like to anchor their learning in case examples. Many applied gerontologists are searching for therapeutic ways of helping that also respect the strengths of their older clients. In this book, the contributors highlight the strengths of older adults and the ways in which therapists can demonstrate respect for their older clients.

The idea for this book was born at the 1997 meeting of the Gerontological Society of America, when Ruth Campbell suggested that several practitioners present papers in a symposium entitled "Creativity in Diverse Populations: Giving Voice to the Unexpressed." Typically, this national gathering of gerontologists focuses on research studies conducted by biological, medical, and social scientists. The symposium that Campbell organized was quite different. At the symposium, practitioners shared their clinical experiences on topics that are relevant to applied gerontologists. The response from the audience was overwhelmingly positive. Many wanted more information about the therapeutic approaches that were presented. Berit Ingersoll-Dayton was impressed by the content of the presentations and the audience's obvious interest. She joined forces with Campbell, and they began to think about the possibility of editing a book that would include case examples and analyses from social workers at the Turner Geriatric Clinic.

The case examples augment the theoretical coursework of students and the clinical experience of gerontological practitioners. The illustrations include men and women from different ethnic groups across a variety of therapeutic settings and important therapeutic issues such as the blurring of roles (e.g., from professional helper to surrogate family member) that occurs when working with clients over a long period of time, how sensitive and confidential matters are handled when working with older people in the context of their families and formal systems, and how one respects older clients' strengths and their reluctance to engage in therapy.

The chapters represent the experiences of different practitioners, so the voices of many applied gerontologists are heard; however, a common set of analytic threads runs throughout the book. In each chapter, the author or authors provide a summary of their intervention and then analyze the therapeutic process using a set analytic framework. Each case is analyzed with respect to six themes:

1. Demonstration of respect for the client
2. Use of the client's strengths
3. Blurred boundaries
4. Changes in the therapeutic relationship over time
5. Benefits and difficulties of the therapeutic relationship for the client and therapist
6. Words of wisdom

The development of a therapeutic relationship over time is a complex process that necessitates growth on the part of the therapist as well as the client. In this book, we are fortunate to hear directly from practitioners about the ways in which they dealt with their own frustrations and the ways in which, in retrospect, they would approach the relationship differently. We have deliberately chosen cases that represented significant challenges to the practitioners involved. In these cases, readers learn how the practitioners creatively tried to address these challenges, often using multiple interventions. Sometimes the outcomes of the therapy are mixed. The chapters illustrate the great variety in individual responses to therapeutic interventions. Some older clients grow, thrive, and make positive changes in their lives despite significant physical and psychological problems; others make few changes but maintain stability through professional support; and still others do not seem to benefit from these interventions. We thought it important to show the variety of responses that most gerontological practitioners are likely to experience.

Although the case examples are based on actual cases, we have been respectful of the clients' confidentiality by making case illustrations a composite of several cases and/or by changing any identifying information. As they were preparing their chapters, the contributors were provided with guidelines for disguising case material that included changing names, locations, physical problems, and other identifying information.

The Delicate Balance is organized in relation to three levels of intervention used with older clients: working with individuals and couples, working with groups, and working with families and systems. After highlighting the importance of the six themes in Chapter 1, attention turns to the three levels of intervention. Chapters 2–6 illustrate individual and marital therapy as well as care management with older clients. Some of the interventions are conducted in home settings whereas others take place in the office. Chapters 7–10 discuss different kinds of group therapy including a cognitive therapy group, an exploring the meaning of life group, a writing group, and an intergenerational memory group. Chapters 11–14 illustrate therapy and care management with family members of the older clients and other larger systems. These systems include work with professionals in other agencies on behalf of older clients in the community. At the end of each intervention chapter, a brief review is included of additional resources that provide information on theory, research, and practice for individuals who are interested in pursuing the chapter's issues in greater depth. Chapter 15 draws upon the six themes to provide suggestions for negotiating the delicate balance between counseling and care management with older adults.

Because readers will see numerous references to the Turner Geriatric Clinic (sometimes noted as "the clinic," "our clinic," or "the geriatric clinic"), we want to provide background on the clinic. It is an outpatient primary care clinic of the University of Michigan Health System's Geriatrics Center for people ages 60 and older. Since its inception in 1978, Turner Clinic has developed into a large primary care clinic serving more than 5,000 older patients with an interdisciplinary staff of physicians, nurses, social workers, and other health care professionals. The Geriatrics Center also hosts neurology, psychiatry, endocrinology, hypertension, and otolaryngology facilities, allowing for collaborations among specialty clinic staff and Turner Clinic staff. In addition to the main clinic adjoining the University of Michigan Hospital, Turner operates nine outreach clinics in senior high-rise buildings and a church in the community.

Turner Clinic's social work department has developed an extensive program in the clinic and the community. There are eight full-time equivalent M.S.W.s, many of whom are funded through grants, contracts, fees, or donations. Social work activities include geriatric assessment, psychotherapy in the clinic (more than 1,000 visits per year), support groups in the clinic and the community (about 20 groups per month ranging from low vision support to one called "New Outlooks"), in-home counseling and care management, nursing facility enrichment groups, information and referral, adult day services, and mental health education in the community. Staff are supplemented by unpaid help in the form of social work interns and students in other fields, as well as help from about 50 peer volunteers who do home visits, facilitate groups, and organize monthly workshops. Referrals for social work services come from the medical staff, community agencies, and the older clients themselves, their families, and their friends.

Turner Clinic social workers collaborate with professionals in other community agencies on both client care and advocacy. For example, the Housing Bureau for Seniors is an independent agency started by Turner Clinic staff and peer volunteers to provide housing information, home sharing, eviction prevention, and other housing assistance. The Learning in Retirement Program

(LIR), developed by clinic volunteers in 1987, has more than 1,000 older adult members and offers a wide range of lecture series, mini-courses, and study groups planned and implemented by its members. LIR was a charter member of the National Institutes for Learning in Retirement network established by the Elderhostel program. The hallmark of the social work program over the years has been to respond creatively to identified gaps in services and to work collaboratively with older adults and others in the community to meet these needs.

Although the Turner Geriatric Clinic setting may be somewhat unusual in providing a wide variety of activities under one umbrella organization, funding pressures and the growth of the older adult population has forced smaller agencies to merge and consolidate programs to offer a wider range of services. The increased commitment to maintain older adults in the community has expanded both the demand for the kinds of services that Turner Clinic offers and the necessity to develop new programs when the traditional ones do not meet clients' and families' needs. In addition, professionals in other disciplines, notably home care workers, nurses, and physicians, are seeking expertise in geriatric counseling and care management. The services that are provided by Turner Clinic social workers provide a model for practitioners as they attempt to meet the challenge of providing comprehensive care for older adults and their families.

The contributors to this book are Turner Clinic social workers with expertise in the use of a variety of social and psychological methods for working with individuals, couples, families, and groups. Several of the contributors present regularly at local and national workshops and have published books, chapters, and articles on working with older adults. Most of them have worked at the Turner Clinic for many years and have worked with clients over an extended time. In some cases, they have assisted clients intermittently through multiple crises and, in other cases, they have provided ongoing counseling and/or care management. Thus, the authors have considerable experience with the challenges that are associated with long-term therapeutic relationships. This book includes both short-term and long-term cases to illustrate contrasting kinds of therapeutic relationships.

Some of the interventions described in these cases were conducted over a period of only a few months, but many took place over a considerably longer time. For example, some of the individual and family sessions took place for several years, and the writing group has met for more than 20 years. This kind of long-term intervention may be difficult to replicate in the current climate of increasing demand for cost-effective and short-term services. When proceeding from a client-centered perspective however, what many older adults want is an ongoing connection with a professional on whom they can call in times of need and unpredictable changes. Such interventions may be intermittent over a long period of time and may decrease in intensity, including sessions that occur once a month or once every few months. In creating a system with various funding sources that is bolstered by the additional resources of students and volunteers, Turner Clinic has been able to maintain stability and flexibility despite the University Hospital system's fluctuations in funding and support. We believe that this creative use of multiple sources of support to provide ongoing therapy and care management is replicable in other agencies that provide services to older adults.

Contributors

Ruth Campbell, M.S.W., is Associate Director for Social Work and Community Programs for the Turner Geriatric Clinic, University of Michigan Geriatrics Center. She is also an adjunct professor at the University of Michigan School of Social Work and a research associate at the University of Michigan Institute of Gerontology. Ms. Campbell has written articles and book chapters on peer counseling, writing groups, and long-term care. She also has authored numerous publications on aging and caregiving in Japan as well as cross-cultural comparisons between the United States and Japan.

Ruth E. Dunkle, M.S.W., Ph.D., is Professor of Social Work at the University of Michigan where she co-directs a National Institute on Aging Training Grant for graduate and postdoctoral students interested in gerontology. She is also co-director of a Hartford Foundation project to strengthen geriatric social work. Dr. Dunkle conducts individual psychotherapy at the Turner Geriatric Clinic. Her special focus is on the health and well-being of very old people as well as racial and ethnic variations in caregiving. She has published extensively on gerontological issues including *Decision Making in Long-Term Care*, *Communication Technology and the Elderly: Issues and Forecast*, and *The Everyday Life of the Very Old: Stress, Coping, and Self-Perception*.

Sally Edwards, M.S.W., C.S.W., works at both Turner Geriatric Clinic and the Washtenaw County Community Mental Health Center. She provides in-home counseling to older people through a grant from the Area Agency on Aging and also co-facilitates cognitive therapy groups for older adults. For several years she has been a facilitator for caregivers of aging relatives support groups; more recently, she began conducting bereavement groups for individuals whose adult children have died.

Janet Fogler, M.S.W., is a senior social worker at Turner Geriatric Clinic who has been in practice for more than 15 years. Her practice includes geriatric assessment, psychotherapy for individuals and couples, and facilitation of groups such as "Exploring the Meaning of Life," cognitive therapy, spouse caregiving, and memory improvement. She has published articles on intergenerational women's groups and diabetes support groups and has presented numerous workshops nationally. She is the coauthor of two books, *Improving Your Memory: How to Remember What You're Starting to Forget* and *Teaching Memory Improvement to Adults*.

Mariko Abe Foulk, M.S.W., A.C.S.W., C.S.W., has been in social work practice for nearly 20 years, many with Turner Geriatric Clinic. Her clinical practice includes psychotherapy with individuals, couples, and families, as well as care management with elderly clients. She speaks fluent Japanese and works as a social worker for the University of Michigan Family Practice Clinic to treat Japanese people who now live in the United States. Her articles on interdisciplinary geriatric care and social work with older adults have appeared in both U.S. and Japanese publications.

Berit Ingersoll-Dayton, M.S.W., M.A., Ph.D., is Professor of Social Work at the University of Michigan where she is co-director of a National Institute on Aging training grant and coordinator of the Specialist in Aging Certificate. In addition, she conducts psychotherapy for individuals and couples at Turner Geriatric Clinic. Her clinical interests include reminiscence, intergenerational family therapy, and services for employed caregivers. Dr. Ingersoll-Dayton has published numerous articles and book chapters on the family in later life and is coauthor of the book *Balancing Work and Caregiving for Children, Adults, and Elders.*

Mary Rumman, M.S.W., is a clinical social worker at Turner Geriatric Clinic. She served as a nursing facility social worker for 10 years before coming to Turner. She provides in-home counseling to older adults through a grant from the Area Agency on Aging and facilitates groups in the areas of low vision, caregiving, and depression. Ms. Rumman also has conducted workshops on low vision and adjusting to nursing facility life.

Karyn S. Schoem, M.S.W., worked in community mental health and family service settings before coming to Turner Geriatric Clinic. Her interests lie in psychotherapy and chemical dependency among older adults. She has presented sessions on care management with elderly clients and on substance abuse among older people at national gerontology meetings.

Lynn E. Stern, M.S.W., is a senior social worker at Turner Geriatric Clinic where she has worked for 17 years. Her areas of focus are individual psychotherapy, group work, family consultation, and supervision of M.S.W. candidates. In addition, she has conducted workshops throughout the country on memory improvement, mental health issues, caring for aging relatives, and enhancing relationships between older adults and their adult children. She is the coauthor of *Improving your Memory: How to Remember What You're Starting to Forget* and *Teaching Memory Improvement to Adults.*

Katherine P. Supiano, M.S., is a clinical social worker at Turner Clinic and has been in practice for more than 16 years. Her practice includes treatment of depression, family relationships counseling, care management, and long-term care issues. Ms. Supiano has published articles on nursing facility enrichment groups, writing at life's end, and care management. She has presented numerous workshops at national gerontological meetings.

Shirley A. Thomas, M.S.W., M.A., has been a social work practitioner for more than 20 years. During this time, she has worked with issues related to family violence, stress, grief, and loss. While at Turner Geriatric Clinic, Ms. Thomas has provided in-home counseling to frail elderly people. Her interests include community health care education with a special focus on the health of African Americans and individuals in poverty.

Acknowledgments

This book is built on many years of collaboration and friendship among the contributing authors. We would like to thank all of them for their enthusiasm, patience, and honesty in writing about and analyzing their own clinical experiences. Without their commitment to working beyond the call of duty, this book would not have been possible. We also want to thank the clients of Turner Geriatric Clinic who have shared their lives with us. These individuals were the inspiration for this book.

In addition, we are very grateful to our colleagues, the Turner Geriatric Clinic interdisciplinary team of clerks, physicians, and nurses, who have supported us and shared their skills and knowledge so freely. In particular, we owe special thanks to three people: Dr. Jeffrey B. Halter, Director of the University of Michigan Geriatrics Center, who has generously supported us both financially and personally; Dr. Neal Persky, Medical Director of the Turner Geriatric Clinic, a strong advocate for social work services; and Florence Tillman, R.N., who, for more than 20 years, has been an indispensable source of information, inspiration, and nourishment. We are grateful to the University of Michigan School of Social Work, which provided us with technical support. At the School of Social Work, Terri Torkko offered invaluable editing assistance, and Diane Devlin and Roxanne Webster helped us meet countless deadlines by correcting, faxing, and mailing manuscripts. We also owe thanks to Mollie Norton for her help in gathering reference materials.

Our colleagues in the geriatric community have also played an important role in the development of this book. In particular, Sandra Reminga and her staff at the Area Agency on Aging IB in Southfield, Michigan, deserve recognition and thanks for their innovative commitment and support of in-home counseling. Without their support, we would not have been able to offer the community the services that are described in this book. We are also indebted to Mary Magnus and Anita McCabe of Health Professions Press, who helped make our vision of this book a reality.

Finally, we would like to thank our families for standing by us through the writing and editing of this book. They gave us encouragement, assumed household responsibilities so that we could write, provided computer mentoring, and offered welcome distractions.

Intervention Issues with Older Adults

1

Berit Ingersoll-Dayton

TO CONTEXTUALIZE THE CASE EXAMPLES THAT ARE PRESENTED IN THE FOLLOWING CHAPTERS, we turn to the writings of gerontological practitioners and researchers. This literature provides a rich foundation for analyzing the cases in relation to the six themes around which this book is organized:

1. Demonstration of respect
2. Use of the client's strengths
3. Blurred boundaries
4. Changes in the therapeutic relationship over time
5. Benefits and difficulties of the therapeutic relationship for the client and the therapist
6. Words of wisdom

DEMONSTRATION OF RESPECT

When home health workers describe the attributes that are necessary for working successfully with older adults, their respect for older clients emerges as a key ingredient (Ebenstein, 1998). Although all clients need to feel respected by the professionals who are helping them, older adults may have a special need to feel respected. Ageism and negative attitudes toward older adults are rampant in American society, making these individuals particularly vulnerable to feelings of low self-esteem (Butler, Lewis, & Sunderland, 1998; Schaie, 1993). Frail and dependent older adults are perhaps the most susceptible of all people to feel undignified and demeaned by others (Moody, 1998); therefore, it is particularly important that older frail clients be treated with respect.

Older clients may elicit from helping professionals a desire to take over and compensate for their limitations. In an analysis of several health and social services organizations as well as a review of fictional and autobiographical accounts, Aronson (1999) observed an orientation toward older adults' "being managed." She pointed out that this orientation further marginalizes older people and casts them in a passive role. Older people who need help are made to feel dependent and then further shamed for their dependence.

One way in which helping professionals can demonstrate their respect for older clients is by appreciating their autonomy. Appreciating autonomy involves providing clients with options and consulting with them about intervention issues (Neeman, 1995). Knight (1996) suggested that practitioners use their clients' frame of reference rather than their own or that of a family member regarding what is painful. Often, family members will bring a client for help and have clear views about how the older adult needs to change. In such cases, clinicians can address older clients' autonomy by focusing on the clients' concerns and asking what they want changed. When helping professionals ask when it would be convenient to provide services and maintain scheduled appointments, they respect their clients' autonomy. Lustbader described how a lack of predictability affects clients' sense of autonomy:

> Just as waiting reminds them minute by minute of their helplessness, firm plans convey a semblance of their former control over their lives. When dependent people can count on events taking place at a set time, they can anticipate them almost as if autonomy were still in their possession. (1991, p. 127)

Helping professionals can show respect by maintaining appointments and routines that the clients have helped to develop.

Another way of demonstrating respect is through appreciating older people's need for privacy. George (1998) conveyed the story of an older woman, a nursing facility resident with advanced dementia, who screamed continuously when she was bathed. The nursing facility staff made every effort to determine why the woman was upset. None of these efforts proved fruitful until a nursing assistant closed the door to the bathing area to talk privately to the staff member who was bathing the older resident. The older woman stopped screaming immediately. George's story illustrates the importance of dignity and privacy to all older people, even those whose dementia is advanced. Helping professionals can enhance the dignity of their older clients by demonstrating respect for their privacy. They can do so in any number of ways, including finding ways of talking privately to their older clients even in institutional settings and maintaining the confidentiality of information that clients share.

Respect for older clients can also be demonstrated by understanding their personal history. Knight (1996) discussed the importance of appreciating the clients' experience as representative of a particular cohort. He urged helping professionals to be knowledgeable about major historical events that may have influenced their clients' lives (e.g., World Wars I and II, the Great Depression). Furthermore, Knight noted that knowledge about music and movies from earlier times can be a means of establishing rapport and showing respect. When therapists do not have sufficient knowledge about a particular historical period, they can demonstrate respect by asking their client questions and expressing appreciation for the older person's experience and wisdom.

USE OF THE CLIENT'S STRENGTHS

A crucial aspect of showing respect for clients is having an appreciation for their strengths. During the 1990s, professionals became increasingly interested in ways of helping clients focus on their abilities rather than on their pathologies (Saleebey, 1996). This approach releases clients from the negative labels that are assigned by others and affirms their dignity and expertise (Sullivan & Fisher, 1994; Tice & Perkins, 1996). This perspective also accentuates the way in which people maintain resilience in the face of stress and adversity (Rutter, 1987). The strengths-based approach does not ignore problems or deny age-related losses. Instead, the approach uses clients' strengths to guide the goals and process of intervention (Sullivan & Fisher, 1994; Tice & Perkins, 1996).

Practitioners and theorists have identified several strengths that are applicable to older adults. One important strength is the older person's wisdom. According to psychological researchers, "wisdom appears to be one of the very few attributes in our mental scenarios about aging that typify positive late-life goals and accomplishments" (Baltes, Smith, Staudinger, & Sowarka, 1990, p. 430). According to Baltes and colleagues, wisdom has a number of facets, including a deep understanding of human nature, knowledge about social relationships, and an understanding about the uncertainties of life. Blazer (1998) noted that Erikson, Erikson, and Kivnick's (1987) conceptualization of integrity as the last stage in human development also has a direct connection to wisdom. Within their formulation, the wisdom of an older person is evidenced by communicating the integrity of human experience to others. When therapists can help accentuate their older clients' wisdom, these clients come to appreciate their own integrity and life experience.

Another set of related strengths is resilience and adaptive ability (Blazer, 1998). Resilience refers to the ability to cope with and recover from difficult situations (Gilgun, 1996). Resilient people do not deny painful life experiences; rather, they persevere in the face of adversity (Saleebey, 1996). They use a flexible set of behavioral strategies, including solving problems and seeking help

(Gilgun, 1996). Resilient people also use cognitive strategies that help to reshape the meaning of negative life experiences. This "management of meaning" (Pearlin & Skaff, 1995, p. 111) is a particularly important coping mechanism for older people, who often experience intractable losses that are not easily changed by solving problems. Clinicians who work with older adults can highlight the ways in which their clients have adapted to adverse circumstances and can enhance resilience through behavioral and cognitive coping strategies.

A sense of control is also an important strength for older people (Blazer, 1998). The aging process involves a number of physical, social, and psychological factors that conspire to deny older adults their sense of control over their lives. Pearlin and Skaff (1995) suggested that feeling masterful helps to mitigate the threat of adverse situations and the resulting feeling of helpless victimization. When their opportunities for control are diminished, frail older people may need to choose certain areas over which they will exert control. According to Pearlin and Skaff, older adults "can selectively pick out specific and usually mundane parts of their daily lives over which they are able to maintain control, and these parts, we believe, replace previous activities as sources of feelings of mastery" (1995, p. 115). Helping professionals can assist older people in identifying areas of their lives over which they can continue to exert control.

Another crucial source of strength for older people is their support networks. Support networks provide "enabling niches" (Taylor, 1993, as cited in Saleebey, 1996), which reinforce people for what they can do well and encourage them to establish strong social ties. Supportive relationships can help buffer people from the stressful effects of adverse events (Cohen & Wills, 1985; Krause & Borawski-Clark, 1994). Supportive others, including family and friends, can provide physical help as well as emotional assistance to older people. Research on social support indicates that support networks are most beneficial when they possess certain characteristics. For example, support networks need to provide the appropriate type of support when difficult problems arise (Pearlin & Skaff, 1995). The ability to give as well as to receive assistance is also an important characteristic of social support (Antonucci & Jackson, 1990; Ingersoll-Dayton & Antonucci, 1988). In addition, the knowledge that support will be available, if needed, is helpful to older people (Hansson & Carpenter, 1994). Clinicians who work with older adults should pay special attention to the support networks of their clients. Practitioners should help their clients identify which individuals can be helpful in times of need and should ensure that clients have the opportunity to engage in mutual exchanges of support.

The strengths perspective acknowledges that there are cultural and individual differences concerning the meaning of strengths and the decision to seek professional help. According to McQuaide and Ehrenreich, "strength is not a culture-free concept" (1997, p. 204). They pointed out the variety of ways in which ethnicity, race, class, and gender affect the interpretation of strengths.

For example, the appraisal of an adaptive coping mechanism (e.g., assertiveness) may vary from one context to another even within an ethnic group. Furthermore, some people who are experiencing difficulties do not want professional help. Older people may react negatively on the basis of past experiences with insensitive or patronizing helpers or may be fearful that involvement with a professional will result in greater dependence (Butler et al., 1998). Older adults' reluctance to accept help can be viewed as a strength. Tice and Perkins suggested that helping professionals ask themselves, "What skills has the client used to progress and survive in life?" (1996, p. 24). Resistance to accepting services may be perceived as an expression of independence, self-reliance, or pride. When their resistance is conceptualized as a strength rather than as a form of pathology, older clients may be more willing to engage in conversation with helping professionals and reconsider the option of accepting assistance.

BLURRED BOUNDARIES

Working with older adults often involves providing services in ways that are different from methods used to help younger people. Helping professionals may work with older people in their homes or in health care settings. Involvement in these settings entails different ways of engaging in and maintaining a therapeutic relationship. Working with older people may also necessitate engaging with their families and other helping professionals. The perspective that is needed to intervene with clients in their homes as well as with their informal and formal supports can be in stark contrast to that of an office-based session involving only a client and a therapist. Thus, the boundaries concerning role responsibilities may become more blurred when intervening with older clients.

Because older clients may be reluctant to work with a therapist (Butler et al., 1998), helping professionals sometimes use nontraditional approaches that differ from those that are provided to highly motivated clients. These approaches may include engaging with reluctant clients as friendly visitors rather than focusing immediately on problem identification and resolution (Edinberg, 1985). The role of friendly visitor involves informality and mutual self-disclosure in which the practitioner seeks to establish a nonhierarchical, nonthreatening relationship. Edinberg suggested that establishing a personal relationship before moving toward a therapeutic relationship can help accentuate older clients' strengths and potential for remaining independent. Blazer (1998) wrote of the importance of providing adequate time for the older client to feel heard as a person by the helping professional. A slow-paced approach may engage clients who otherwise would not be amenable to therapy. Edinberg cautioned, however, that clinicians who begin their work with clients in an informal, friendly manner may be challenged in their attempts to move toward a more therapeutic relationship. When the boundaries between "friend" and "professional" are blurred, it may be difficult to encourage clients to discuss significant clinical issues.

The blurring of the friend–professional boundary is exacerbated when practitioners meet with clients in their homes or in nonoffice settings. Knight observed, "The environment of the therapeutic relationship changes when the site of that relationship is moved from the therapist's office to the client's home" (1996, p. 57). Home-based counseling often involves the presence of other people as well as the intrusion of the television and the telephone. On the one hand, practitioners are provided with a much more accurate assessment of the client's living situation. On the other hand, they need to find ways of maintaining confidentiality, separating the therapy portion of the visit, and establishing the limits of the therapeutic relationship. Such blurred boundaries can make therapists extremely uncomfortable when they are accustomed to office-based intervention with clients (Knight, 1996).

Another source of blurred boundaries is the multiple roles that are played by helping professionals. In addition to the provision of therapy, professionals who work with older adults often provide a number of other services, including care management (also referred to as case management), advocacy, and serve as a liaison and negotiator among older clients and their families and other professionals (Edinberg, 1985; Williams, 1990). Professionals who experience multiple role expectations and a blurring among their role responsibilities are prone to burnout (Barber & Iwai, 1996). Furthermore, conflict may occur among professionals who are not clear about their respective responsibilities and therefore disagree about the "ownership" of specific clients (Wacker, Roberto, & Piper, 1998). The ability to form partnerships with other professionals and to work as a team is a crucial skill for practitioners who assist older clients.

The blurring of boundaries results in a number of challenges for clinicians. Snyder and McCollum (1999) wrote about the concerns that were raised by student therapists who conducted in-home family visits. Although their work focused on families with young children, the issues that they encountered are equally relevant to families in later life. One challenge that arose for the interns concerned the issue of who was in charge of the therapy sessions. Snyder and McCollum observed,

> Being in the family's physical territory "on their turf"—changes the usual balance of power. The interns were used to treating clients with respect in the office, of course, and supporting the clients' autonomy and competence. However, interns also maintained control of certain aspects of the sessions in order to facilitate intervention. In the home, interns felt noticeably less in charge. (p. 233)

When meeting with clients in the office, the interns were accustomed to deciding on seating arrangements and directing the therapeutic process.

However, when meeting in clients' homes, the clients often assumed control over these basic decisions. In addition, the interns felt unable to limit distractions caused by visitors, despite their agreement at the beginning of therapy to meet with their clients in a private area.

A second challenge resulting from blurring of boundaries concerned confidentiality. At times, friends or neighbors were present in clients' homes during therapy sessions. The interns felt uncomfortable discussing private matters with the family members when other people were present. One of them described this reaction: "Sometimes there are situations ... which feel so strange, leaving me with an unsettled, 'Oops, did I do something wrong?' feeling" (Snyder & McCollum, 1999, p. 235). On other occasions, the interns contended with their discomfort in sharing information with other helping professionals. They received permission from the clients' families to share information with these other collaborators. Nevertheless, "the regular sharing of information at staff meetings or in other informal encounters felt 'out of bounds' to the interns, compared to the usual experience of exchanging information with other professionals only periodically through telephone calls or written documents" (p. 234).

A third challenge that emerges from the blurring of boundaries concerns the timing or pacing of sessions. When clinicians meet with clients in their offices, they have more control over the therapeutic time. Snyder and McCollum's (1999) interns found that it was difficult to keep track of time because many times there were no clocks in the clients' homes and they felt self-conscious about continually checking their watches. Furthermore, because there were so many distractions and interruptions, it was often difficult to bring closure to their in-home sessions. Their time with clients frequently extended well beyond the time allotted for an office session.

When working with older clients, such challenges often require that practitioners redefine their notion of appropriate boundaries. Like the interns in Snyder and McCollum's (1999) study, practitioners who work in nonoffice settings and with other professionals must find a new "comfort zone." Helping professionals must think about the areas over which they need to exert control, how to handle issues of confidentiality, and how to pace interventions in the clients' home. Developing this comfort zone requires considerable experience as well as supervision from valued colleagues.

CHANGES IN THE
THERAPEUTIC RELATIONSHIP OVER TIME

Older adults' resilience may ebb and flow during the aging process. The same stressor (e.g., poor health) may evoke successful coping mechanisms for an older adult at one point in time but may be experienced as extremely aversive at another time. According to Rutter, "if circumstances change, resilience alters" (1987, p. 317). Older adults and their families may need professional help during times of low resilience. Intervention from a helping professional may be required for only a single session or may entail many years of assistance.

Some interventions with older adults involve relatively brief encounters. These kinds of sessions may characterize work with older adults who are very ill or near death or for whom access to a practitioner is limited (Butler et al., 1998). The time-limited nature of the session may make the therapeutic work particularly intense. Butler and colleagues (1998) recounted a story about Florida Scott-Maxwell, a Jungian analyst who worked for a single session with a woman whose life had been tragic. This woman approached Scott-Maxwell because she wanted to confide in someone whom she respected and to determine whether there was anything that she could do about her situation. At the end of the session, the analyst asked the woman whether she would like to return. The woman seemed surprised and answered, "There is no need. I've told you everything" (p. 353). Sometimes the presence of a helping professional who affirms the pain and the strength of a client during a single session is sufficient.

Other interventions with older adults may evolve over a much longer period. Clients may need intermittent help during periods of low resilience or may need ongoing support. The helping relationships between some clients and practitioners can continue for years. In a national study of care management described by Wacker and colleagues (1998), older adults were retained as clients for an average of 32 months. Reasons for termination included relocation, institutionalization, and death. Butler and colleagues contended that

> *Older persons need the opportunity for continuing support and easy availability of services, even when a particular problem has been resolved. ... With older people it may be necessary and totally appropriate to continue treatment and care, varying it according to changing conditions until a quite different termination—death. (1998, p. 224)*

Ongoing intervention with older adults may be primarily therapeutic, may be care management, or may involve a combination of counseling and care management.

Practitioners whose interventions are primarily therapeutic may use different methods with clients depending on their changing needs. Hansson and Carpenter (1994) described a number of different therapeutic modalities that are appropriate for working with older adults. One modality is individual psychotherapy. Older clients in individual therapy are afforded the opportunity to explore clinical issues within the context of a special kind of one-to-one relationship with a therapist. Another modality is group therapy, which can be particularly helpful for older adults who need support with social functioning and changing behavior patterns. A third modality is family therapy. Although under-used by gerontological practitioners, family therapy may be especially helpful for older adults because families often play a supportive role in later life. These three modalities can be used independently or in conjunction, depending on the client's needs.

As therapeutic modalities and goals change, so does the relationship between practitioner and older client. Ryan and Doubleday (1995) described a group for isolated older adults that began as a short-term, psychoeducational group and evolved over a period of 4 years into a long-term therapy group. Initially, to encourage isolated older adults to join the group, the facilitators took a very active role in reaching out to clients. They conducted an extensive telephone outreach and, as a further inducement, prepared lunch for the participants. They had minimal expectations of the group members, except for consistent attendance. In the beginning, the older adults generally directed their conversation toward the group facilitators rather than toward each other. Over time, group members developed more trusting relationships and felt more comfortable disclosing personal information to one another. After the group decided to meet on a long-term basis, group members took increasing responsibility for the group process. They negotiated new roles that included sharing in the preparation of lunch. The content of the therapeutic conversation deepened and included working through feelings about their own aging (e.g., grieving losses, fearing death) and about their group leader (e.g., reactions to her impending vacation). Over a period of 4 years, the relationships between the facilitators and the group members evolved from a tentative connection that was initiated by the facilitators to a mutual process that involved shared commitment and responsibility among all participants.

Therapeutic relationships may be different depending on whether practitioners are working with clients on a short- or long-term basis. Knight (1996) suggested that in short-term therapy (12 sessions or fewer), the relationship between the therapist and the older client is influenced by the real differences between them. During short-term interventions, differences in age, gender, and personality may have the greatest effect on the therapeutic relationship. For example, in an early session with a younger therapist an older client may query the therapist about his or her age (Herr & Weakland, 1979). According to Knight (1996), in longer-term therapy, a different set of factors influences the relationship. When practitioners and clients have worked together over time, their real differences are less important and relationship distortions become more prevalent. Clients in long-term therapy may identify their therapists with individuals from their family of origin (i.e., transference). By exploring these transference reactions, it is possible to help clients gain additional insight into their thoughts and behaviors. Likewise, therapists may identify their clients with individuals from their own past who have been emotionally significant (i.e., countertransference). Therapists can use their countertransference responses to help gain empathy for the client's situation.

BENEFITS AND DIFFICULTIES OF THE THERAPEUTIC RELATIONSHIP FOR THE CLIENT AND THE THERAPIST

Relationships between practitioners and their older clients can be deeply rewarding as well as challenging. Knight observed, "The therapeutic relationship is a two-way street" (1996, p. 68). Both the helping professional and the older adult are influenced by the relationship that they build and the process of their work together. For older clients, working with a caring professional can be deeply satisfying; however, such work can also inspire intense negative feelings. For therapists, working with older adults can make them face their own concerns about aging, which can be both helpful and terrifying.

Older clients experience several benefits from psychotherapy. For example, counseling can help older adults cope with the losses that are inherent in aging. Such losses include the death of family members and friends as well as physical losses (Butler et al., 1998). Through exploration with a therapist, older people can begin to acknowledge the anger and grief that are associated with such losses. An understanding of their own feelings can result in the development of coping strategies that enhance the older person's resilience. Reminiscing about early experiences can also provide an enormous benefit for older people (Butler, 1963; Haight, Michel, & Hendrix, 1998). Wong contended, "The emotional baggage and the scars we carry can sap our energy and reduce our sense of well-being. But the reservoir of memories can also serve as a storehouse of wisdom, meaning, and solace" (1995, p. 23). Reminiscing with a therapist can help clients accept negative experiences from the past and, when integrated into the present, achieve a sense of coherence. By reminiscing, the older client can draw from past difficulties by identifying previous sources of strength and resilience and then apply these lessons to present problems (Wong, 1995). In addition, involvement in psychotherapy can provide clients with the opportunity to start fresh. According to Butler and colleagues, "Older people often express a wish to undo some of the patterns of their life, to unritualize behavior and give some newness to their experiences" (1998, p. 350). As older clients talk with their therapists, they may begin to feel less stuck in their current patterns, start experimenting with new ways of relating to others, and discover new interests and abilities.

Clients can also derive numerous benefits from care management. The care managers' knowledge of community resources and their ability to link services with clients may provide the key to the client's ability to live at home. According to Wacker and associates, "[Care] managers serve as navigators, guiding older persons in their pursuit of services that will foster their independence" (1998, p. 307). Help with negotiating the confusing bureaucracy that is associated with Medicaid and Social Security or the paperwork that is involved with insurance and hospitalization can provide an enormous relief for older clients (Mellor & Lindeman, 1998). Because younger family members may not live nearby, care managers often assist in the communication between older adults and family members, thus allowing family input in major decisions (Mellor & Lindeman, 1998). The kinds of hands-on services (e.g., bathing, housekeeping) secured by care managers can alleviate the need for family members to fulfill these activities and thereby allow them more time to provide emotional support to their older family members (Aneshensel, Pearlin, Mullan, Zarit, & Whitlatch, 1995).

Working with a helping professional may be problematic for older adults. For some, relying on a professional connotes dependence and loss of control. The need to be dependent on another person can result in feelings of humiliation and guilt (Lustbader, 1991). A social worker expressed her frustration that despite her attempts to empower and advocate, "my professional presence in the life of a client indicates that some funding source in society deems her needy and inadequate in some way" (Rojiani, 1994, p. 149). Knight (1996) noted that one form of transference among older adults is to perceive their therapist as a powerful authority figure. This transference can result in the fear that they will be deprived of their independence. Indeed, care managers and therapists need to be vigilant to ensure that their desire to be helpful to older adults does not result in their clients' increased dependence. When clients have established a relationship with a practitioner, they often become strongly attached. In such cases, the termination of services may be particularly difficult for older adults who have few other individuals with whom they feel intimate. For these clients, termination of the helping relationship may represent another significant loss (Edinberg, 1985). Edinburg noted that before termination, practitioners should spend considerable time preparing clients for the end of therapy and help them identify other social relationships in which they can invest. Furthermore, he suggested that practitioners consider ways in which they might maintain contact (e.g., friendly visits) with older clients after terminating the therapeutic relationship.

Working with older adults is also beneficial for helping professionals. Intense involvement with clients who are old, disabled, and dying inevitably affects practitioners (Katz, 1990). To the extent that professionals can acknowledge their feelings and cope with their fears, they can begin to understand themselves better. Urging professionals to acknowledge the feelings that are evoked by their aging clients, Katz wrote, "When we can face our own intense emotional reactions and their meaning without feeling too threatened, we can engage in a responsive therapeutic relationship that enables us to grow as persons and professionals" (1990, p. 19). Working with older adults also affords helping professionals the opportunity to identify individuals who can serve as role models for their own aging. Listening to how older adults persevere in the face of adversity often provides illustrations of the kinds of strengths that are needed to cope with aging (Levine, 1996). In a study of home care workers for older adults, Ebenstein (1998) described the workers' appreciation for what they learned from their older clients. Similarly, when Williams (1990) provided care management services to a dying client, she learned how to face death. Williams identified the client with her own mother, whose long, painful death she continued to mourn. Initially, because of her own countertransference reactions to this client, Williams avoided her. Eventually, however, she began to talk to the client about her illness and about her treatment options. Her client decided not to accept further treatment, to reunite with her husband, and to die with dignity. Williams wrote, "In her last days, she became a wonderful teacher, showing me how to let go of her as a person in the present and to take another step in letting go of the past loss of my mother" (p. 140). Working with older clients affords practitioners the opportunity to discover role models among older adults and to work through feelings about disability and dying.

Such work can be extremely difficult for helping professionals. Whereas older adults may be able to adjust to their own mortality, most of their practitioners are younger and less equipped to grapple with their feelings about disability and death. Knight (1996) observed that many young therapists have not thought much about death, whereas their middle-age counterparts often are actively engaged in avoiding aging. Negative countertransference feelings evoked by their clients may result in practitioners' inability to help clients face their own fears about dying. In addition, Williams (1990) pointed out that positive countertransference can be detrimental to the helping relationship. She described a case in which she assessed the needs of an older couple for care management. She felt very positive about this couple and wanted the initial interview to go smoothly. Her positive feelings for the couple resulted in her overlooking the possibility of spouse abuse. This case illustrates the need for practitioners to ensure that their identification with clients' positive qualities not result in blind spots and inadequate service provision.

Another problematic area for practitioners concerns the termination of services. Knight (1996) contended that practitioners have even more difficulty than clients in saying goodbye. He explained that therapists often worry about whether their clients will feel lonely and deserted. They feel personally affected by the relationship and want to cross the subtle boundary between professional and friend. As they consider termination with a client, helping professionals may want to seek supervision to find ways to address their clients' needs rather than their own.

WORDS OF WISDOM

Many of the issues that emerge when intervening with older adults are complex. As illustrated in this chapter, mental health experts do not always agree about which approach is most beneficial for older clients. When considering termination, for example, Edinburg (1985) urged practitioners to make the transition from the role of therapist to that of friend, whereas Knight (1996) cautioned against this approach. When deciding how to intervene in problematic situations, helping professionals can turn to the practice and research literature as well as ask the advice of valued colleagues. By integrating the wisdom gained from multiple sources, clinicians can better serve their older clients.

In the following chapters, experienced practitioners discuss the therapeutic issues that they have encountered in their work with older adults. Using the themes introduced here, the authors analyze their clinical examples. At the end of each chapter, they provide words of wisdom to help guide other professionals who are interested in helping older people and their families.

REFERENCES

Aneshensel, C.S., Pearlin, L.L., Mullan, J.T., Zarit, S.H., & Whitlatch, C.J. (1995). *Profiles in caregiving: The unexpected career*. San Diego: Academic Press.

Antonucci, T., & Jackson, J. (1990). The role of reciprocity in social support. In I.G. Sarason, B.R. Sarason, & G.R. Pierce (Eds.), *Social support: An interactional view* (pp. 173–198). New York: John Wiley & Sons.

Aronson, J. (1999). Conflicting images of older people receiving care. In S.M. Neysmith (Ed.), *Critical issues for future social work practice with aging persons* (pp. 47–69). New York: Columbia University Press.

Baltes, P.G., Smith, J., Staudinger, U.M., & Sowarka, D. (1990). Wisdom: One facet of successful aging? In H.R. Moody (Ed.), *Aging concepts and controversies* (pp. 427–431). Thousand Oaks, CA: Pine Forge Press.

Barber, C.E., & Iwai, M. (1996). Role conflict and role ambiguity as predictors of burnout among staff caring for elderly dementia patients. *Journal of Gerontological Social Work, 26*, 101–115.

Blazer, D. (1998). *Emotional problems in later life*. New York: Springer Publishing.

Butler, R.N. (1963). The life review: An interpretation of reminiscence in the aged. *Psychiatry, 26*, 65–76.

Butler, R.N., Lewis, M.I., & Sunderland, T. (1998). *Aging and mental health: Positive psychosocial and biomedical approaches*. New York: Macmillan.

Cohen, S., & Wills, T. (1985). Stress, social support, and the buffering hypothesis. *Psychological Bulletin, 98*, 310–357.

Ebenstein, H. (1998). They were once like us: Learning from home health workers who care for the elderly. *Journal of Gerontological Social Work, 30*, 191–201.

Edinberg, A. (1985). *Mental health practice with the elderly*. Englewood Cliffs, NJ: Prentice-Hall.

Erikson, E.H., Erikson, J.M., & Kivnick, H.Q. (1987). *Vital involvement in old age*. New York: W.W. Norton.

George, L.K. (1998). Dignity and quality of life in old age. *Journal of Gerontological Social Work, 29*, 39–52.

Gilgun, J.F. (1996). Human development and adversity in ecological perspective: Part 1. A conceptual framework. *Families in Society, 77*, 395–402.

Haight, B.K., Michel, Y., & Hendrix, S. (1998). Life review: Preventing despair in newly relocated nursing home residents, short- and long-term effects. *International Journal of Aging and Human Development, 47*, 119–142.

Hansson, R.O., & Carpenter, B.N. (1994). *Relationships in old age*. New York: The Guilford Press.

Herr, J.J., & Weakland, J.H. (1979). *Counseling elders and their families. Practical techniques for applied gerontology.* New York: Springer Publishing.

Ingersoll-Dayton, B., & Antonucci, T. (1988). Reciprocal and nonreciprocal social support: Contrasting sides of intimate relationships. *Journal of Gerontology,* 43, 65–73.

Katz, R.S. (1990). Using our emotional reactions to older clients: A working theory. In B. Genevay & R.S. Katz (Eds.), *Countertransference and older clients* (pp. 17–25). Thousand Oaks, CA: Sage Publications.

Knight, B.G. (1996). *Psychotherapy with older adults.* Thousand Oaks, CA: Sage Publications.

Krause, N., & Borawski-Clark, E. (1994). Clarifying the functions of social support in later life. *Research on Aging,* 16, 251–279.

Levine, L. (1996). "Things were different then": Countertransference issues for younger female therapists working with older female clients. *Social Work in Health Care,* 22(4), 73–87.

Lustbader, W. (1991). *Counting on kindness.* New York: The Free Press.

McQuaide, S., & Ehrenreich, J.H. (1997). Assessing client strengths. *Families in Society,* 78, 201–212.

Mellor, M.J., & Lindeman, D. (1998). The role of the social worker in interdisciplinary geriatric teams. *Journal of Gerontological Social Work,* 30, 3–7.

Moody, H.R. (1998). *Why dignity in old age matters. Journal of Gerontological Social Work,* 29, 13–38.

Neeman, L. (1995). Using the therapeutic relationship to promote an internal locus of control in elderly mental health clients. *Journal of Gerontological Social Work,* 23, 161–176.

Pearlin, L.I., & Skaff, M.M. (1995). Stressors and adaptation in later life. In M. Gatz (Ed.), *Emerging issues in mental health and aging* (pp. 97–123). Washington, DC: American Psychiatric Association.

Rojiani, R. (1994). Disparities in the social construction of long-term care. In C.K. Riessman (Ed.), *Qualitative studies in social work research* (pp. 139–152). Thousand Oaks, CA: Sage Publications.

Rutter, M. (1987). Psychosocial resilience and protective mechanisms. *American Journal of Orthopsychiatry,* 57, 316–331.

Ryan, D., & Doubleday, E. (1995). Group work: A lifeline for isolated elderly. *Social Work with Groups,* 18, 65–78.

Saleebey, D. (1996). The strengths perspective in social work practice: Extensions and cautions. *Social Work,* 41, 296–305.

Schaie, K.W. (1993). Ageist language in psychological research. *American Psychologist,* 48, 49–51.

Snyder, W., & McCollum, E.E. (1999). Their home is their castle: Learning to do in-home family therapy. *Family Process,* 38, 229–242.

Sullivan, W.P., & Fisher, B.J. (1994). Intervening for success: Strengths-based case management and successful aging. *Journal of Gerontological Social Work,* 22, 61–71.

Tice, C.J., & Perkins, K. (1996). *Mental health issues and aging: Building on the strengths of older persons.* Pacific Grove, CA: Brooks/Cole Publishing.

Wacker, R., Roberto, K., & Piper, L. (1998). *Community resources for older adults: Programs and services in an era of change.* Thousand Oaks, CA: Pine Forge Press.

Williams, I. (1990). Case management: Awareness of feelings. In B. Genevay & R.S. Katz (Eds.), *Countertransference and older clients* (pp. 136–147). Thousand Oaks, CA: Sage Publications.

Wong, P.T. (1995). The processes of adaptive reminiscence. In B.K. Haight & J.D. Webster (Eds.), *The art and science of reminiscing: Theory, research, methods, and applications* (pp. 23–35). Washington, DC: Taylor & Francis.

Working with Individuals and Couples

I

Choosing Loneliness over Rejection

2

Mariko Abe Foulk

CLIENT'S BACKGROUND

A COMMUNITY AGENCY CONTACTED THE CLINIC ONE FRIDAY AFTERNOON AND ASKED ME TO CALL HELEN, a woman in her late 70s. Helen was living alone in an apartment, and the agency was concerned because she seemed to be very depressed and suicidal. Helen had a few previous contacts with the agency when she was trying to arrange chore services. She had various medical conditions, including diabetes, osteoporosis, chronic pulmonary problems, recent weight gain, and water retention. Because of her shortness of breath and back and leg pain, her physical capabilities had become increasingly limited, but she had a hard time asking for help.

Helen was raised in a fundamentalist Christian family and was the oldest of five children. She recalled her parents fondly and with great admiration. She described her mother, whom she adored, as a graceful socialite. Helen felt like a failure because she did not have her mother's social skills or inclination to be sociable. Her mother wanted her to be a "very good Christian girl" who obeyed teachers at school and never questioned their authority. Helen recalled how she protected her younger siblings from unreasonably strict teachers at school yet felt guilty that she did not live up to her beloved mother's standard of good manners. Helen remembered her father as someone who had been stubborn but fair and who had always kept his feelings hidden. She saw herself as resembling her father.

As an adult, Helen worked as a teacher until she was forced to retire in her late 50s because of physical problems. Despite these problems, she continued playing the family caregiver role. When her siblings got sick, she went to help care for them no matter how far away they lived. She provided hands-on care

19

and negotiated with health care workers when she believed that her family members were treated poorly by them. A few years before I met her, Helen had helped her sister with a financial crisis by taking out a loan from a credit company. Consequently, over the years Helen's debt snowballed as she tried to pay the minimum balance by borrowing from multiple creditors. She was deeply worried about her finances but was too embarrassed to mention her financial concerns to anybody.

Helen had been a loner most of her life, although she longed for close relationships. She did not think that she was attractive enough for others to enjoy her company and chose to avoid people rather than risk rejection and humiliation. In her early 30s, Helen developed a relationship with a man who wanted to marry her. They decided to marry, but after they returned from the honeymoon, he left her, and she never understood why. She remembered vividly how she waited in vain for him with the table set for supper. It was weeks before she could tell her parents because she felt so ashamed. She tried to get the marriage annulled by her church but was unsuccessful, so she never remarried. She did not want people to know that she was no longer married, so she had kept her husband's last name.

Helen was the sole caregiver for her father in her own home for 11 years until he died from Parkinson's disease. After his death, her younger sister, who also lived with her, suddenly became paralyzed. Believing that the medical care that her sister was receiving was inadequate, Helen took her to a prestigious out-of-town medical institution for consultation. The consultation revealed that her sister's medication was negatively affecting her sister's condition. Thus, Helen's fight against the local medical community started. She spent many lonely and frustrating months advocating for her sister's care. Helen was so furious with the way in which the physicians treated her sister that she sued the hospital and the staff after her sister's death 4 years later and received a settlement. While Helen was involved in these crises and in caring for her family, her mental health was stable. However, when she was relieved of her caregiving duties, her depression surfaced.

INTERVENTION SUMMARY

Because the original referral was related to a crisis, I called Helen immediately and talked to her on the telephone for almost an hour. I had to assess her suicidal feelings and determine whether a psychiatric emergency outreach team should be involved. She stated, "I don't see why I should still be alive," but denied having any concrete plan of action, as she wanted to be "a good Christian." After assessing that she was not at risk for suicide, I simply listened to her painful story. She stated that she had never gotten over her sister's death and had been crying a lot, feeling hopeless, "self-pitying," and "out of control." When I invited her to come to the clinic to continue our discussion, she agreed to set up an appointment for counseling. Because she was a regular patient at our medical clinic, I scheduled our session just before her medical appointment the following week. Later, she called me to reschedule our appointment. Her sister-in-law, who lived in a nearby town, wanted to accompany Helen to her medical appointment and Helen did not want her sister-in-law to know that she was getting counseling. She revealed that she was crying a lot but believed that she had to hide her feelings from her siblings. She did not want them to worry about her and wanted to maintain her image as the proud, strong, and independent older sister.

Perhaps my telephone crisis intervention helped her to visit me for counseling because I later discovered that her primary care physician had recommended counseling numerous times, but she either had refused to try such services or went to one appointment and then stopped. Her physician also had prescribed antidepressants, but she had refused them as well.

Helen visited me 1 week after her original appointment for the initial therapy session. Although her clothes were plain, she had good color coordination and looked almost fashionable. She had a nice smile and seemed perky. The primary focus of the first session was the illness and death of her sister. Helen talked in great detail about the medical care that her sister received and expressed her anger at the medical establishment. When she talked about the last years of her sister's life, she became absorbed with the story and seemed to appreciate having an audience. Her discussion was dramatic and animated. Then, she broke down in tears, saying, "I am not like this," and, "I am usually in control." She admitted that she had been depressed and that it had been difficult to get out of bed for some time. She admitted to wanting to "quit with life" but denied having active suicidal thoughts. She refused antidepressants but agreed to try weekly psychotherapy sessions.

I have worked with Helen for almost 3 years, meeting with her an average of twice a month. Despite her initial reluctance to see a counselor, she was always on time for our sessions. We worked on a series of psychological and care management issues. The three major issues that emerged were relationships, housing and finances, and self-esteem.

Relationships

For the first several sessions, Helen continued to talk in great detail about her sister's illness and the medical care that her sister received. She even brought meticulous documentation with her to back up her stories. Helen was very angry with the medical community for failing to notice that her sister's problems were worsening as a result of her allergic reaction to medications. She also was resentful toward her other siblings, who did not offer much help while she cared for her father and sister. According to Helen, they criticized her for not placing her father and sister in a nursing facility. She believed that she was not supported by the physicians, who also told Helen to place them in a nursing facility. She believed that nobody understood her commitment to the care of her family and consequently felt very alone. She spent all of her time caregiving, which isolated her from the rest of the world.

After several sessions, Helen began expressing how lonely she had felt as she cared for both her father and sister for 15 years. My task at this stage was to listen actively to her stories; validate her anger; and tune in to the underlying frustration, sadness, and vulnerability. When she talked about her sister's illness, her energy seemed to return. She told the same stories about her sister over and over. At times, I wondered whether she was using her memory of her sister's illness as a buffer against facing her painful present. I decided to move slowly to build trust within our relationship before pursuing my hypothesis.

Helen was angry with herself for not standing up for her sister early enough to postpone her death. I helped her work through her feelings of guilt and accept her limitations as the oldest sibling and the caregiver. I tried cognitive restructuring to help her understand her irrational expectations of herself. I asked her what she would say if she saw another woman taking care of her family in the same way that she did. She said that she would think that the person did a pretty good job; through this, I helped her realize that she tended to have extremely high expectations of herself and that they were unrealistic. It took several months, but Helen eventually accepted that she did the best that she could at the time.

However lonely she might have felt while her father and sister were alive, she at least had a relationship with each of them. After their death, she believed that she had nobody. She stated, "I am carrying an empty hole," "I lost the purpose of life," and, "I lost the mission." At one point she said, "I feel like I am swimming in deep water without knowing which direction to go." She reminisced about her happy childhood with her parents and siblings. It seemed that such reminiscing gave her some strength. I did not confront the quality of her "perfect" family as I listened, for I was sure that Helen would begin to reveal other sides of her family as she began to trust me and to feel safe in disclosing them. She also grieved the loss of her beloved family members and the loss of her dream to raise a family. I listened to and affirmed her heritage, happy memories, disappointments, and despair.

After about 3 months, she said that she would like to "get on with my life," but that "I have nothing to do, nowhere to go, and no friends to visit." She said that she would love to have people visit her but had no one to invite. At this point, I thought that she was ready to start rebuilding her life. Helen said that it would be nice to have company with whom she could enjoy a cup of coffee. I suggested that she meet with one of the peer volunteers from our clinic. She agreed, and I arranged for a volunteer to make home visits. Helen did not accept potential volunteers right away. When a volunteer called her to set up a date, she always had reasons why she could not meet, thus making the volunteer feel unwelcome. After a few unsuccessful telephone calls, the volunteer stopped calling her, and Helen decided that the volunteer was not really interested in her. This inability to make a positive human connection was another indication to Helen that she was not worthy of anyone's attention.

I discussed with Helen her interactions with the volunteer as a way of examining her interactions with other people, but she stuck to the story that she was busy and that the volunteer was supposed to call her back but did not. She refused to see how she might have contributed to turning off the volunteer. The volunteer coordinator who was arranging for another peer volunteer questioned Helen's motivation to have volunteer visits. She stopped looking for other volunteers and suggested that I work more with Helen.

After three volunteers failed to make connections with her, I hand-picked a volunteer with whom I thought she might get along well. I arranged for this person to meet with both of us after we had our session at the clinic. In this way, I was able to prepare Helen for the meeting, and she could interact with a stranger while I was present and she felt safe. Once she met the volunteer, she was able to work with her. They enjoyed conversation over a cup of coffee and had lunch together. The volunteer also helped her with various errands. In addition, I arranged for a few college-student volunteers to do occasional errands for Helen. I discovered that she did well with students and younger volunteers because, as a former teacher, she believed that she could contribute to their development. In addition, she felt less vulnerable to their rejection.

In an effort to develop other outside interests, Helen and I started looking at a local monthly publication that prints all of the events in town. I wanted her to start exploring her interests and identifying which activities she might enjoy. One day Helen brought in a book about church rituals that she published when she was in her 30s. I was very impressed. This book gave me a clue that Helen might enjoy writing. Our clinic offers several writing groups, which also function as support groups (see Chapter 9 for a description of one of these writing groups). I arranged for her to join a writing group, which she wanted to try. She sat in the group for the first hour but left at the break and never went back. According to her, there were a couple of snobbish "country club–type" women in the group, and she could not bear to be with them. She believed that they looked down on her and did not want her in the group. When I talked to the group facilitator, she could not recall any incident that might have made Helen feel rejected. I asked Helen about other members whom she liked and tried to help her understand that she would fit into the group if she wanted to. The group facilitator even called to invite her back, but she refused to return.

Her inability to make meaningful connections in the present suggested that we needed to explore her previous relationships. As we talked about her past, Helen related that she always took care of her younger siblings. At school, she was busy protecting her younger siblings from unreasonably strict teachers. She did not believe that she fit in at school and did not think that her teachers understood her. We explored these beliefs further, and she remembered one musical in high school in which she was to sing a major role. She practiced her part very hard; then the teacher in charge switched the parts and gave hers to another girl. Although she got a new part, she did not want to do it because she was so hurt by the teacher's unfairness. At the rehearsal, Helen still refused to play the new part. The teacher called her mother, who, in turn, pleaded with Helen to take on the new role. This incident left her feeling rejected by the teacher and misunderstood by her mother.

As we reviewed her relationships, it became clear that Helen distanced herself from others for fear of being rejected in social situations. Helen told herself, "They don't care about me," "I am not likable," and, "I don't fit in." We examined how her negative thinking and confrontational style served as a buffer against her vulnerability. We reviewed times when she felt rejected by friends, and together we explored whether she had any distortions in her inter-pretation of these past events. Helen had a hard time accepting those whom she believed did not adhere to her values, and her judgmental tendencies sur-faced. She believed that she had to condemn those whose actions she did not approve of and thought that accepting or forgiving those people would mean that she would have to compromise her moral values. I tried to help her under-stand why people might react differently to an event, as each one had different experiences. I helped her to see how being judgmental hurt her ability to con-nect with others. Helen was able to see the limitations of being judgmental but was not willing to modify her style. She declared that if her style would cause her to be isolated, then it would be fine with her.

Because so many of her interpretations involved cognitive distortions, I referred her to a 10-session cognitive therapy group (see Chapter 7 for details about this group). I was not sure whether she would follow through with the group, but she accepted my suggestion to try it because she was "tired of being depressed." Also, I was the co-therapist in the group and this gave her a sense of security. Helen did not participate much during the interaction among group members. She said that she could not speak up when it was her turn because she felt uncomfortable letting others see her problems and weakness. She told me that when she was about to say something in the therapy group, she recalled her high school musical episode. The episode reminded her of what would happen when she tried to assert her feelings. She thought, "I should keep my mouth shut, or I will get in trouble." She was too scared to let down her guard. Helen described this feeling: "I create a wall, and behind the wall I hide. Then nobody knows how I feel. I can't be embarrassed." Despite her lack of participation in the group, Helen gained some insight into her tendency to feel criticized and to overreact by shutting herself off or getting angry.

Throughout her group therapy sessions, we continued to meet individu-ally. I thought that she needed the support to continue with the group and that she might find it helpful to discuss her experiences with me. She had some positive interactions with group members who were more verbal about their depressive symptoms. She seemed to enjoy talking with them after the ses-sions, but she never shared her vulnerabilities. She told me later that she was exhausted from trying to be social and helpful. Her positive experience with particular individuals did not seem to influence her negative views of others in general. She did not want to change her confrontational style either. Helen tended to take general comments personally and to feel attacked. On such occasions, she either stayed quiet and felt rejected or angrily snapped at the other person.

Financial and Housing Concerns

Several months after we began working together, Helen started expressing anxiety over her financial situation. She stated that worrying about her finances kept her awake for many hours at night. She was spending half of her monthly income on rent for a spacious two-bedroom apartment. I suggested that Helen discuss her options with staff at our local senior housing bureau. I encouraged her to learn about local resources and hoped that living in an apartment building for older adults might help her to interact with more people. She met with the staff a couple of times. I helped her weigh the benefits of moving to an apartment building for older adults, where she could meet others more easily. She longed for company. In addition, she was able to see the financial benefit of moving to a subsidized apartment. I suggested that she visit some apartments for older adults, and she agreed. She considered various options but felt overwhelmed at the thought of moving. She stated, "I sometimes want to just give it all up," and, "I am waiting for God to call me home."

When I observed that her anxiety was keeping her from acting on her desire to visit potential apartments, I offered to accompany her on these visits. She originally refused my offer, stating that I was too busy to help her in this way and that she could not ask that much of me. With my reassurance, she accepted my offer. We visited some clinic patients who lived in subsidized apartments for older adults, and she seemed to enjoy the visits very much. I asked her to visit other patients because I wanted her to see older adults in circumstances that were similar to her own. They modeled for her the ability to survive through their moves and adjust well to the new environment.

Helen was discouraged to see that their rooms were much smaller than those in her apartment. She worried about whether there would be enough space for her favorite furniture. Despite her worries and with my encouragement, she placed her name on waiting lists when she realized that it did not commit her to moving. She vacillated between the choices because she did not want to part with her familiar furniture. The pros and cons of each option were discussed repeatedly. We talked about her fears of making such a big decision. We talked about the worst-case scenario, and I wanted her to understand that even the worst situation could be reversed. During this period, I reassured Helen that I would be with her throughout the move.

The care management skills that I used in this phase were as follows: 1) carefully assessing her situation, 2) empowering her to use available community resources, 3) helping her to understand her options, 4) assisting her in the decision-making process, and 5) providing emotional support to help her cope with her anxiety. With 1 month's notice, Helen was informed of the availability of an apartment. She started packing. With her permission, I arranged for a couple of student volunteers to help her pack and a local senior services agency to move her boxes and furniture. When one of her nephews volunteered to move her belongings, Helen was delighted to know that her family cared enough about her to help when needed. She canceled the arrangements I had made and accepted her nephew's offer. In return, Helen gave him a lot of her furniture as a token of appreciation. However, the nephew was unreliable and postponed the moving date several times. As she desperately wanted to maintain her relationship with her nephew, Helen decided to wait until he was available. Her anxiety reached a high point as the lease on her current apartment was coming to a close. She was totally overwhelmed and frightened about her uncertain future. I decided to intervene in the moving process. With her permission, I contacted her nephew, confirmed that he would appear with his truck by a certain time, and mobilized several available volunteers, including my high school–age son, to move her boxes in time.

Shortly before the move, Helen disclosed that she had a huge credit debt. She was so ashamed that she had kept it secret from everyone. She stated, "I will have no choice but to sell all of the furniture and move out of my apartment and get a small room at the YMCA. I won't let anyone see me that way." First, I tried to help relieve her immobilizing shame. Although she was embarrassed about the debt, Helen was proud of the cause of her debt: She had borrowed money to relieve the financial crisis of one of her siblings. I helped Helen to remind herself about her good intentions at the time that she had borrowed the money. I also educated her about the aggressive marketing strategies of credit card companies and how easy it is to get more credit cards to pay for other debts, which in turn escalated her problem. Second, I helped her to explore her options. She decided to make an appointment for free credit counseling. Each time that she made an appointment, she canceled it. She explained that her anxiety was so high that she could not face the credit counselor. I reminded her several times of the benefit of credit counseling but was unable to convince her to go. I believed that a crisis would have to occur for her to take a risk, and because the nature of this crisis was not a matter of life or death, I thought that we could wait. It took another year before she was able to go to credit counseling and tell someone other than her therapist about the state of her finances.

As the appointment date approached, her anxiety over her finances increased and she became more and more hopeless. She started having vague suicidal ideations. I asked her, "What would happen if you died?" She stated, "I won't have to face the humiliation of my debts." I then asked her, "How about your brothers and sisters?" She said, "They will be sad if I died." I again asked, "What about the debts?" Helen hesitantly replied, "They will find out about my debts and will be shocked." I asked, "Would you like that to happen?" The embarrassment that she would feel if her siblings discovered her debts was sufficient motivation for her to keep her appointment. To help ease her discomfort, I offered to accompany her. The financial adviser recommended filing for bankruptcy; it took a few more months for her to file. I worked with her repeatedly to minimize her guilt and embarrassment and kept talking with her about her options. We searched for and found a sympathetic lawyer who was willing to work with her for a minimal charge. During this period, Helen became so depressed, humiliated, and fearful at the thought of filing for bankruptcy that she again became suicidal. She believed that suicide would be "the only way out." She confided that she had a bottle of Valium that had been prescribed for her deceased sister and that she was thinking of taking an overdose. When I carefully assessed her suicidal thoughts, she stated that she would not act on this impulse. I asked her to promise to call me if or when her impulse got stronger and more tempting. She was frightened by the thought of creditors knocking on her door. I encouraged her to check out this fear with her lawyer. She was told that creditors would not pursue her. I asked Helen to remember this whenever she became fearful. Throughout the process, I empathized with her fear and supported her ability to tackle challenges. I accompanied her to her lawyer's office for her first visit and to the bankruptcy court for her hearing. Because Helen was a deeply religious person, she was helped a great deal by the Bible verse (Deuteronomy 15:1) that debts are forgiven in the seventh year. I encouraged Helen to think of this verse when she became anxious, and she found that it helped make her feel calmer.

Self-Esteem

When I started seeing Helen, she blamed her recent weight gain for all of her problems. She said that she had gained 40 pounds in the past 5 years. She weighed herself every day, read articles on weight loss, went to Weight Watchers, did exercises, and restricted her diet. Her weight did not decrease, and she became very frustrated. Helen was angry with medical staff for not paying enough attention to her weight. Talking about her weight problems triggered the anger that she had felt at the medical community when battling with them over her sister's illness. She would start her session saying, "My whole body feels bloated to the max and I cannot go on like this anymore." She continued, "I feel fat and ugly and hopeless about my weight." I showed an interest in her concern by looking at the literature that she brought regarding weight loss and listening to her. I pointed out the nice color coordination of her clothes and admired her fashion sense. As we discussed the issues further, she realized that her depression, weight problems, and poor self-esteem might be related.

Underneath her strong, proud façade, Helen had a vulnerable inner self. She did not think that she was likable or useful. This was an ongoing issue in our therapy sessions. I wanted her to reexamine her self-image. At times, I challenged her by asking her questions such as, "N*obody* liked you?" or, "You were not useful to anyone?" At other times, I gave her specific homework assignments and brainstormed with her. One assignment was for her to develop a list of her strengths. Helen could not identify any strengths during our session, but she brought to her next session a list that included faith, compassion, and kindness. We explored what each strength represented. She was able to see these traits in her stories about helping her sick and troubled siblings as well as in her devotion to her students. I encouraged her to notice her positive qualities.

She also talked about her failed marriage and stated, "I should have known better," and blamed herself for the outcome. She said that all of her "pride and self-esteem were washed away." I acknowledged that the failed marriage was in fact a trauma and validated her belief that it was a very painful event. I helped her to understand her own struggle and to accept herself. We also reviewed her unrealistic expectations that she alone could have changed the outcome, that instead marriage requires that both spouses work for change. I also redirected her focus from blaming herself to examining ways in which her husband's problems may have contributed to the end of the marriage. She was able to reexamine her irrational statements and evaluate her husband's problems.

During our work together, Helen came to appreciate a few meaningful relationships. She maintained positive close relationships with her siblings and enjoyed her volunteer's friendship. She also took pleasure in chatting with a few neighbors who lived in her apartment complex. Despite these gains, she continued to find it hard to reach out to people. She tended to avoid meeting other residents in her apartment by going to the lobby to pick up her mail at times when most people were eating dinner.

INTERVENTION ANALYSIS

My therapeutic work with Helen combined counseling and care management. There are two reasons why I chose to integrate these roles. One was that Helen needed help with securing resources, and the other was that Helen was intelligent but not psychologically oriented. If counseling were the only method I had used, then I believe that Helen would have left therapy before having acquired the kind of skills that she needed to cope with her crises in a timely fashion. That she refused to take any medication for depression or anxiety further limited her ability to cope.

Demonstration of Respect

I listened to Helen's anger, despair, and frustration and validated her feelings. I moved at her pace and waited for her to be ready to tackle issues about which she was extremely embarrassed (e.g., her financial difficulties), thus respecting her pace of change. I remained sensitive to her pace through careful observation of her verbal and nonverbal expressions. I respected her desire for control. This was manifested in the following two situations. First, I supported her plan to rely on her nephew rather than on my arrangements for her move to the apartment complex for older adults, although I was not sure whether her nephew was reliable. Helen was happy that a family member cared about her enough to help, and following her lead was worth the risk.

Second, I respected her choice of physicians, although sometimes I disagreed with her choices. I communicated the pros and cons of her options but never tried to pressure her to take any particular suggestions. I respected her values, although at times they were not practical in her struggle. For example, tending her parents' graves was so important to her that it was worth pushing her body, although we both knew that she would have aches and pains for the next few days. I made sure that her choices and their consequences were clear to her, but she was the one who made the decisions.

I respected her desire for independence and that she had a hard time accepting help because it made her feel useless. When our clinic was given a new walker with a basket and a chair attached to it, she was happy to try it. We asked her to be a tester and to record her feedback rather than make her feel indebted. She was proud to monitor a new product.

Use of the Client's Strengths

A main focus of the therapy with Helen was to highlight the strengths that emerged in her life stories. She was a bright woman who was determined to live independently and wanted to maintain control over her life. She was interested in law, politics, and current events. Others often interpreted her sense of independence as stubbornness, but it was her persistence and tenacity that kept Helen going. I wanted her to appreciate her own tenacity and hoped that such strength would give her the energy to combat her depression.

Helen was able to appreciate her ability to help others. I offered her opportunities to play the part of a home-visit client in our clinic's training program for graduate students. She happily volunteered and welcomed the students, beaming. Helen enjoyed helping.

She respected and valued her family of origin. Helen was extremely giving with her family, and they, in a limited way, reciprocated her care. When Helen was hospitalized for hip replacement, her sister-in-law stayed at her bedside, and Helen very much appreciated this support. When Helen was entertaining suicidal ideation just before going to a credit counselor, I pointed out her love for her family. I asked her to imagine what her family would think of her and her debts if she killed herself. The thoughts that this question provoked were powerful enough for her to reconsider suicide.

She also had a sense of humor. She was able to laugh at herself when she recalled getting in trouble with teachers during her childhood or when she confronted some authoritative physicians. She was very good at mimicking the statements of such individuals and described how they struggled to find the right words to respond to her. We shared a good laugh, and it seemed to help lift her spirits, if only briefly.

Helen had a variety of artistic talents, including interior decorating, painting furniture, and writing. I encouraged her to pursue her interests. I read her book and admired her talent. I wanted her to remember that she was still the same person who had accomplished so much in life. When she moved to the new apartment and filed for bankruptcy, I commented that she did it using all of the resources that she had. I wanted her to feel proud of her accomplishments.

She also revealed that she prayed to God every morning and night and that it was important to her to be on good terms with God. I listened attentively to her declaration of faith and to her anger and disappointment as the rituals in her church changed over time. Helen often told me that she prayed for me and my family every morning. I made a point of letting her know how much I appreciated such prayers.

Blurred Boundaries

Through my work with Helen, I became a crucial source of support. I took her to see apartments, helped her move when her plans fell apart, and arranged for my son and volunteers to help move her boxes. I took her to credit counseling, lawyers, and bankruptcy court.

Why did I become so actively engaged in assisting Helen? Besides persistent depression, Helen experienced marked anxiety about going to new places, meeting new people, and facing uncertain situations. Her anxiety kept her from going places unless she was with someone she trusted, and unfortunately there were few people whom she trusted. Helen had a brother in the area who was willing to help and sisters living out of state who were willing to come in times of crisis. However, Helen did not want to damage the image of herself as the strong oldest sister and refused to share with them her debilitating anxiety, depression, or financial problems. Thus, I stepped into the role when no one else was available.

Asking my son to move furniture for Helen was an unusual blurring of boundaries. I made this arrangement after her nephew failed to help her and after I contacted a community agency, which was unavailable. It was relatively easy for me to arrange for my son to help, I believed that it would be a good act of community service for him, and I thought that Helen would accept this kind of help from a young person. I also knew that it was urgent that we complete the move before her lease ran out; and although using one's own family members is unorthodox, I knew that I had more flexibility with and control over my son than I would with a stranger.

Even while the boundaries were blurred in some ways, in other ways they remained clear. For example, I never gave Helen my home telephone number. We also had the understanding that she would come to the clinic for counseling unless she was sick. When she did not feel well enough to travel, I offered her home visits. Helen knew that I lived in town and that my telephone number was listed, so she could have easily found my telephone number. However, she was careful not to step into my private life. In the beginning of therapy, I established clear boundaries, not knowing how Helen would use or abuse them. As I learned that she was able to maintain a professional relationship with respect to certain boundaries, I trusted her judgment and was able to provide her with assistance in a more relaxed manner. Because Helen's personality was different from my own or my family members', it was relatively easy for me to maintain my professional stance with her.

Changes in the Therapeutic Relationship over Time

Although Helen may never completely resolve her feelings concerning her sister's death, she now believes that she did the best that she could at the time. This understanding has made her feel less guilty and self-critical. She has not felt suicidal since her bankruptcy procedure was completed. Her depression is less acute but worsens when her physical health deteriorates and when she must depend on others for assistance. On such occasions, she still feels useless and sees no meaning for her continued existence.

She moved to an apartment complex for older adults, which more effectively met her needs, and she got rid of her debts as she successfully completed her bankruptcy procedure. This new start helped to reduce her stress and despair and made it possible for her to purchase some gifts for herself and others whom she wished to thank.

She has formed friendships with a volunteer and with a resident at her apartment complex. She has conflicts with them from time to time but basically enjoys their friendship. These two relationships represent significant progress, although she still avoids most other people. She has maintained her amicable relationships with her siblings. Although she would rather be the caregiver than the care receiver, Helen gracefully accepted and expressed her appreciation for her sister-in-law's help when she was hospitalized. However, Helen continues to feel uncomfortable discussing her vulnerabilities with her family, including her depression and anxiety.

As for the changes in our therapeutic relationship, Helen started out seeing me as yet another medical professional who might or might not help her. As she began to trust me, she saw me as a person who understood her and advocated for her. Because I am considerably younger than she, Helen might also have seen me as the idealized daughter she never had. She now calls me

her best friend, yet she continues to give me the kind of respect and appreciation that she pays to other medical professionals.

Benefits and Difficulties of the Therapeutic Relationship for the Client and the Therapist

Because Helen was so distrustful of others, it was good for her to have someone like myself, with whom she felt safe disclosing her dilemmas. She was able
to vent her anger to me and did not have to worry about losing our relationship. Through her connection to me, she experienced some of the benefits of a
positive relationship and the feeling that she was capable of sustaining a relationship. She was able to come up with solutions for concrete issues, such as
finances and housing. As Helen relied on me, she worried about my well-being
whenever I traveled. She prayed, for example, that my plane would land safely.

I was reluctant to challenge Helen's perception of her mother as flawless
because she had put both of her parents on a pedestal and believed that any
criticism would be an insult to their souls. I provided some suggestions concerning alternative ways of perceiving her mother, but Helen continually
rejected my suggestions. I believed that our therapeutic relationship would be
at risk if I confronted her further in this area.

The difference in our races might have served as a benefit. I am Asian and
Helen is Caucasian. For Helen, who had a long list of negative relationships
with people of her race, my being "different" might have given her a fresh start.
Since we started working together, Helen has formed relationships with her
favorite medical resident and her favorite volunteer, who are both Asian. At one
point, she stated that she had a special appreciation for Asian people because
they "come from a culture that respects elders." The influence of the cultural
background of the therapist is also demonstrated in the way I understood
Helen's caregiving style. She totally embraced caring for her deceased father
and sister, which often was regarded by medical professionals and her siblings
as unhealthy. Because I come from a culture that endorses such caregiving, it
was probably easier for me to understand Helen's caregiving style than for
some helping professionals who might interpret her approach to caregiving as
dysfunctional.

It has been a challenging but satisfying experience for me to work with
Helen. I am pleased that we were able to develop a trusting relationship,
because she had few such relationships in her life. I was able to find her positive qualities despite that other professionals found her stubborn and difficult.
Through her, my horizons expanded. I learned about such concrete services as
bankruptcy procedures and, more important, how to help a client who was
reluctant to accept help. Helen did not want to feel useless, and she wanted to
reciprocate. I was able to acknowledge that by praying for me and my family,
Helen gave me a valuable gift.

Words of Wisdom

Sometimes a crisis needs to occur before clients will change. Helen was able to take risks when her mental state became so intolerable that she wanted to kill herself. Her first crisis enabled her to begin counseling and form a relationship with me. Later, when she feared that she would become destitute, she took the risk of moving to another apartment and undergoing bankruptcy proceedings. My presence was a symbol of security, stability, and hope for her so that she knew that she would survive the risks that she took.

I knew that her situation eventually would come to a crisis point if she kept stalling and avoiding facing her problems. I was able to wait patiently for her readiness to change because I respected her rate of progress. I helped her to understand the issues and options, but I was able to tell myself that if she refused to take antidepressants or if she continued worrying about her finances without taking action, it was her choice. In other words, I was aware of my limitations as a helping agent. There is another important element that is worth mentioning: I knew that I had the support of my colleagues and that they would work with Helen even if she had a crisis while I was out of town. All of these elements made it possible for me to take the risk of waiting for her to be ready to change. I think that is why I did not perceive Helen as stubborn and frustrating.

As mentioned previously, I was reluctant to confront Helen's image of her mother as perfect. However, if Helen can be helped in the future to see that it was her mother who failed to accept Helen as she was rather than Helen's failure to meet her mother's expectations, it might diminish her sense of being a misfit. When she can accept her mother's flaws, Helen can be helped to forgive her mother. I think that this understanding and forgiveness of her mother might help Helen to see herself and others less judgmentally. Because I am still working with Helen, this indeed might be an approach that I can take in the future.

In the Turner Clinic setting, I have the flexibility to continue to see Helen to provide support and counseling as changes occur in her life. For some clients like Helen, who are vulnerable and have few other supports, the relationship with the therapist/care manager can be ongoing, even if meetings are less frequent during stable periods. As I continue to work with Helen, I need to help her to consider how her physical disabilities may have an impact on her future. More disappointments about her unrealized dreams may surface along with her sense of mortality. I would like to help her to realize that she does not always have to be a caregiver to her siblings and that she can receive care from them. She can maintain her worth as a person and as a proud older sister. In so doing, she can prepare for the time when she no longer is able to live independently.

ADDITIONAL RESOURCES

Although there are numerous articles and books on psychotherapy or care management, there are few that incorporate both interventions. The theoretical framework that fits well with my work with Helen is a strengths-based model that is described in a book by Tice and Perkins (1996). This book describes how ecological theory provides a useful framework for thinking about people in relation to their environment. Furthermore, the strengths-based model emphasizes the uniqueness of individuals and their dignity and self-determination.

Several books and articles address various issues raised within this case. In the book chapter "Building Rapport with the Older Client," Knight (1996) provided many helpful hints, starting with educating clients about therapy. The chapter illustrates rapport-building techniques using therapist–client dialogues. For crisis management and psychotherapy, a book chapter by Kahana (1987) may be helpful. It addresses psychological crises through the life span and characteristics of crisis management in older adults. It also touches on psychotherapy beyond crisis management. An article by Klausner and Alexopoulos (1999) reviewed the effectiveness of existing psychosocial interventions for a variety of older populations and caregivers. It concluded that combining techniques to target problems that are relevant to older adults is especially beneficial. It also pointed out that we should expend increased efforts to recognize and treat geriatric depression and anxiety in primary care settings as older adults with emotional problems prefer such settings.

There are a number of resources available for grief counseling. One of them (Worden, 1991) gives an excellent overview on this topic and is useful as a handbook for mental health practitioners. It describes a wide range of losses, mechanisms of grief, and procedures for helping clients grieve. Worden explained how unresolved grief can lead to problems that require psychotherapy. He also talked about grief among older adults and grieving special types of losses.

An article by Delon and Wenston (1989) provides the broad perspective that is needed to work with depressed older clients and integrates role theory with Erikson's psychosocial theory. *Feeling Good* (Burns, 1980) is the book that Helen read as part of her cognitive therapy group homework. It is a self-help book for those who experience depression and anxiety. It is easy to read and offers a clear and entertaining presentation. Helen enjoyed the book very much.

As I discussed previously, my Asian heritage might have influenced my ability to understand Helen's caregiving style. Long (1996) examined Japanese women as nurturers and caregivers through a social anthropologist's eye. She stated that the full and undivided attention of the caregiver has become the cultural ideal in Japan and is found in both child care and eldercare. The chapter provides insight into diverse cultural perspectives on caregiving.

REFERENCES

Burns, D. (1980). *Feeling good: The new mood therapy*. New York: New American Library.

Delon, M., & Wenston, S.R. (1989). An integrated theoretical guide to intervention with depressed elderly clients. *Journal of Gerontological Social Work*, 14, 131–145.

Kahana, R. (1987). Geriatric psychotherapy: Beyond crisis management. In J. Sadavoy & M. Leszcz (Eds.), *Treating the elderly with psychotherapy* (pp. 233–263). Madison, WI: International University Press.

Klausner, E.J., & Alexopoulos, G.S. (1999). The future of psychosocial treatments for elderly patients. *Psychiatric Services*, 50, 1198–1204.

Knight, B.G. (1996). *Psychotherapy with older adults*. Thousand Oaks, CA: Sage Publications.

Long, S.O. (1996). Nurturing and femininity: The ideal of caregiving in postwar Japan. In A.E. Imamura (Ed.), *Re-imaging Japanese women* (pp. 156–176). Los Angeles: University of California Press.

Tice, C.J., & Perkins, K. (1996). *Mental health issues and aging: Building on the strengths of older persons*. Pacific Grove, CA: Brooks/Cole Publishing.

Worden, W. (1991). *Grief counseling and grief therapy*. New York: Springer Publishing.

Redefining the Role of Victim

3

Ruth E. Dunkle

CLIENT'S BACKGROUND

DOUGLAS THOMPSON, A MAN IN HIS MID-70S, WAS REFERRED TO THE CLINIC BY A FRIEND who used it for medical care and knew about the social services department. Douglas complained of feeling depressed and victimized in many areas of his life and was having trouble sleeping as a result of a recent partial retirement and long-standing marital problems. He was in good health and wanted to be able to enjoy his life more.

Having owned his own gravel business and having worked 7 days per week for 50 years, Douglas found it difficult to cut back on his work. He had always been self-employed and enjoyed working. His wife had retired because of health problems and needed to spend several months a year in a warmer climate. He did not want to leave work but did not want to be separated from her either. He worried about how he would fill his time and who would run the business during the months when he was away.

Douglas had been married previously and had two children. His first wife died when his children were young, and he remarried shortly after her death. His second marriage of 35 years had not been happy. He believed that he and his wife had never been partners in this marriage, as she expected him to bear the financial responsibility for her life without giving him any of the money that she had inherited. Furthermore, he believed that his wife had prevented him from having a satisfying relationship with his two children as well as her son. He believed that she wanted to control the relationship that he had with these children. This had caused resentment because he saw less of the children than he wanted. He also believed that his children resented their stepmother.

37

INTERVENTION SUMMARY

I worked with Douglas for 3 years. We met weekly, except for short periods during the winter months when he was in Arizona. We discussed what he hoped to accomplish in counseling. There were two areas of concern: He wanted to be able to sleep and not feel depressed, and he wanted to fight less with his wife. Overall, he wanted to enjoy his life. We set two goals: 1) to decrease his depression and insomnia and 2) to improve his marital relationship.

Building a therapeutic relationship during the first several months of treatment was not easy. Douglas frequently posed questions about his reactions to situations as though he were looking for insight. For instance, he asked me why I thought that his wife had yelled at him earlier in the week. My initial tack was to ask him his thoughts. He said frequently that he just did not know. If I ventured to suggest what might be happening, he would refute my interpretation by saying, "Yes, but ... ." When I pointed out this pattern to Douglas, my observation was also met with, "Yes, but ... ." Eventually, I handled his reaction by attempting to draw on his own explanation. For instance, when he had talked about his wife's feeling that he did not care for her, I would mention this explanation as a possible reason for her being upset with him. If he believed that the idea was his, then he could embrace it.

I found some of Douglas's interaction styles intimidating. For instance, he frequently commented on my appearance, saying how attractive I was. At first, I ignored these comments, but he persisted. I attempted to point out the irrelevance of his statement, but he would smile and then reiterate his comment about my appearance, insisting that it was true. I began to make direct statements in reply such as, "What is important in our relationship is that you feel that I am on your side and able to help you reach the goals that you want out of counseling." Although his sexualizing comments did not stop completely, they greatly diminished after this discussion.

His anger was also intimidating. For example, one day I was going to hang up his coat, which he had draped across the chair. He momentarily resisted when I offered to do this. As I lifted the coat toward the hanger, he told me in a loud voice, "I told you that I do not want my coat hung up!" I apologized, but believed that his anger was inappropriate in this circumstance. At this point I chose not to explore this behavior with him because of my feelings of intimidation. Over time, I grew to understand Douglas, and I felt less intimidated. He struggled for control in all of his relationships, and ours was no exception. As I began to understand his behavior as resulting from his sense of vulnerability, it was easier for me to provide the support that allowed him to feel in control.

Initially, he also insisted on giving me gifts to show his appreciation for my time. He would bring to each session fruit from the market or bread from a local bakery. At first I was polite, thanked him for the fruit or bread, and told him that it was not necessary to repay me with gifts. I emphasized the therapeutic nature of our relationship and reminded him that he was already paying for our time together. Gradually, he stopped bringing these weekly gifts but continued to give me a gift at the holidays, which I accepted because I thought that it was important for him to feel that he could give something to me.

Depression and Insomnia

Victimization, coupled with abandonment, was the theme of Douglas's story. He felt victimized by his father's alcoholism, the death of his first wife from liver cancer, the accidental death of his business partner, and his second wife's health problems that forced him to retire partially. His childhood memories were colored by his father's drunken behavior. He believed that he and his siblings, as well as his mother, were victims of his father's verbal and physical abuse. As a boy of 8 or 9, he could not concentrate in school because of the many occasions that the household was awakened in the night by one of his father's drunken rages. He also felt victimized by his first wife's early death and being left with two young children, ages 10 and 12, to raise. He met his second wife on a blind date, and they were married 4 months after his first wife's death. He knew that he remarried too quickly after her death, but he did not believe that he could be a single parent and manage his business. He said, "My children needed a mother."

About 10 years after his first wife's death, his business partner died of food poisoning; this left Douglas to run the business alone. He found this stressful, as he had no one with whom to talk about business matters. He felt abandoned.

When his second wife, Mary, retired as a result of health problems and needed to spend winters in a warmer climate, he felt further victimized. In general, he believed that his wife was controlling his life because "she gets cool" when she is unhappy with their relationship. Eventually, he accepted the blame for whatever had happened to resume sexual contact with her. Douglas blamed his wife's behavior for his depression and insomnia; he was unaware of any connection between these problems and his feelings of victimization in childhood.

One therapeutic goal was to help him understand the root of his victimization and to gain control over his life as an adult. We began to develop insight into this problem by revisiting his childhood, specifically when he had been awakened by his parents' arguing. I asked him to remember waking up and to describe how he felt. He remembered feeling frightened and wanting to protect his mother but not wanting to make his father angrier, so he stayed in bed. Once the fighting subsided, he was unable to get back to sleep. He remembered how tired he was in school the next day.

Over time, Douglas came to see his sleeping problems as beginning in his childhood. As an adult, when he woke up in the night, he felt a sense of alarm but could not connect these feelings to those nights in his childhood. We then focused on his awakening in the night as an adult and it was quiet in the house. I asked him why he was afraid in the night when all was quiet. Douglas explained that his feelings were similar to those he experienced as a child, and he gradually began to connect these feelings to events in his childhood. He began to see the irrational response to awakening in the night as an adult when there was nothing to fear.

Like other children of alcoholic parents, the sense of abandonment was a part of Douglas's life. It was important for him to recognize what choices he made in his life and what events were matters of chance. I helped Douglas to realize that he was no longer a child who had little or no control over what happened to him. We discussed the major events of his life and separated the ones that life brought (e.g., the deaths of his wife and business partner) from the situations that he had created through his own decisions (e.g., fighting with his wife, seeing his children less than he wanted).

Although this could have taken on a tone of "I victimized myself," instead, Douglas began to justify his decisions on the basis of his own needs. He could talk about his desire to see his children and reluctance to mention this to his wife for fear of an argument. His fear of his wife's anger resulted in his not seeing his children as often as he wished and feeling deprived. Gradually, he understood that he played an important role in the decision not to see his children. As he connected his decision making with his emotions, he began to feel more in control of his own life and actions.

Marital Relationship

We worked on helping Douglas relate more effectively to Mary. Douglas and I discussed the need to communicate feelings with a partner, but he and his wife found this difficult. Douglas tried to guess why his wife was upset but did not ask her. He was better at telling her why he was upset. He described this as "asserting myself." He also began to tell her when his feelings were hurt. Douglas and Mary struggled for control in their relationship and frequently talked of divorce when their frustrations mounted. Douglas felt happier when he spent time as he wanted and with whom he wanted.

I discussed with Douglas the advantages of his wife's coming to the therapy sessions with him, but she rejected his invitations. On one occasion, however, she did come of her own volition, without an invitation. It was the morning after a particularly bad argument, and she arrived unannounced at the waiting room of the clinic. She came to the clinic separately from her husband. Douglas was surprised and glad that she was there. During this session together, Mary was able to help her husband to understand their relationship from her perspective, which was that she did not feel that he cared for her. I asked her to give her husband concrete examples of his behavior or spoken words that made her feel this way. I also asked her to give examples of what her husband could do to make her feel that he cared for her. She said that he yelled at her, which upset her. She wanted him to tell her that he loved her so that she could feel that he cared. When she was able to give him concrete examples of the types of behavior that would help her feel as though he cared, Douglas was receptive. For the first time, he understood the root of her anger toward him. He was surprised by what Mary told him and said that he did care for her. He promised to try his best to do some of the things that she thought would make her believe that he cared for her. He began to change his behavior toward her the same week that she came for counseling. Unfortunately, Mary never returned to another session even though her husband invited her to come, and I subsequently called to encourage her to join us. As she explained to us during that single session, she believed that her husband needed to talk about his feelings, but she did not.

The main area of marital conflict regarded Douglas's children. According to Douglas, neither child felt particularly close to Mary, although she had been their stepmother through their adolescent years. He attributed this conflict to their loyalty to their biological mother, saying, "No one could replace her." Douglas believed that he would have had a better relationship with his children if their mother were still alive. When I asked what this relationship with his children would be like, he said, "We would do more with them and their families—it would be a more natural bond." I asked him what stopped him from seeing his children, and he said that his wife interfered because she was moody. After they got home from visiting his children, she would "become cool," meaning that she was not friendly and not interested in sexual contact. We discussed the possibility of his seeing his children without his wife. Through several sessions, we discussed the trajectory of the anger in his fights with his wife. When he could acknowledge that Mary always got over her anger toward him, he gradually started to go to his grandchildren's sporting matches and birthday parties without her. He said that he had a much better time and that he was less bothered by her "emotional coolness" when he returned. His ability to separate himself from her displeasure resulted in his feeling more in control of his own happiness.

Marital discord also played out through financial issues. One issue was their children's inheritance. Douglas believed that his children deserved what money he had. Mary believed that her son deserved what Douglas had as well because she had been married to him for 35 years. This incongruity led to deception. Douglas opened bank accounts and purchased gifts and insurance policies for his children, unbeknownst to his wife, to give them more of his assets than his wife thought was fair. I told Douglas that I did not think that this financial maneuvering was helpful to his marriage and recommended honesty with his wife about what he was doing. He decided not to tell her and risk that she might find out on her own. He did not believe that he owed her an explanation for how he spent his money.

Gradually, we began to explore the roots of Douglas's concern for his children's financial condition. Douglas explained that his family lived in poverty as a result of his father's drinking habits. He did not want his children to have to struggle and scrimp in their lives, as he had done. He would have been willing to give more of his assets to his stepson if he believed that he needed it. When I pointed out that need was not a factor when he worried about his children's future, he asserted that he was their only parent and that he and their mother had begun the nest egg that he hoped to pass on to them. I wondered aloud if he thought that this would keep the children connected to their mother. Was it his way of helping them deal with the loss of his wife and their mother so many years ago? Did it help him with his guilt in marrying his second wife so soon after burying his first wife? Douglas had not considered these possible inter-pretations. After these conversations, he did spend more time talking about his first wife and how different his life and his children's would have been if she had lived. There was no doubt that his children clung to her memory and that this made it difficult for his second wife to feel as though she were part of this fam-ily. Conversely, Douglas believed that Mary clung to the memory of her deceased husband, as did her son. Overall, there were really three families liv-ing in this house: two involving the dead spouses and the one formed by Douglas and Mary.

Financial concerns also affected daily life with his wife. When Douglas vacationed in Arizona with his wife, he worried about the business that he left behind. His general sense of financial insecurity was exacerbated by this worry and affected his relationship with his wife. When she wanted to purchase a house, he told her that they could not afford it, although he admitted that this was not the case.

We discussed his financial condition, trying to separate his fears from the financial reality. What he could never determine was the extent of the demand that would be made on his financial resources in the future. He saw his wife as a significant demand on his financial resources, one that he needed to control. He also did not know how long he would live or what financial demands he would face for health care. He acknowledged that both his sister and his brother worried about finances. He knew that, realistically, none of them had to worry. He understood that his siblings were consumed by their worry and did not want to follow their pattern. He wanted to enjoy himself while he was able to do so. Gradually, he began to realize how significantly his childhood poverty had affected him and his siblings. This realization helped him to acknowledge that it was their insecure childhood that had caused all of them to respond in similar ways.

Frequently, I asked him to recount the areas of his life in which he felt for-tunate, mainly having good health. I usually did this after he had told me unfor-tunate things that had happened with friends and relatives. This contrast between his good health and others' health took on greater salience for him as he saw more illness and death among close friends. Wallowing in his problems seemed like a waste of energy on his part as time went by. The result was a reordering of priorities and lessening of financial worries.

Throughout the course of counseling, there was not much need to link Douglas or his family to other services. He was capable of connecting with needed services. He discussed with me concerns such as his fears as he faced cataract surgery, but he had no difficulty finding a doctor and making the appointment. On one occasion, I encouraged him to see a urologist to understand better his complaints of sexual dysfunction. His erratic sexual functioning made him wonder whether the problem was physiological or psychological. In the end, it seemed that his functioning was related to both sets of factors. His sexual function ebbed and flowed but never was consistently good in his estimation.

There were times during the 3 years of treatment when Douglas seemed to be handling his life better. On a few occasions, I suggested that we move toward ending our counseling sessions, but Douglas resisted this suggestion. Although he believed that he was having less trouble sleeping and felt depressed less often, he thought that he could not handle life by himself and that talking about his fears related to daily activities was helpful to him.

In the last year of counseling, his wife had increasing memory and health concerns. Although I thought that her health problems would make Douglas more anxious, they had the opposite effect. He seemed calmer and to feel in greater control of his life than he had when his wife was not having memory problems. He orchestrated their daily lives and enjoyed these responsibilities.

Mary's increasing health and memory problems as well as the death of friends helped Douglas to focus on how lucky he was to be alive and in good health. Gradually, his depression lifted. The last time we saw each other was the second week that he was back from an extended winter trip to Arizona. During the previous winter, I had heard from him either in a letter, in which he would tell me how poorly things were going, or at an appointment that he would make on trips back to town to check on his business. This was the first winter that I had not heard from him at all. At the first appointment, he recounted some of the significant events that had occurred over the winter and that brought him back to town for a family gathering. He had not made an appointment to see me on this visit as he had always done in the past when he was in town. I pointed out how unusual this was, and Douglas acknowledged how well he thought he had been doing. I agreed and asked whether he thought that the time had come to say goodbye. He just smiled at my suggestion and insisted on making another appointment. During the next session, Douglas continued to describe how well things were going. At the end of the session he said, "Well, I think it *is* time to say goodbye." Douglas thanked me for my help, and I told him how hard I thought he had worked to develop his sense of confidence.

I think that Douglas recognized his own capacity to manage his life without counseling. As with other changes in our therapeutic relationship, although initially rejected, my suggestion to terminate therapy ultimately was embraced. Throughout the last several months of therapy, I helped Douglas to identify several indications that he was functioning well. When Douglas could embrace these ideas as his own, he decided that he could manage on his own.

INTERVENTION ANALYSIS

At the end of 3 years of counseling, Douglas was sleeping better and having fewer bouts of depression. He felt in greater control of his life; was more assertive; and felt less victimized by situations at home, with his friends, and at work. He was able to talk about his feelings rather than bury them only to have them surface again later.

His relationship with Mary improved as well. I think that her increasing dependence on him as a result of her memory and health problems may have been beneficial for him. She posed less of a threat to him and the decisions that he wanted to make about their financial future. In addition, his wife's increasing health problems may have provided him a chance to grieve for his first wife as he anticipated the death of his second wife. Douglas worked hard to rationalize why he had married his second wife so soon when he had not had adequate time or emotional space to say goodbye to his first wife. During counseling, he spoke of his first wife only in terms of what her death had meant to his children. As he began to realize that he would in all likelihood be widowed again, he had the freedom to examine the pain of his first wife's death and begin to shore himself up to face the possibility of his second wife's dying before he did.

Demonstration of Respect

Respect is a critical component of successful treatment. Although I found Douglas's behavior intimidating at times (e.g., his "yes, but ..." commentary, frequent gifts, sexualizing of our relationship by commenting on my appearance), I tried to understand his need to do this in a counseling context. In an effort to show respect, I did not express the anger that I felt initially. Rather, I explained the inappropriateness of these behaviors in a counseling relationship and the barriers that this created in helping him to solve his problems.

I also showed respect for him by going at his pace, allowing him time to make connections and not pushing my own interpretations onto him. At times, he was not willing or able to discuss events in his life, such as his first wife's death, and I respected his choices. On many occasions, I found that I needed to make my point with examples from his own life. The examples I chose needed to be concrete and not too abstract.

Respect was also demonstrated by not dwelling on circumstances that I believed would cause further problems in Douglas's life. For instance, I believed that his wanting to make financial decisions without his wife's knowledge was something that would come back to haunt him in the years to come.

Although I did not hesitate to give my opinion on such behaviors, I understood his reasons for doing so. My obligation was to point out the risks involved in these decisions.

Last, respect was best exemplified by my accepting who Douglas was and what his therapeutic goals were. He wanted to feel better about himself and fight less with his wife. He did not want a more intimate emotional relationship with his wife, but he was willing to hear her concerns about their relationship. By my accepting who he was and providing support for him to talk about his fears and concerns, he was able to meet his goals.

Use of the Client's Strengths

Douglas approached each counseling session by describing his week and his sense of failure in interactions with family and friends. He believed that he was not able to assert himself and take control of the situation. Gradually, I helped him to understand the choices that he was making to give others power over him. For instance, he complained about his brother, who he said was wealthy but manipulated him into paying the bill when they went out to eat together. He learned to avoid becoming a victim to his brother and took control by suggesting that they spend time together in his apartment rather than in a restaurant.

Whenever possible and relevant to the discussion, I pointed out the successes in his life. I underscored Douglas's business success as well as his ability to maintain two long-term marriages. Despite his sense of financial insecurity and frequent dissatisfaction in his second marriage, he was committed to maintaining his marriage. He was also a dedicated father and grandfather. He worked hard to overcome the obstacles to seeing his relatives and tried to be a part of their lives.

Douglas wanted to be more comfortable with himself as he grew older. As he recounted his earlier life, it was clear that he had weathered a tremendous amount of loss, such as the death of his first wife and of his business partner, much of which he continued to struggle with. He had been able to bury his feelings by working long hours. When he was forced into partial retirement, he had to confront some of these feelings and did not like the resulting emotional upheaval. However, he was determined to enjoy his life, and he did.

He had been a fine businessman, a good father, and a faithful husband. He had many friends to whom he was loyal, and he took good care of his children, grandchildren, and siblings by spending time with them and taking an interest in their lives. Whenever possible, Douglas helped them financially. Frequently, I discussed his relationship with his children and friends in an effort to underscore the strength of these commitments.

I admired Douglas's ability to describe his wife in respectful terms, although he was frequently angry with her. He thought that she was an honorable person, and he appreciated her honesty. He believed that their relationship had made him a better person. In many ways, he realized that his wife made positive contributions to his life. She was a resourceful person; she had long-term friends and many hobbies. He believed that he had learned some of these same abilities from her during their marriage.

As a couple, they had many good friends whom they saw regularly. Some of them came from Douglas' and Mary's previous marriages. I told Douglas that this capacity to accept friends from his wife's past and to make new friends as a couple was a testament to the depth of his character.

Blurred Boundaries

The boundaries between therapist and friend merged most acutely in relation to gift giving. In the initial therapeutic period, Douglas wanted to give me numerous gifts in an effort to persuade me to like him. With insight provided through peer supervision, I was able to help Douglas to understand that these gifts were not necessary for me to find him acceptable. I saw this gift-giving pattern played out with his children numerous times, when he gave them money or bought his grandchildren gifts. I helped him to understand the connection between his gift giving and his desire to be liked both by his family and by me.

It took several weeks to end his weekly gifts, and I attribute this prolonged period to my own discomfort with the seemingly ungracious behavior of not accepting a gift. I found peer supervision with the other therapists at the clinic to be helpful in dealing with this behavior. In particular, when I felt angry with him for his unwillingness to accept the limits that I wanted in the relationship concerning gifts, my colleagues were helpful in validating my right to these feelings and suggesting comments that would be appropriate in meeting this challenge.

Gift giving is a complicated behavior. Douglas wanted to establish a relationship through giving gifts in return for the counseling that he received. I tried to move Douglas away from the giving of gifts by underscoring that there was no need to repay me for our therapeutic relationship. What had been weekly gifts became annual holiday gifts. I thought that these yearly gifts were important for Douglas to feel more equal in the therapeutic relationship. However, it is important that gift giving not be used to manipulate the therapist into liking the client or allowing him or her to avoid the painful work of change. Often, older clients who are uncomfortable with a therapeutic relationship attempt to put therapy in a framework that seems more natural. Giving a gift to someone you appreciate, someone who has helped you, makes the relationship seem more acceptable.

Changes in the Therapeutic Relationship over Time

Mary's memory and health problems positively influenced Douglas's mental health. They helped him to feel in control. This influence was most salient in relation to Mary's memory problems. I thought that Douglas would be concerned about the issues of caregiving and the financial expense possibly related to her poor health, but he was not. In fact, he seemed much calmer after these problems began. Possibly, her health problems relieved his fear of abandonment that could have resulted from his wife's frequent threats to leave him when they were fighting. Maybe her poor health allowed Douglas to reconnect with his feelings of grief related to his first wife's death, which he had rushed to stifle by marrying his second wife so soon. Although his first wife was not ill for long, he had been actively involved in her care. During this time, his children were small, and he was anxious about their care. Although he felt more in control being close to his wife in her final days, he felt more out of control with his uncertain future for himself and his children.

Vacationing in Arizona each winter and not coming to weekly counseling sessions probably contributed to his growing belief that he was able to manage on his own. Douglas and his wife spent more time in Arizona each winter. He had time to realize that he was living his life successfully independent of a weekly therapy session.

Benefits and Difficulties of the Therapeutic Relationship for the Client and the Therapist

As I reflect on the years of therapy with Douglas, I wonder whether the time could have been shortened if I had been more assertive with him. Because insight was difficult for this client, I adopted an approach of pointing out therapeutic messages in a concrete manner. When he described an event and how he handled it, I drew parallels with our previous conversations. He always marveled at my memory for the details of his life, but I think that he had not looked for connections of meaning in his life to gain a greater understanding for himself. In addition, when he did gain insight as with the impact that his father's drinking had on his sleeping difficulties as an adult, he used this single insight to explain a large number of his previously unexamined feelings.

Throughout therapy with Douglas, I saw significant changes. At first, I wondered what progress I would be able to help him make. He was controlling of our time together, and I found him intimidating. I believe that my initial sense of intimidation by this client slowed our therapeutic process. I tiptoed around his anger as I tried to build a more open relationship with him. I felt too intimidated to discuss his anger as a therapeutic issue, which would have been the appropriate thing to do. As I got to know him better and understand the roots of his behavior, I realized how hard he was working to change and that his intimidating style was a cover for his feelings of vulnerability. He did not want to continue to feel victimized; instead, he wanted to feel in control and enjoy his retirement years. In the last year of Douglas's therapy, Mary had several illnesses as well as noticeable memory problems. These problems brought about compassion in Douglas toward his wife. He was less combative and was willing to attribute her sharp comments and belligerent manner to her poor health. He displayed great patience in handling her memory problems, and he willingly repeated information to her several times if necessary.

Words of Wisdom

It is important to consider the impact of gender differences between therapist and client as well as a significant age disparity. There was a 40-year difference in our ages; Douglas and I were raised in different eras. Under these circumstances, it was likely that Douglas felt uncomfortable with these differences and the power differential between us as the therapy began. His intimidating manner and initial gift giving could have resulted from his effort to gain control in a therapeutic relationship with a younger professional woman. The relationship moved from one in which he was trying to be friends to a more professional relationship. If the relationship had not moved in this direction however, then it would have been important to address these differences. Raising the issues in a direct manner is the beginning approach. Couching these comments in their historical relevance can minimize the feelings of being attacked personally. The therapist should view this as an educational experience and not as a crusade. If this is not successful, then changing to an older, male therapist might be in order. This decision should be based on therapeutic goals as well.

It takes time to integrate the past with the present for all people in counseling, but it may take longer for individuals who are unaccustomed to thinking in this manner. Older male clients may have a more difficult time building trust with a therapist, experiencing their feelings, and describing their feelings in words.

Consideration also should be given to the issues of transference and countertransference, dynamics of relationships that are often a component of therapeutic relationships. My sense of intimidation early in the relationship with Douglas was an example of parental countertransference. I found his direct and aggressive style similar to my own father's, and I responded as a child would to a parent. It is important not to act on these feelings but to examine them in the context of the therapeutic relationship. When these reactions are conscious, the therapist can obtain greater distance from these feelings by discussing them with a supervisor and thereby gain insight into handling them to the benefit of the client. When these feelings interfere with treatment, it may be necessary to transfer the client to another mental health care professional.

In Douglas's case, he could have seen me as his deceased spouse, as we were similar in age, thus having transference toward me. Spousal transference can provide a mechanism to resolve guilt feelings and, in Douglas's case, to gain contact with a period in his life when he felt more in control.

ADDITIONAL RESOURCES

Depression is a problem that many older people face. There is substantial literature that identifies factors related to depression. One sixth of the older adults in the United States experience clinically significant symptoms (Lebowitz, 1996). Even when symptoms do not meet the DSM-IV criteria for major depression, depressive symptoms are common among older adults (Unutzer, Katon, Sullivan, & Miranda, 1999). An article in *The Milbank Quarterly* described factors that contribute to depression in older adults as well as successful treatment approaches (Unutzer et al., 1999).

I have identified a few articles on transference that may be helpful to clinicians who work with older people. In Knight's (1996) book *Psychotherapy with Older Adults*, there is a chapter entitled "Transference and Countertransference with Older Clients." This chapter identified patterns that frequently emerge between the clinician and the older client using case examples, which clearly illustrate the issues at hand. A chapter entitled "The Inner World of the Therapist of the Elderly" in Muslin's (1992) book *The Psychotherapy of the Elderly Self*, is of value for its focus on the inner reactions of the therapist toward older clients, a neglected area. This author underscored the ubiquity of these "self intrusions" and identified common reactions that therapists have to older clients. Numerous and detailed case examples are presented to illustrate these reactions.

Last, it is important to consider the role of gender in the therapeutic relationship. An article by Levine (1996) focused on women in situations in which the client is older and the therapist is younger. Levine readily identified different expectations that arise from the age discrepancy between therapist and client when one holds prefeminist-era values and beliefs and the other does not. The cultural milieu in which people are raised has a profound impact on values and beliefs. This aspect of the client's and therapist's life should always be examined in the therapeutic relationship.

REFERENCES

Knight, B. (1996). *Psychotherapy with older adults*. Thousand Oaks, CA: Sage Publications.

Lebowitz, B. (1996). Diagnosis and treatment of depression in late life: An overview of the NIH consensus statement. *Journal of Geriatric Psychiatry* 4(Suppl. 4), S3–S6.

Levine, L. (1996). "Things were different then": Countertransference issues for younger female therapists working with older female clients. *Social Work in Health Care*, 22(4), 73–87.

Muslin, H.L. (1992). *The psychotherapy of the elderly self*. New York: Brunner/Mazel.

Unutzer, J., Katon, W., Sullivan, M., & Miranda, J. (1999). Treating depressed older adults in primary care: Narrowing the gap between efficacy and effectiveness. *The Milbank Quarterly*, 77(2), 225–256.

Recognizing Our Professional Limits

4

Shirley A. Thomas

CLIENT'S BACKGROUND

MARIE SMITH WAS AN INTELLIGENT, INDEPENDENT, AND DETERMINED 74-YEAR-OLD AFRICAN AMERICAN WOMAN. She had raised three children and worked in a large medical center until she resigned because of rheumatoid arthritis. Over the past 15 years, her health had deteriorated, but she had managed her own health care at home. Mrs. Smith was bedridden and could not move without assistance. She was incontinent and had diabetes and hypertension. As a result of her lack of movement and her diabetes, her legs and feet often were swollen with blisters and lesions.

Mrs. Smith was a widow and had one son and two daughters, none of whom were able to provide help. Both daughters lived out of state, and although her son lived in her basement, he was rarely home and provided little assistance. A nurse checked her blood pressure and blood sugar level and provided wound care several times a week. A home health aide cooked her meals, bathed her, and provided light housekeeping. A college student lived with her and was available to help in the evenings.

Mrs. Smith had reached her insurance limit for custodial care; as a result, her home care services had been reduced drastically. She was upset because her insurance company did not believe that she qualified for skilled care. In addition, the company reduced the number of home care hours for which they were willing to pay from 8 to 4, and social work services provided by the home health care agency were terminated. Mrs. Smith believed that she still needed the services and could not afford to pay for them herself. To complicate matters further, her live-in college student moved out.

Mrs. Smith was frustrated and decided to switch home care agencies; however, other home care agencies were setting the same limits on services. Because the insurance company had assessed that she was not in need of skilled care and she had exhausted her money for in-home services, they could not offer her services. She qualified for Medicaid; however, Mrs. Smith believed that the allocation from Medicaid still did not provide enough help. Although she had two insurance policies, neither company would pay for the extra hours. They told her that if she needed additional help, then she should consider a nursing facility placement. The home health care agency involved in her care made this assessment as a result of her inability to care for herself, the lack of family support, and her dwindling financial resources. For Mrs. Smith, a nursing facility placement was absolutely unacceptable. A referral was made for in-home counseling after Mrs. Smith reported to the home care social worker that she was depressed.

INTERVENTION SUMMARY

I provided in-home counseling to Mrs. Smith for approximately 4 months. Initially, we met weekly; after 6 weeks, the home visits were reduced to twice a month. Although there were several collateral contacts with social services agencies and numerous conversations with home care aides, the home visits primarily involved working with Mrs. Smith. The intervention goals were to help Mrs. Smith work through her depression, assess the feasibility of her living situation, and, if necessary, assist Mrs. Smith in making the transition from her home to a nursing facility.

Several consistent themes emerged during my work with Mrs. Smith, including the nature of providing in-home counseling, the thin line between care management and counseling, and the client as her own care manager. The intervention demonstrated how cultural similarities and spirituality could be used to enhance the therapeutic intervention process.

The first theme concerned the nature of in-home counseling. Providing in-home counseling to clients who are older and frail can be challenging. Often, the presence of relatives and/or caregivers can hinder the development of an open and trusting relationship. Likewise, when professionals such as nurses and home health aides are present, it is difficult to engage the client, and this can impede progress. The description of my first home visit with Mrs. Smith illustrates how visits often can be filled with unexpected interruptions. Remaining focused can be difficult for the client as well as for the practitioner.

Just before my first visit to Mrs. Smith, I called to let her know that I was on my way, and she indicated that I could come. When I arrived, however, the house was very busy. The telephone rang repeatedly, and the house was full of other helping professionals. Mrs. Smith was giving directions to the home health care aide and finishing up with the nurse when I entered the room.

Mrs. Smith's bedroom was nicely decorated. At the head of the bed stood a table that held her speakerphone and a blue plastic basket that contained her important papers. Several feet from the bed was her portable toilet beside which was a chest of drawers. There was a chart on the wall explaining the symptoms of low and high blood sugar levels. When I first met with Mrs. Smith, she was in her bedroom, sitting on the side of her hospital bed. She appeared small and frail. Her legs were stretched across a straight-back chair that was pushed up against the bed. Several feet across from the bed was another straight-back chair. This was the chair in which I sat for all of my visits.

After about 10 minutes, the nurse left and things seemed to quiet down; the aides were in the kitchen fixing Mrs. Smith's lunch. When I had the opportunity to talk with Mrs. Smith alone, the aides kept interrupting us with questions concerning her lunch. During my brief time alone with her, I informed Mrs. Smith that her previous social worker reported that she was depressed. I asked her whether she felt depressed. In a distracted manner, she responded that she had been a little down. I told her that I was there to provide in-home counseling concerning her depression. To this she said, "I remember now—she told me about you."

Mrs. Smith introduced me to both aides. After each introduction, she said, "Tell them where you're from, sweetie." One of the aides explained that she was no longer going to work with Mrs. Smith and that the other aide was in training to take her place. Mrs. Smith stated that she would miss her aide and remarked that it seemed as if "once you get them trained, they leave." The aide also explained that the little girl with her was her daughter. I asked her whether her daughter came with her every day, and she said no. At this point, Mrs. Smith stated that she did not mind the aide's bringing her daughter because she liked children.

Initially, Mrs. Smith was polite and friendly although somewhat guarded, and she seemed a little suspicious. She was in the middle of a crisis—finding more help. Although she seemed to be completely in control of the situation via the telephone, I observed her to be anxious and frustrated with a flat affect. Mrs. Smith asked me several times which agency I was from, and I repeated the information, including more detail each time. She also asked me whether the clinic was a part of the university hospital. I answered affirmatively, and she began to explain that she worked at the hospital for years and now they were "cutting me off." Because the university was her former employer, she believed that it had cut her off from services.

The second theme of our intervention also emerged during that first session: Gerontological practitioners often merge the roles of care manager and counselor. The very nature of in-home counseling as a method of intervention affords us an effective way to witness our clients' daily activities and observe their strengths in meeting daily challenges. In Mrs. Smith's case, her unmet physical needs contributed to her feelings of depression. As I attempted to help relieve her depression, I became involved in providing both care management and counseling. Although my role as care manager has been more extensive in other cases, with Mrs. Smith my care management included frequent calls to home health care agencies and insurance companies as well as numerous calls to try to assist Mrs. Smith in finding live-in help.

To assess the extent of her social support systems and to determine whether anyone else could be available to help her, I asked about relatives, friends, and church members. She told me that she had some friends, although her closest friends also were sick. Members of her church dropped by on occasion; however, according to Mrs. Smith, "When you are sick for as long as I have been, they forget you." I asked whether there was anyone she wanted me to call who could help her. In a very formal manner, she said, "Not at this time."

Mrs. Smith's desire to maintain control over the help that she was receiving was the third recurring theme in this case. Clients such as Mrs. Smith may need help but still exert considerable control over their own lives and, in fact, serve as their own care manager. This point was made clear to me during my first visit with Mrs. Smith, who talked on the telephone to try to arrange services with several agencies while I was present. After I was there for about 30 minutes and continually interrupted by her aides, I decided to come back when we could have more privacy. I told her that I would return and stay for about 1 hour. As an afterthought, Mrs. Smith asked me whether our conversations would be confidential. I told her that all of our conversations would be confidential. To this statement she nodded her head approvingly, and we decided on our next meeting time. The telephone rang again. She took her extender and hit the talk button and told me that she had to talk with this person; I excused myself and told her that I would be back in a week. She again demonstrated her control by asserting, "Okay, honey, we'll talk then."

On the way out of the house, I said goodbye to the aides; as her aide walked me out, she told me that she was glad that I was coming back because Mrs. Smith had been "real down lately." The aide also reported that she enjoyed working with Mrs. Smith. As I left her home, I remembered thinking that Mrs. Smith was denying the gravity of her living situation. I hoped that her current crisis would make her recognize her limits, face the reality of her situation, and reconsider a nursing facility placement. However, encouraging her to reconsider this decision while maintaining her sense of self and independence would be challenging.

An example of my providing care management was when Mrs. Smith asked me to discuss her situation with the various agencies that were involved in her care in the hope that I could convince them not to terminate her services. In a follow-up conversation with the home health care social worker, I was told that although Mrs. Smith reported that she was depressed, the agency referred Mrs. Smith to me because they believed that I could help her to make the transition from her home to a nursing facility. The previous social worker believed that Mrs. Smith's depression was probably the result of her beginning to realize that without a great deal of help, she was not going to be able to stay in her home much longer. The social worker reiterated to me that she had not met any of Mrs. Smith's children. She further stated that it was her understanding that Mrs. Smith's son was an alcoholic, which was why she could not depend on him consistently for help. I also discussed the case with a nurse from the home health care agency. The nurse reported that Mrs. Smith needed special care and that if her son or another family member was available, then they could be trained to dress her wounds as well as check her blood pressure and blood sugar levels. It should be noted that the conversations with the various agencies did not require me to violate Mrs. Smith's confidentiality because Mrs. Smith requested that I work with them on her behalf. Furthermore, the conversations did not require me to provide any additional information concerning Mrs. Smith.

At this point, I felt overwhelmed by Mrs. Smith's physical condition, and I was beginning to feel anxious and desperate about getting her additional help. I not only felt sad for her but I also felt inadequate because I was not able to do anything to help her with her most pressing problem—getting more help so that she could stay in her home. On the date of my next home visit, I again called Mrs. Smith before I left the clinic. This time she told me not to come because she was busy. She told me that she wanted me to come soon and talk with her about her depression but that she needed to work out her "help problem" first. Two weeks later, she was ready to see me.

Mrs. Smith and I decided that the purpose of my visits would be to allow her to talk and express her frustrations about not being able to find the help that she believed she needed. I believed that the most immediate issue for me, as the social worker, was to establish a relationship with Mrs. Smith and to assess the nature of her depression. Also, on a more personal note, I believed that it was important for me to remain flexible and spontaneous during our home visits, especially given the number of people coming in and out of her home. For me, being flexible and spontaneous meant not planning our time together. I believed that this was important for two reasons. First, reminding myself to remain flexible allowed me to relax during our time together. Second, by remaining calm, I enabled her to relax during our sessions as well.

To remain flexible and spontaneous proved to be the most challenging goal, particularly when I started working with Mrs. Smith. With so many agencies contacting her, she could not remember which agency I was from or which services I provided. This made it difficult to form a relationship with her and hard to get her to discuss her feelings. Several times when I arrived, she was frustrated from a conversation with the insurance company or home health agency. No matter how carefully we scheduled the home visits, a nurse or home health aide was always interrupting us. To handle these interruptions and to gain her respect and trust, I allowed my visits to be unstructured. The conversations were free flowing, and I followed her lead as to the topics we covered. Initially, I did not mention her need for a nursing facility placement because she had told me that she did not want to consider that option.

For several weeks, I let myself in through the unlocked front door and went back to her bedroom, calling her name to let her know that it was Shirley coming through the front door. Before I sat down, she often asked me to open her blinds and then we talked about her concerns. If anyone else came in, I remained seated until my time was up and then I left.

I always made a point of arriving and leaving on time to set boundaries around my time. Therefore, I was flexible to whatever circumstances were presented to me during our session and simultaneously set limits concerning my time. For example, Mrs. Smith asked me to look through all of the papers in her blue basket to find the telephone numbers of two insurance companies. This was not a difficult task because Mrs. Smith had asked the aide to alphabetically organize and date each letter. Although typically the home visits were not for this purpose, I did call the insurance agencies from her home for a fact-finding conversation that took place over the speakerphone. My involvement in this task served several purposes: It provided me with a clearer picture of what the companies were actually saying to her, it provided me with the opportunity to advocate for her, and it helped me to interpret for her any information that was not clear. I believed that this unstructured approach helped Mrs. Smith to expect my visits and realize that I was not leaving until my time was up. Also, this approach caused a change in Mrs. Smith's behavior: Eventually, she began not to allow our visits to be interrupted and began to discuss her sadness.

I also used self-disclosure to gain Mrs. Smith's trust. This may have been easier for me than it might have been for others because Mrs. Smith and I both are African American. Often, sharing with clients similarities such as race minimizes barriers. Sharing with clients similar languages and cultural practices can expedite establishing a therapeutic relationship, which was true for Mrs. Smith and me. For example, during one of my initial home visits, Mrs. Smith asked me where I lived, how long I had been in the area, and how long I had been working with older people. I explained to her that I came to the area to attend graduate school. She responded that she was proud of me. She also assumed that I knew little about the community. I explained that I had a lot of relatives in the area. To this she responded, "I think I may know your family." Although we did not specifically discuss my family members, my self-disclosure enhanced our therapeutic relationship because it resulted in a connection between us; as a result, Mrs. Smith seemed to be more relaxed during the visits.

Mrs. Smith rarely discussed her children, although I did meet her son. During several of the home visits, she repeated that she could not count on him; however, she never revealed why he was so unavailable except to say that he was out a lot. After a while, she told me that he got a job working at night and that she was pleased that he had a job. Mrs. Smith was estranged from her youngest daughter, whose husband was in the military, and she informed me that, the last she had heard, her daughter lived in North Carolina. Mrs. Smith never discussed her relationship with her youngest daughter or why they were estranged. Once she told me that "sometimes things happen that you cannot change."

During one home visit, she told me that her primary desire was to have her oldest daughter come to live with her; there was just a 14-year age difference between them. According to Mrs. Smith, they were very close, and, although they spoke frequently by telephone, Mrs. Smith missed her terribly. In exploring further the idea of her daughter living with her, she indicated that it was out of the question because her daughter also was very ill. When I asked about her daughter's illness, Mrs. Smith just said, "She has the same thing I have." I asked Mrs. Smith whether she was worried about her daughter because she was so sick. I wondered whether she wanted her daughter to live with her to be able to see for herself how her daughter was doing. To this, Mrs. Smith replied, "Mothers worry about their daughters and daughters worry about their mothers." I asked her whether her daughter knew the graveness of Mrs. Smith's situation, and she assured me that she did. I asked whether she thought that it would help if I called her daughter. She said no. On other occasions, I asked for her daughter's telephone number but she would not give it to me; she did not flatly refuse, she simply replied, "I will have to get it for you." These conversations were another example of how Mrs. Smith maintained control in managing her life and how I respected her wishes.

My home visits with Mrs. Smith primarily provided support to her as she discussed her frustrations and sadness concerning being sick and not having help. Working with her, I observed that Mrs. Smith was a sharp and articulate woman. She was in charge of her health care and the management of her living situation. Furthermore, her depression was related to situational adjustment rather than to clinical depression. Often, I complimented Mrs. Smith on her ability to manage as well as she did, given her limitations, to which she responded, "I have no choice. I can't just give up."

During the home visits, I suggested to Mrs. Smith that a lot of her sadness was related to her feelings of inadequacy about not being able to fulfill her own needs because of her deteriorating health. She explained that she was not sad often and that her faith sustained her. I asked her what happened that was different when she was sad and when she was not sad. She informed me that fighting to keep her help made her depressed. During the home visits, I began asking Mrs. Smith to articulate her exact thoughts as to when she began to have feelings of sadness. To maintain this focus was difficult for her. When she did, Mrs. Smith's thoughts always centered on the circumstances surrounding having a chronic illness without any help. After several weeks, her anxiety and anger decreased and her mood elevated tremendously. This change was largely the result of her finding another woman to live with her, and although she was getting only 4 hours of help per day, she felt more optimistic.

I remained concerned about her safety and the amount of time that Mrs. Smith was alone with the door unlocked. On the days of my visits, she would be alone for 3 hours, and on the remaining days, she could be alone for up to

4 hours. The door had to remain unlocked until the aide arrived because if the door was locked, the aide could not get into the house. However, giving the aide a key was not a good idea, according to Mrs. Smith. This concern was exacerbated by the unpredictability of the home health aides. They did not always come as planned, and a replacement could be slower in coming and often difficult to arrange. Also, her body remained in the same position until the arrival of an aide who could turn her. I ensured that she was as comfortable as possible before I left. For example, one afternoon, Mrs. Smith asked me to put on gloves (because of the blisters and lesions on her feet and legs) and move her feet from the chair to the floor because she was tired of her legs stretching out across the chair.

Often, therapeutic goals must be redefined on the basis of clarifying the needs of clients as well as changing circumstances. This was the case with Mrs. Smith. It was clear to me that helping Mrs. Smith make the transition from her home to a nursing facility was no longer a goal, especially given our conversations concerning her desire to live at home. Our conversations concerning nursing facility placement took place primarily because the home care agency that was providing her care called me several times to complain about Mrs. Smith's being too demanding and difficult. In addition, several of the new aides who were assigned to her refused to provide care. In discussing this situation with Mrs. Smith, she stated that the new aides that the agency sent were not trained. She reported the home care agency's behaviors and billing practices to her attorney, and then she changed agencies. Mrs. Smith assured me that when the time was right, she would go to a nursing facility.

I asked her to explain, given all of her frustrations concerning services, why she chose not to go to a nursing facility. She informed me that she was aware of the care that people received in nursing facilities and that as long as she was able, she would fight to stay in her home. I again told her that my concerns were for her safety, especially during the times when she was alone, sometimes at night and often with the doors unlocked. Mrs. Smith did not believe that my concerns for her safety were necessary because she had been alone before and there were no problems. She remarked once that she knew how to dial 911. By this point, Mrs. Smith had me convinced that living in her home was best for her at the time, particularly because she had hired another live-in person. I understood her determination to stay in her home and assured her that I would provide whatever support I could, which seemed to me at the time very little.

It has been my experience that within the African American community, the use of spirituality is a coping strategy, especially for older people. While working with Mrs. Smith, I recognized how important her spiritual beliefs were and decided to incorporate these beliefs into her treatment. I asked Mrs. Smith to explain her beliefs to me and used her interpretations to help achieve the goal of reducing her sadness. It seemed that as a very religious woman, she felt guilty about feeling sad, which I determined was the basis for her depression.

This issue came to the forefront after several weeks during which I encouraged her to express her sadness. Her therapeutic task was to schedule time to feel sad. This time was to be used for crying, praying, envisioning what she wanted to happen, or thinking about any regrets. After several weeks of discussing what emerged during her scheduled "sadness time," she shook her head, laughed, and said, "I did not schedule it." She explained how she felt guilty for feeling sad because God had blessed her; after all, she was not in a nursing facility. I asked her whether she believed that God knew her every thought. She said that she did. I then asked her why God did not know that she was already sad, and she started to laugh. She said that she thought I was right, because God knew her every thought. I pointed out that because God knew that she was sad, there was no need to hide it from him. I helped her to understand that it was acceptable to feel sad by explaining to her that when one's basic needs are not being met, it is difficult to "keep the faith." The important thing was to find ways to help her get out of her depressed moods. Together, we explored activities that she could do to help her when she felt "a little down." I gave her several suggestions, and she had some of her own that she believed would help (e.g., listening to books on tape, calling a friend, praying) when she was feeling sad.

Some of our visits were intense; however, I believed that humor kept the sessions from being too overwhelming for her and for me. During our visits, Mrs. Smith and I laughed often. After our discussion about feeling guilty about feeling sad, our visits were not as intense and she did not focus as much on the circumstances of her situation. Ultimately, Mrs. Smith informed me that she had decided that it was acceptable to feel sad about her situation every now and then, although not too often.

At this point, Mrs. Smith and I decided to see each other twice a month. It was also at this point that Mrs. Smith gave me her daughter's telephone number and permission to call. I believe that Mrs. Smith was ready for her daughter to come and that is why she told me I could call her. I informed Mrs. Smith that I would call her daughter the following week; however, when I returned, her daughter was already living with Mrs. Smith. Mrs. Smith explained that she had taken the initiative to call her and that she was relieved and pleased that her daughter was with her. Although Mrs. Smith was limited in what she could give to her daughter, she was still a mother. She believed that her daughter was with her because her daughter needed her. Her observation illustrates that clients who need help themselves may also be helping others.

Her daughter Naomi was very ill and seldom said much to me when I visited her mother. I informed Naomi about the services that my clinic offered. I asked her whether there was anything I could do for her, and she told me to "just see about Mom." It was clear that she believed that I was there for her mother and not for her. After her daughter's arrival, my visits were more sporadic, primarily because Mrs. Smith's health was deteriorating and she required more hospitalizations. According to her daughter, both of Mrs.

Smith's legs were infected and the infection was spreading, but Mrs. Smith refused amputation.

Mrs. Smith and I never really terminated our sessions. I visited her once in the hospital, and she informed me that she would call me when she needed me. Occasionally, she calls me when her services are not working and she needs some advocacy or she wants me to help her locate another live-in helper. When she does call, I make a "check-up" visit. I have noticed that when she returns home after each hospitalization, for a short period of time she receives additional assistance from the home health care agencies.

Mrs. Smith has a strong desire to continue to manage her own care. Running her household was an excellent way to remain in control of her situation. In the end, I agreed with her decision to remain in her home because of her managing skills and because she was willing to live with the consequences of her own choices. She had no regrets. According to Mrs. Smith, she would make the same choices again.

INTERVENTION ANALYSIS

This therapy began with my own assumptions about Mrs. Smith's inability to care for herself and to manage her home. My assumptions were fueled further by the information that I had received from the many social services agencies that were involved in her care. Mrs. Smith's case is a reminder to practitioners to remain open and sensitive to their older clients' desires. In general, the intervention is an example of the limits of clients in managing their own care as well as our own limits as helping professionals. This case illustrates how recognizing these limits is fundamental in providing services to older clients.

The lack of resources and the fragmentation of services prevent older adults from feeling as though their basic needs will be met. Although Mrs. Smith had access to more resources than most of my more impoverished clients, this in-home intervention demonstrates how the lack of resources that are available to older adults interferes with their emotional health and could lead to premature nursing facility placements. My brief intervention taught me many lessons in providing in-home counseling, working with multiple agencies, and providing culturally relevant intervention.

Demonstration of Respect

Although I doubted Mrs. Smith's ability to maintain her living situation, from the day I met her she had my respect. I demonstrated this respect by understanding her persistence and determination to control her destiny. I recognized that we were working in Mrs. Smith's home and took her lead as to whom she wanted in the room while we were talking and I allowed her to direct the home visits.

I also recognized that because Mrs. Smith was African American, it was important for me to demonstrate respect by not calling her by her first name, not telling her what to do, and never making her feel as though I thought I knew everything. Although these indicators of respect may be salient for all older adults, they are especially important for African Americans. Given their experience with covert and overt racism, many older African Americans remember not having their needs addressed when they received services from medical institutions in the past, and some are concerned that this lack of respect will continue. Although I am African American, I represented the health care institutions that discriminated against African Americans in the past, and I had to acknowledge this history.

Use of the Client's Strengths

Although Mrs. Smith's body had limitations, she was not bound by those limitations. I was amazed by her ability to manage her home and to fight for services despite her health problems and the lack of resources. Mrs. Smith used her religious faith to anchor her through difficult times. When she was not fighting for services, she was quick-witted and had a great sense of humor and a gentle spirit. Also, Mrs. Smith was aware of the resources that were available to her and did not mind asking for help when she believed that she needed it. In addition, she was capable of making the best decisions for herself and recognized her limits, as illustrated by her daughter's not coming to live with her until she believed that they needed each other. I believe that it took strength to live with a chronic and debilitating disease such as rheumatoid arthritis and face the challenges that she had for so many years. It was her faith and her need to be in charge of her own destiny that enabled me to assist her in working through her most depressed time.

Often, regardless of their circumstances, clients need an external source to validate that they have the capacity to achieve their goals. In this case, Mrs. Smith's goal was to stay in her home as long as possible. I used her strengths by reminding her of how her past resourcefulness had enabled her to overcome hardships, which fostered her sense of control over her present situation. Also, I used Mrs. Smith's spiritual beliefs to diminish her depression by helping her to understand that occasionally feeling sad did not mean that she was losing the essence of her faith. Furthermore, by recognizing Mrs. Smith's strengths, I was in a position to support her goal without as many reservations.

Blurred Boundaries

In my work with Mrs. Smith, there were many blurred boundaries. For example, most of my work in the community involved working with older African Americans; as a consequence, many of my clients knew each other, which was true in Mrs. Smith's case. This situation made it more difficult for me to protect her confidentiality. On occasion, I came into contact with clients who would talk about Mrs. Smith with me. They were concerned about Mrs. Smith and asked me to get her some help. I assured them that if she had been ill for as long as they said she had been, then I was sure that she had the services that she needed. Sometimes they shared with me information that I was tempted to discuss with Mrs. Smith. This approach was not appropriate because she had never discussed the matter with me herself. Once, I met with one of her former health aides. The aide told me about her frustration concerning the unavailability of Mrs. Smith's children. In this case, I changed the topic by shifting the focus to something more general, such as the availability of reliable in-home care, without disclosing any information about Mrs. Smith.

Another blurred boundary concerned the client's self-determination versus the therapist's assessment of those needs. In this case, Mrs. Smith believed that her depression was related to her lack of resources, and she had no desire to discuss any other therapeutic issues. For example, Mrs. Smith rarely discussed her children. Every time she did, it was in response to my questions. I kept encouraging her to explore her relationship with her son and her estranged daughter to determine whether there was a way to enhance their involvement with her and thereby provide her with more support. Mrs. Smith was reluctant to discuss this topic with me, and it became clear that it was futile to press her. Nevertheless, I was sometimes frustrated by believing that I could help her with this issue but not having her cooperation to do so. This frustration indicated to me that the boundary was blurred between Mrs. Smith's self-determination and my assessment of additional therapeutic issues.

A blurred boundary also emerged concerning who was my client. I was Mrs. Smith's social worker, but I also wanted to help her daughter, Naomi, despite Naomi's reluctance to accept my assistance. When I came to see Mrs. Smith, Naomi usually was lying on the couch in obvious pain. Mrs. Smith asked me to try to help her daughter. When I offered my assistance to Naomi, she indicated that she did not need my help. I offered my assistance more than once but eventually decided that continuing to pursue Naomi would not be respectful of her autonomy. I reasoned that she was aware of our services and capable of requesting help if she needed it.

Changes in the Therapeutic Relationship over Time

With many African Americans, the "helper" becomes integrated into an extended family role. This kind of role change occurred during my work with Mrs. Smith. Over time, Mrs. Smith became relaxed with me and much more trusting of me. Instead of viewing me as an outsider, I became her ally. She no longer needed to be told my name several times before recalling who I was, and she began to place limits on the people who could interrupt our visits. Mrs. Smith went from not remembering my name to telling her neighbors and close friends about the help that I provided her. In addition, Mrs. Smith did not want me to call her daughter. After her daughter arrived, however, Mrs. Smith wanted me to help her as well.

I believed that our therapeutic goals had been addressed. Mrs. Smith understood her feelings of sadness, and she no longer felt so upset when these feelings reemerged. Mrs. Smith was able to discuss her sadness without feeling guilty. Although she did not like the decisions of the insurance companies with which she worked, she was more accepting and not as angry as she was at the beginning of our work. Although we did have several conversations about it, Mrs. Smith never conceded to a nursing facility placement. It was my assessment that Mrs. Smith knew her physical and emotional limitations and that she would decide to make the move when she reached her limits. All of these changes were related to changes in our therapeutic relationship. Our work together changed our perceptions. Mrs. Smith's perception of her circumstances changed, particularly as it related to the insurance companies. My perceptions changed as to her ability to decide when she needed to go to a nursing facility. These changes in perception altered our therapeutic relationship and further opened the doors of communication between us.

Benefits and Difficulties of the Therapeutic Relationship for the Client and the Therapist

I believed that the home visits had a positive impact on Mrs. Smith because she needed someone who was supportive to whom she could vent her feelings and frustrations concerning the lack of help for her. Mrs. Smith told me on several occasions that she enjoyed our talks. I believed that she viewed me as a confidant and trusted me not to betray her confidence.

My work with Mrs. Smith had a tremendous impact on me. I learned a lesson in recognizing my own limits while allowing a frail client to make decisions about her own limits. Working with Mrs. Smith provided me with yet another example of how spirituality is woven into African American culture and serves as an important source of sustenance for many clients. Understanding the strength of her religious faith made it easier for me to identify with Mrs. Smith's determination and persistence against great odds. When I first met Mrs. Smith, I felt somewhat sorry for her. She was fighting so hard, and her desire to stay at home seemed so futile. I felt helpless and overwhelmed because there was little I could do to change her situation. After working with Mrs. Smith, however, I was able to acknowledge my professional limitations and to listen to and accept the decisions of my clients.

Words of Wisdom

Overall, I believe that my work with Mrs. Smith was a lesson in limits: the limits that we have as professionals in providing the resources needed to add to the quality of life for our clients and the limits that we experience as professionals when other agencies and family members want us to change our clients. In addition, this intervention demonstrates the limits that clients have in negotiating their own care as well as the repercussions that occur when anticipated support from insurance companies or family members begins to dwindle.

Often, social workers lose sight of a fundamental principle of practice: client self-determination. When we work with so many clients with similar problems, it is easy to assume that we know what is best for them. Even if we do not know what will work best, we know what will work better. My words of wisdom are just reminders that will enhance our intervention with some of our more challenging clients.

The first reminder is that practitioners need to apply a basic social work principle: Help clients to help themselves. Often, we forget this when working with frail clients. To this end, we must recognize the purpose of our intervention as the client sees it. As helping professionals, we may be able to comprehend the broader issues. However, intervening when our help has not been requested can be experienced as intrusive by our clients and may prevent clients from turning to us when they are ready to address other issues. Although it is important for us to have goals, these goals must be interwoven with those of the client and must occasionally be reevaluated to ensure that we are on the same path.

The second reminder is for helping professionals to be creative and flexible while they provide services. Intervention with clients cannot always be based on traditional therapeutic models, particularly when providing in-home counseling. The environment in the home has a tremendous impact on the therapeutic process. For example, it would have been easy to misinterpret Mrs. Smith's behaviors at the beginning of our working together as a form of resistance. Instead, I viewed them as part of the reality of her living situation and incorporated this situation into my work with her by allowing her the time that she needed to solve her "help problem" before we actually began working together.

The third reminder is to respect differences by allowing our interventions to be culturally relevant. This does not suggest that a helping professional must know all there is to know about the many cultures in the United States. It is a suggestion that we admit that we do not know everything and that we are willing to learn from our clients.

The final reminder is that a lack of resources creates an environment of anger and resentment. Furthermore, being told as a client that you do not know what is best for you further intensifies the situation. Some groups of older people are especially vulnerable because they do not have adequate financial resources to meet their needs. As a result, they may be overlooked. Such individuals need additional advocacy as well as frequent reminders that they also have our support and that we consider their needs in program planning.

ADDITIONAL RESOURCES

There are numerous resources that may enhance social work practice with clients who are similar to Mrs. Smith. Those interested in developing a strengths-based practice may find a book chapter by Saleebey (1997) helpful. Saleebey discusses the elements of strengths-based care management and illustrates how these principles can be applied when working with individuals, families, and communities. A book chapter and a training manual by Fast and Chapin (1997 and 2000, respectively) and an article by Sullivan and Fisher (1994) discuss the strengths-based care management model and how this approach can be applied to working with older adults. The authors encourage social workers to devote attention to the abilities and strengths of older adults rather than focus on their pathologies. Also, a book by Cox and Parsons (1993) discusses empowerment, one of the essential elements in providing strengths-based social work practice. This book is particularly important for practitioners because it not only discusses the external forces that impede the well-being of older adults but it also provides practice strategies that can be used to help to empower clients.

Several resources are available to practitioners who want to develop a better understanding of the challenges of living with a chronic illness. Wells's (1998) book A Delicate Balance: Living Successfully with Chronic Illness not only is helpful to practitioners but also can be shared with clients. This book is a personal account of the author's experiences with chronic illness as well as the experiences of others with chronic illnesses. This book discusses the need to maintain a balance between giving in to disease and denying that the illness exists. Another book, Psychosocial Aspects of Chronic Illness and Disability among African Americans (Belgrave, 1998), written from an academic perspective, discusses chronic illness among African Americans. Although the book does not focus on older adults in particular, it does provide the basis for an understanding of the unique psychosocial aspects of living with a chronic illness for African Americans.

A number of resources can assist helping professionals in developing culturally competent interventions for African American women. Boyd's (1990) chapter in The Black Women's Health Book: Speaking for Ourselves (White, 1990) discusses the need for African American women to work with culturally sensitive therapists and explains how psychotherapy can be more culturally diverse. The book is useful for practitioners and can be shared with clients of color who are reluctant to participate in therapy. Another helpful book chapter by Davis (1990) addresses depression and also may be shared with clients. The chapter is a powerful story of the author's own encounter with loss and depression. Although the focus of the chapter is not on the losses that accompany aging, the chapter is useful in providing a cultural perspective to the grief process. Davis also provides therapists with helpful suggestions on how therapists can improve their cultural sensitivity in working with African American clients and provides strategies that assist therapists.

Spirituality can be a particularly important source of strength for older African American women. A growing number of resources are available to practitioners who want to incorporate spirituality into their practice. Among these references, an article by Casio (1998) is especially helpful in explaining the differences between religion and spirituality and provides strategies for spiritual intervention.

REFERENCES

Belgrave, F.Z. (1998). *Psychosocial aspects of chronic illness and disability among African Americans.* Westport, CT: Auburn House.

Boyd, J. (1990). Ethnic and cultural diversity in feminist therapy: Keys to power. In E.C. White (Ed.), *The black women's health book: Speaking for ourselves* (pp. 226–234). Seattle: Seal Press.

Casio, T. (1998). Incorporating spirituality into social work practice: A review of what to do. *Families in Society, 79*(5), 523–531.

Cox, E., & Parsons, R. (1993). *Empowerment-oriented social work practice with the elderly.* Pacific Grove, CA: Brooks/Cole.

Davis, B.M. (1990). Speaking of grief: Today I feel real low, hope you understand. In E.C. White (Ed.), *The black women's health book: Speaking for ourselves* (pp. 219–225). Seattle: Seal Press.

Fast, B., & Chapin, R. (1997). The strengths model with older adults: Critical practice components. In D. Saleebey (Ed.), *Strengths perspective in social work practice* (2nd ed., pp. 115–131). New York: Longman.

Fast, B., & Chapin, R. (2000). *Strengths-based care management for older adults.* Baltimore: Health Professions Press.

Saleebey, D. (1997). Introduction: Power in the people. In D. Saleebey (Ed.), *Strengths perspective in social work practice* (2nd ed., pp. 3–19). New York: Longman.

Sullivan, W.P., & Fisher, B.J. (1994). Intervening for success: Strengths-based case management and successful aging. *Journal of Gerontological Social Work, 22*(1–2), 61–74.

Wells, S.M. (1998). *A delicate balance: Living successfully with chronic illness.* New York: Insight Publishing.

White, E.C. (Ed.). (1990). *The black women's health book: Speaking for ourselves.* Seattle: Seal Press.

Playing Multiple Roles in Home-Based Therapy

5

Mary Rumman

CLIENT'S BACKGROUND

GRACE REED WAS AN INTELLIGENT WOMAN IN HER MID-70S WHO WAS RETIRED FROM TEACHING HIGH SCHOOL HISTORY. She had been married and had two children, now grown. Her oldest, John, was married and lived across the country. Her youngest, Julie, was also married and lived about 2 hours away in an adjoining state. Grace had been widowed for 20 years, at which time she experienced a period of depression but successfully went on with her life with support from friends and family. After retirement, she threw herself into many activities, including short trips and bingo. With her love of the arts, she joined a writing group and wrote many creative stories as well as some memoirs.

At 70, Grace experienced weakness in her legs and began to fall frequently. She was diagnosed with amyotrophic lateral sclerosis (ALS), a progressive, fatal neuromuscular disease that attacks nerve cells and pathways in the brain and spinal cord. It causes physical deterioration of all limbs, speech, swallowing, and breathing and eventually leaves people paralyzed but with their minds unaffected.

Grace quickly found it challenging to get around and needed a walker. Her speech became more difficult to understand. Consequently, she received some speech and physical therapy services at home. She also frequently experienced severe headaches. Although Grace was emotionally close to her son, he worked all day and could not care for her. Instead, she moved to her daughter's apartment to live with her and her husband. This move was the most sensible solution because her daughter did not work outside the home and her son-in-law's business sent him on frequent trips. She moved to their two-bedroom apartment and had her own room and bathroom. They shared the common living areas. Most of Grace's furniture was put in storage, except for her bedroom furniture and her piano. They had one car, but Grace could not get into it without help and there was no public transportation near their apartment.

After the move, Grace began to see a geriatrician and a neurologist at the hospital in a nearby town. The neurologist authorized physical and speech therapy services in her home through a local home health agency. A social worker from the agency also visited her every other week. Her physician prescribed an antidepressant medication for her. When the in-home Medicare benefits ended, a referral was made by the visiting social worker for in-home counseling services because Grace continued to be depressed and tearful. The social worker also noted that Julie had trouble coping with her caregiving role.

It was at that point that I began seeing Grace in her home. My visits were funded by a grant administered through the Area Agency on Aging that allowed me to do in-home counseling with county residents. We did not charge a fee but informed clients that they could make donations. Grace was also a patient at our geriatric medical clinic, which would ease future coordination of care. I worked with Grace for about 9 months.

INTERVENTION SUMMARY

During our initial sessions, Julie was at home, but later she used that time to do errands. Sometimes I talked with Grace in the living room and sometimes in her bedroom, depending on where Julie was. Grace was a small woman with a welcoming smile and a keen sense of humor. On the couch, she was surrounded by her necessities, including a box of tissues, a tray with water and her crossword puzzle book, and her cane.

It was clear from the beginning that ALS already had begun to affect her speech. Speaking took great effort; when Grace spoke, she was difficult to understand, especially when I first met her. Luckily, she was accommodating and willing to repeat herself when I did not understand what she said. Also, she lived in a very quiet place where there were no distracting noises with which to compete. Because of the laboriousness of communication, I found it a challenge to condense my questions so that they could be answered briefly. Eventually, Grace wrote instead of spoke her thoughts to me. She was always eager to communicate and did not let her communication problems get in her way if she could help it.

Grace's therapy and goals were tied closely to the changes in her disease process and her associated coping or coming to terms with each stage. At the beginning of therapy, she expressed a goal to regain her independence and vitality. Grace clearly had been an independent person who had led a full life up until her illness. Although she was grateful to her daughter for taking her in, she was not ready to succumb to her illness and wanted to keep doing as much as she could for herself. Her daughter, conversely, was ready to serve her and was overly solicitous at times and did not always give her mother sufficient opportunity to be independent.

Grace loved to read, and early on I was able to connect her with the local library and its home delivery program. She also liked bingo but could not play at the apartment complex because the stairs to the clubhouse were prohibitive. Unfortunately, I was never able to find a way for her to go out to play bingo because she lived in an area where there was no public transportation or senior centers that were close enough to arrange a ride for her, especially because she required help. Grace also cooked many of the meals for the family as her way of contributing, even though Julie would have to set out the food for Grace to prepare as Grace's ALS progressed.

Grace wanted to continue to walk. When we began our therapy sessions, she used a cane but soon moved to a wheeled walker. Even with this, she could go only short distances. Although she was encouraged by health professionals to walk to maintain endurance, her daughter was fearful that she would fall and did not like to walk with her. Grace said that her daughter wanted her to wait until she got stronger. Grace expressed frustration to me about this situation but at the same time did not want to make Julie do more than she felt able. Grace preferred not to impose on her even if it was detrimental to herself (Grace). Julie became nervous when she expressed concern about her mother.

Because I knew that, without regular exercise, strength can wane quickly and that decreased mobility can lead to decreased independence, I wanted to intervene but felt limited by Grace's concerns about her daughter. With Grace's permission, I educated Grace (who was already aware of this) and Julie about the benefits of exercise and the increased risks that are associated with decreased mobility. I tried to do this in a matter-of-fact way so that Julie would not feel criticized. I also went on a brief walk with Grace each time I visited, both to give her exercise and to model to Julie the importance of walking. Grace was always glad to get out as she was virtually homebound except for doctor's appointments. This intervention was somewhat helpful, and Grace took walks by herself on nice days. Julie remained fearful that her mother would fall, both because she did not want her to break any bones, thus becoming more disabled, and because she tended to panic in emergency situations. She would go on walks with Grace only occasionally. As the weather got colder, however, Grace's walking decreased again, and a few months later, her disease had progressed to the point that she needed a wheelchair.

Grace and I also discussed her depression and the ways in which she coped with it. She told me that some of the ways she fought her own depression were to "get busy," "talk myself out of it," and to exercise. I tried to use her identified strength of "get busy" in therapy by exploring her talents and interests and encouraging her to use her creativity therapeutically. For example, I encouraged her to continue to play the piano as she had done previously. She was an accomplished pianist but had rarely played since moving in with her daughter. She expressed concern about bothering her son-in-law, who sometimes slept during the day. Despite these obstacles, I encouraged her to play for me one day when we had the apartment to ourselves. She clearly enjoyed the experience, and her playing was expressive. I suggested that she play more regularly because it relaxed her and was a way for her to express her emotions through music. She could choose pieces that matched her mood (e.g., a loud, fast piece through which she could work out anger) or those that helped her to change her mood (e.g., a happy or playful piece). She agreed that playing the piano was something she missed and that it helped her to relax. As a homework assignment, she agreed to play the piano twice a week. She followed through on this assignment and chose times when nobody was home. She reported that playing was helpful to her and was a good way to release some of her pent-up emotions. At times while playing, she cried.

Crying became a theme in our counseling. Grace felt a lot of sadness as a result of her losses and became tearful easily. Because of the nature of our conversations, she discussed this sadness in therapy, and there were times when crying was good for expressing this sadness. When she cried, however, it sometimes was problematic because the tears combined with the excess saliva from ALS would leave her susceptible to choking, a symptom of her disease process. Also, crying further compromised her already-difficult communication. She was self-conscious about keeping up a good front for her daughter and told me that she did not like for her daughter to see her cry. Again, she was concerned about not putting too much of a burden on her daughter, partially because if her daughter knew that she was sad, then she would become overly concerned.

In working with Grace, I always needed to strike a delicate balance between encouraging her to express how she felt and protecting her desire to maintain composure for her daughter's sake. Other than her son, who lived far away, I was the only person with whom she could safely "let it out." When I wanted to conduct more in-depth discussions, I chose days when Julie was out of the house, and I made our therapeutic conversations less intense on other days. I also asked Grace's permission to discuss certain topics on certain days. During one memorable session when she played the piano for me, she broke down crying and stopped playing, saying, "My daughter is going to be home soon. I don't want her to see me crying."

As Grace's disease progressed, her initial goals of increasing independence were not as realistic and the goal to maintain her abilities and stay in the apartment became more realistic. My counseling role became augmented by care management tasks. I helped her get information about obtaining the needed assistive devices to maintain her independence, including a raised toilet seat and a TTY (a teletypewriter), which allows someone to have a telephone conversation with another individual through a special telephone relay center by typing a communication and having it verbally transmitted to the other person. I brought Grace information on equipment that she could purchase and how to obtain it. I believed that it was important to assist with locating these items, especially because they related to Grace's goal of staying at home.

Grace talked about her condition each time I saw her and reviewed all of the changes that had taken place. Some weeks she had severe headaches; during other weeks, her speech was worse. At one point, she was concerned about decreased tongue action. Subsequently, I contacted her doctor to discuss speech therapy, and her doctor authorized a few more sessions. Grace was diligent about doing her exercises.

As her condition worsened and it became clear that it was not going to improve, we used her creativity in a different way through a modified life review process. During this time, she began to pull out and read some of the things that she had written in her creative writing class or earlier in her life. This activity was sparked by my questions and interest in her writing. By looking at these writings together, she could review many of the highlights of her life. Because she had already written many stories about her life, I did not ask her to generate new ones, as might be done in a more traditional life review, but rather reviewed what she had already written and encouraged her to talk about their meaning. This modified life review process was a strong validation of her self-worth. I praised her for her work, which was well written and often comical. This, in turn, inspired her to show me more and share her pride in her accomplishments (e.g., being a published author). This process reinforced her as a person and put the disease in a secondary role.

In sharing her writing, her natural strength as a giving person came through. During our therapy, I had told her that my 6-year-old son was learning to play the piano. During one of our sessions, she pulled out a musical composition that she had written for a small child and asked me to give it to my son. She was excited to share her composition and enjoyed hearing about his response later. I also told her that I was leading a short-term writing group for older adults for the first time. At the next visit, she was ready with materials from her own writing group that she hoped I could use. By allowing myself to be the student and Grace to be the mentor, we found a comfortable way for her to continue to give and teach, which was her life's work. It was one way in which she could pass her legacy to the next generation and remain connected with the world around her. It was also during these sessions that she gave me a necklace with an "R" on it, an initial we both share. Although agency policy suggests that we not accept gifts from clients, I accepted graciously because this was a clear symbol to me that she was putting her life in order.

As was expected, Grace's condition declined as we entered the third phase of therapy. Her abilities were inconsistent: On some days she could dress herself and get to the bathroom, on others she could not. During one visit, I had to help Grace into the bathroom and transfer her onto the toilet because she was not able to do this on her own. Her daughter, although kind-hearted, continued to feel nervous about the very real events that could occur (e.g., her mother's falling, having to suction her throat if she began to choke, having difficulty with getting her to the bathroom). Because of these concerns, Julie began to feel more inadequate and scared about her caregiving role. On a number of occasions, I talked with her about other resources that could help her, and she did hire some home health caregivers to help in areas such as bathing. Julie had also attended an ALS support group and had contact with the social worker through that group as well.

It was during this time that Grace asked me about feeding tubes. An unfortunate consequence of her ALS was the potential for choking that could require suctioning. Grace had been suctioned before, but the need to do so was increasing. Part of the difficulty was that the muscles in her throat lost their resilience and her swallowing was altered. Whenever there was increased saliva in her throat, she was susceptible to choking. It was hard for her to eat and get enough nutrition for her daily needs. By eliminating eating from her lifestyle, she had less chance of choking. I checked with her doctor and brought Grace articles and information about feeding tubes and their pros and cons, which we discussed in some depth. As in many conversations before, she weighed the advantages and disadvantages in light of the stress that it would create or alleviate for her daughter. Although Grace clearly was concerned about the procedures involved with a feeding tube and the additional loss of eating and tasting, she was most concerned about decreasing the potential of choking. The final decision to accept the feeding tube came after a terrifying incident in which she began to choke during dinner and her daughter had to suction her throat. Grace did not want to put her daughter through this stress, and the potential of choking was frightening to both of them.

To me, the most important turning points in our therapy had less to do with specific therapeutic interventions than with the progress of her disease. Although I had introduced at the beginning of our therapy the subject of her disease being progressive and eventually terminal, it was not our main focus. Rather, it was a backdrop to the losses that she was experiencing. I played a supportive role as her understanding and acceptance of ALS progressed. Grace was a strong person who had survived many hardships, but because she experienced the grief in this case on so many levels (e.g., physical losses, lifestyle changes, the anticipation of her own death), her previous coping skills were now insufficient and required another person to keep her focused on the tasks of grief in a healthy way. I provided through this process the emotional support that her daughter could not. I could listen to her pain and accept it as a necessary part of grieving, whereas Julie perceived the pain as something she needed to fix, thus stifling her mother's grieving process. Ultimately, however, I found Grace to be the leader in her coping process. I found this inspirational as I watched her and supported her through each change.

After the incident in which Grace choked at the dinner table and Julie had to cope with an emergency situation, Julie investigated nursing facilities with the help of the support group social worker. During a therapy session, Grace told me that she was going to live in a nursing facility, and she was resigned to the decision. She did not want to leave home but at the same time was concerned about the stress that caregiving placed on her daughter. Unfortunately, the nursing facility chosen was in another county and funding did not pay for the continuation of my counseling services. When I realized that funding for counseling would terminate, I told Grace that I would try to visit her occasionally, but I knew that the amount of time would be significantly reduced, because we had been having sessions almost weekly. I found a peer counselor volunteer, Norma, who was associated with our clinic but lived in the town to which Grace was moving. Grace agreed to allow this volunteer to visit her on a regular basis. Norma had been a speech therapist before retirement, so she was comfortable with the speech issues that she would encounter with Grace. She was also fairly comfortable in medical settings, which was a real advantage.

Over the next few months, I visited Grace three times and Norma went a few times per month. I was in regular contact with Norma and was able to send messages to Grace through her. As mentioned previously, Grace and I shared a love of music. A nearby opera house was being renovated, and I told Grace that I was going to see an opera there. Grace remained interested in the outside world until her death. Through Norma, I sent Grace a copy of the program showing the newly renovated opera house. She received this program a few days before she died.

My visits to the nursing facility were different from my visits to her home. First, it was more difficult to have privacy, especially because she had to be in bed some of the time. Even when the door was closed and her roommate was out of the room, staff would interrupt occasionally. In addition to being there in a supportive role, I played an advocate role at times. For example, Grace described an experience with a nursing assistant who spoke harshly to her. I found the supervising nurse and reported what Grace had told me. Although initially defensive, in part because she did not know me, the supervisor said that she would address the situation. Later, I followed up with the supervisor, who said that the nursing assistant had been confronted about her behavior. Through Norma, I found out that Grace's relationship with this nursing assistant had improved and she had apologized to Grace.

Although Grace preferred to be at home, the nursing facility provided socialization opportunities that she had not had at the apartment, and she was finally able to join in some bingo games. Grace adjusted fairly well to being in the nursing facility and prepared for her death as her illness progressed. I was not with her when she died but was thankful that Norma saw her only a few days before.

INTERVENTION ANALYSIS

There were many interesting facets to my work with Grace. For one, issues of loss and grief were central to the counseling process as she prepared for her death. Also, the specific disease progression of ALS affected the way in which the therapy was conducted and the education that was necessary for both of us. Another factor was the special accommodations in the therapeutic relationship that were made within a home setting versus an office setting and the family's interaction. Finally, we experienced a break in our therapeutic relationship as a result of her making the nursing facility decision.

Demonstration of Respect

I showed Grace respect in various ways. First, I gave Grace ample time to communicate her thoughts and adjusted my communication on the basis of what her needs were that day. It was a challenge to me to alter my questions so that they could be answered briefly while addressing the crucial issues. I tried not to intrude too quickly but found that I sometimes talked more than I would in a typical session and framed questions in a slightly mFore leading manner. I did this in part because I wanted to conserve Grace's energy and use of words. I welcomed feedback from Grace and observed her cues, verbal and facial, if I asked questions too fast or if the questions were too personal. As noted previously, I also tried to respect her need to maintain her composure by choosing only the totally private sessions in which to focus on deeper issues. I frequently asked her permission to discuss certain subjects, for example, how she was feeling about her illness, her death, and her relationship with her daughter.

Another way in which I respected Grace was to let her direct how to work with Julie. Although there were times when I believed that Julie's approaches did not maximize Grace's potential, I did not interfere. It was clear that one of Grace's primary concerns was protecting her daughter from stress, and it would have been counterproductive to interfere. I let Grace be her own advocate with her daughter. A third way in which I showed Grace a great deal of respect was during the life review process when we shared Grace's writing. Through this process, I validated who she was as a person.

Use of the Client's Strengths

One obvious strength was that Grace had been good at coping with other challenges and losses in her life, and it was only the intensity and multiplicity of these new losses that required additional support. Another strength was her strong family ties. Not only did she have two caring children but she also had two siblings living in the state, both of whom she saw during the months that I worked with her. She told me about a visit with her brother in which they laughed the whole weekend. Her son gave her a fax machine, and she corresponded frequently with him. Because Grace could manipulate her pencil more easily than her mouth, writing down her thoughts was an ideal way for her to communicate with him and with me. She and her son viewed the world more similarly than she and Julie did, and she was able to express her emotions more easily with him without fear that he would become overly concerned.

Grace's creativity clearly was a strength and was put to use many times during our sessions. She enjoyed reviewing her writing and being validated for her work. In retrospect, it may have been a good tactic to encourage her to write to express herself as a therapeutic intervention. I did not do this, partly because of the enjoyment that she seemed to get from looking at the past. At this point in her life, she seemed to be tying up loose ends and reviewing her life rather than wanting to generate new ideas. As noted, her writings often were humorous and served as comic relief to some of her physical struggles. She displayed a strong sense of humor that we both used to full advantage.

Another strength was Grace's fierce independence, which allowed her to persevere even when her health diminished. At one point, she told me that she was strong like her mother. She was interested in the world around her up until her death. She continued to do things for herself as long as she could and always wanted to help in the home setting as much as possible (e.g., by cooking).

Blurred Boundaries

I really liked Grace. We had many common interests, including music, theater, and writing. Had we met under different circumstances, perhaps cast in a play together, we would have become fast friends. She was easy to like, and we shared a sense of humor, making our visits sometimes more fun than one would normally ascribe to a therapy session. We both found that laughter was therapeutic when coping with Grace's serious illness. Together we laughed at her stories and I sometimes shared anecdotes that I thought she would enjoy. More important, she had an ability to laugh at herself and find humor in her struggles. This is a strength that not everyone has, and I encouraged her to use it to her advantage. For Grace, humor was therapeutic because it took her focus away from the negative and led her to a greater acceptance of her situation and losses. Also, laughing felt good.

As noted previously, Grace gave me a silver necklace with an engraved letter on a glass-like pendant. I struggled with whether I should accept this gift, as it blurred the professional boundaries. On one level, this felt uncomfortable to me because gift giving is not considered appropriate within a therapeutic relationship, but on another level, it was important to her because it was a way in which she could give. In this case, I also believed that refusing would interfere with her process of tying up loose ends.

In general, I have found that with older clients, the professional boundaries do become slightly more blurred than with younger clients. Sometimes to gain trust, helping professionals need to give older people a sense of who they are, especially when coming into a client's home. To gain their trust, I sometimes reveal a little more about myself than is "textbook appropriate." For me, this disclosure usually revolves around minimal family facts and interests. In

Grace's case, I told her that I was married and had a son, that our family is musical, and that I was going to the opera (bringing a little of the outside world in). Sometimes I reveal to a client the general area where I live, especially if he or she is from the same or a nearby town, because it can help the client to know that I am local and have a good sense of their roots. I rarely give out my home telephone number unless I feel confident that it will not be abused and there is a specific need for it.

Providing therapy in someone's home and being on the client's turf can be very different from a traditional therapeutic approach. You do not have the control that you have in an office setting. With Grace, we sometimes had privacy when Julie left on errands. At other times Julie was at home, which limited our conversation and prevented Grace from fully expressing herself for fear that she would lose control with her daughter nearby. In later months, our sessions often took place in Grace's bedroom, bringing up questions about where to sit and what is proper etiquette in a bedroom. Although it is preferable to sit in a chair, there were times when I could not do this because of the layout of the bedroom and the need to be close enough for Grace to write notes to me.

Another issue that emerged was Grace's increased care needs. Out of necessity, I found myself doing things that are not normally done in a traditional counseling setting, such as getting a tissue to clean up saliva, taking her on walks, walking her to the bathroom, and helping her with minor dressing such as putting on shoes and socks. Having worked in a nursing facility for years, I felt comfortable with this blurring of roles, but it was not always easy for Grace because it stripped her of more independence. I let her know that I felt comfortable helping her but would wait for her direction, be it a hand gesture or a written note, about when she wanted help.

Refreshments sometimes were an issue. Especially at the beginning of our therapy, Grace always had at her side a glass of something to drink and offered me the same thing. It is a polite thing to do, and I accepted. I have been to the homes of other clients when it has not been so easy to accept refreshments because of unclean conditions, insects, and so forth, and I have struggled with what to do. Sometimes to be polite, I have taken a "doggie bag" home with me to avoid eating something on the spot.

Another way in which the home setting was different was that on at least one occasion, I needed to call my office for messages and had to ask Grace's permission to use the telephone. I try to avoid this as much as possible, but when on the road for a period of time, it is sometimes necessary to use a telephone. On a few occasions, I had to avoid letting her cat out or was asked to let the cat out. Although I am not a pet lover, this was a minor request.

Changes in the Therapeutic Relationship over Time

Our relationship was affected by two main factors: the physical decline precipitated by Grace's ALS and her move to the nursing facility. Because of the changes in her physical condition, Grace's goals also changed from wanting to increase independence (by walking and cooking more) to maintaining independence (by transferring herself independently to the toilet and cooking with food set out for her) to coping with further decline and preparing herself for it (by learning about adaptive devices and feeding tubes). She continued to strive for her maximum potential despite the changes that she encountered, and I supported her efforts at independence. As the inevitability of the disease became manifest, she began to consider her own death and legacy within the safety of the counseling relationship. It was at this point that the counseling relationship moved from a focus on grieving her losses to reviewing her life and putting the pieces in place.

Another shift in our relationship occurred when Grace moved to the nursing facility. I tried to remain supportive, but our visits were constrained by the setting and centered on her adjustment there and her physical decline. As noted previously, I added the role of advocate as I tried to intervene with the staff when Grace expressed concerns. It was hard for both of us when I had to decrease our visits because I had been available to her as an emotional support through so many physical and emotional changes. Fortunately, I was able to find through our agency a peer counselor who lived near her and could visit her. Through this volunteer, I was able to maintain contact with Grace and she could keep in touch with me. Unfortunately, I was able to see Grace only three times after she moved into the nursing facility until her death.

Benefits and Difficulties of the
Therapeutic Relationship for the Client and the Therapist

Probably the biggest benefit for Grace was to have someone with whom she could express her feelings. She was not able to share much with her daughter, and her son lived too far away to talk with him consistently. The difficulty was finding the right time to have more in-depth discussions when her daughter was not nearby. This frustrated me at times, especially when I believed that Grace would have had more to share if her daughter were not so close. At the beginning of and through the whole therapeutic process, I served as a good listener and guided Grace through her grieving process. As her condition worsened and she began to tie up loose ends, her natural bent as a teacher and giver emerged and I was sometimes the recipient. By adding another set of roles, she became a mentor and I was her student, which gave her a feeling of usefulness and control. Another benefit was that I was able to share information about her disease and help her make some difficult decisions. In addition, sharing humor proved important to Grace because, at her daughter's apartment, the atmosphere was fairly serious.

For me, the benefits of our relationship were many. I became very attached to Grace and enjoyed working with someone with whom I had so much in common. A close family member of mine had recently died from ALS, so I felt a special kinship with her and perhaps a deeper understanding of what this disease was like for her. I lived too far away from my family member to be intimately involved in his care, so Grace's case was an opportunity for me to support someone else. I was pleased with my ability to let Grace guide her own therapy. Even though I took the lead in asking her questions because of her difficulty in communicating, I followed her lead about what she wanted to discuss. For example, by observing Grace, I was gentle in my interactions with Julie. Even though I believed that at times Julie inhibited her mother, I had to learn to respect the choice that Grace made to live in this setting.

Grace also demonstrated for me how to live with adversity. ALS presents a terrifying disease progression, and although she struggled through it, she maintained a deep caring for others and was concerned about how her illness affected them. She was interested in life and continually wanted to learn new things, even near her death. She did not succumb to despair even though it would have been reasonable, given her rapid disease progression. She was able to call on her strengths to help her through the difficult times. She was an impressive role model.

Words of Wisdom

Counseling someone in his or her home is different from counseling in an office setting. The therapist has much less control over the environment, and being a guest in someone's home means respecting his or her rules. In addition, the home environment can muddy the therapist/client roles somewhat, making it easier for a client to perceive the therapist more as a friend or a friendly visitor. This blurring of roles can have advantages and disadvantages. One advantage is that being seen initially as a friendly visitor (e.g., "Is it okay if I come to see you?") is sometimes the only way to connect with someone who is hesitant about undertaking a therapeutic relationship. Another advantage is that it can provide an easier and more casual way of meeting family members and friends and thus viewing the whole picture in a short time. One disadvantage, of course, is that clients may not take the suggestions or directions that the therapist offers as seriously as they might in an office setting. It sometimes requires the therapist to remind the client of the purpose of the visits and to refer to the therapeutic goals. I have found that maintaining a balance between these roles can be helpful.

In the same vein, in-home counseling can lead to establishing other roles. Had my relationship with Grace been conducted strictly in an office setting, I would not have seen as easily her physical deterioration and how it affected her daughter. I would not have seen the joy that she felt when going through her boxes of writings. I would not have perceived as clearly her lifestyle and the barriers in her living situation to keeping up with her walking, piano playing, and so forth. For that matter, I would not have discovered how playing the piano helped her to release her emotions. By witnessing these aspects of

Grace's life, I was drawn into other roles, such as detective, resource expert, walking partner, concert goer and reporter, student, and helper. I believe that these additional roles served to enrich and strengthen our therapeutic relationship.

A few other issues have presented themselves to me during home visits. One is smoking. Being a nonsmoker, it is sometimes difficult to enter the homes of clients who smoke. If they came to my office, then I would ask them not to smoke and tell them where it is appropriate to do so, but when the session takes place in their homes, I do not believe that I have the right to do this. Fortunately for me, most of my smoking clients have been sensitive to nonsmokers' issues and have asked if I would prefer that they not smoke.

Another issue that has come up for me during home visits is television. Many people have the television on in their homes for much of the day. I find it distracting during a visit, not only for my client but also for me. I have dealt with it by saying something such as, "Could we turn it down a little bit because I'm having trouble hearing you?" Some clients volunteer to turn it off. On one occasion, though, watching a television show took half of the session: I happened to arrive at a client's home just as the space shuttle carrying John Glenn was being launched. She was excited about this historic moment, ushered me to a chair, and called her son from another part of the house to watch. The three of us watched the launch in her bedroom, and our session could not begin until it was over.

It often becomes necessary when providing in-home counseling, as well as working with older adults in general, to assume the role of care manager. Because I was the only outside professional coming to Grace's home at that time, I helped her to maintain her independence and sense of well-being by seeing things that she needed and helping her get them (e.g., raised toilet seat, library services). In this case, meeting most of her needs was well within my expertise and jurisdiction, because I worked in the clinic where she received her medical care. I would have been negligent if I did not help Grace with these needs. There have been times, however, when care management issues have overwhelmed the counseling issues. One client had such significant financial problems that unless I paid attention to those first, counseling could not occur. In that case, I assisted with the financial issues that I could and made sure that the appropriate agencies helped her with her other needs.

Although I believe that I followed Grace's wishes in dealing with Julie, in hindsight, perhaps I should have more intentionally supported Julie. As it was, my outward support of Julie was left to brief discussions at the door and giving her resource information. Another way in which I supported Julie was by giving Grace an outlet to express her concerns, an area that was difficult for Julie to handle. I did not want to overwhelm this emotionally fragile woman by making demands on her, but at the same time, it is possible that Grace's quality of life could have been improved had I worked harder to give Julie the support that she needed to help her mother. Were I to do this again, I would, with Grace's permission, have attempted to schedule a session or two with Julie or with Julie and Grace together to discuss caregiving issues.

Peer counselors are incredibly important when working with older adults. In social work, it is tremendously helpful to be able to match a client with a caring individual who will forge a friendship. In this case, the peer counselor in essence took my place by extending the work that I had started with Grace. In other cases, I have used a peer volunteer for friendship and companionship while I continued the therapeutic relationship with a client.

As I look back over Grace's case, I realize that many of the turns in the therapy were precipitated by changes in Grace's illness, not by my therapeutic interventions. In the final analysis, I recognize the worth of just being there. It seems so simple, but the fact is that sometimes being there to hear someone express his or her pain is the most important part of helping someone grieve. I gave Grace a safe place to release her emotions, losses, and fears. By doing so, I encouraged her to find her natural strengths and to use them to carry on with the task of grieving.

ADDITIONAL RESOURCES

ALS is a disease that is not as widely known as some, although it has been popularized in the press through the debates about the work of Dr. Jack Kevorkian and physician-assisted suicide and by the best-selling book *Tuesdays with Morrie* (Albom, 1997). The ALS Association provides excellent information in the form of suggested reading lists, tips for family members and people with the disease, and a number of "Living with ALS" manuals that focus on areas such as preserving mobility, coping with change, and swallowing/speaking difficulties.

Two other articles may be helpful to someone who is counseling a client who has ALS. The first (Young & McNicoll, 1998) compiled data from a series of interviews with people with ALS who coped well with the disease. They found that good coping skills included maintaining a positive attitude, having a good sense of humor, having good family/friend relationships, putting to use problem-solving skills to cope with ALS, and maintaining a high level of intellectual stimulation. In another journal article (Sebring & Moglia, 1987), family members of people who had ALS were interviewed. Most ALS patients were cared for at home until the last few months of their lives. The researchers found that loss of mobility was the most difficult part for both family and patients to cope with. Many families felt ill equipped for the caregiving tasks and believed that they had inadequate information. They concluded that the counselor's role should be to provide two essential services to patients and their families: information and emotional support.

As already indicated, counseling homebound older adults is different from counseling in the office setting. Kerson and Michelsen (1995) focused on this issue in an article that provided case examples of counseling four different homebound clients, one of whom had ALS. The counseling goals were to support the highest level of independence for the clients. The researchers' conclusions, which supports my own, noted that the provision of concrete services cannot be separated from counseling services and that each reinforces the effect of the other. They also pointed out that in all cases with homebound older adults, issues of loss surpass all others. (With Grace, this certainly was true as new losses were addressed throughout the course of therapy.) Another theme that they discussed was the constant weighing of the wish for autonomy against the desire for safety. With any homebound client, the issue of moving to a care facility looms even if it is not directly addressed. Finally, they recognized the power that the use of reminiscence and life review can have in helping a client to come to terms with the life that he or she has lived.

Peer counseling is a wonderful intervention to use with a homebound client. Various programs (Becker & Zarit, 1978; Campbell, 1995) have effectively used peer counselors with older clients and have demonstrated the benefit to older peer counselors of continued growth and responsibility after retirement. Bratter and Freeman (1990) recognized that older adults often talk more freely to peer counselors who can also serve as role models.

REFERENCES

Albom, M. (1997). *Tuesdays with Morrie: An old man, a young man, and life's greatest lesson*. New York: Bantam Doubleday Dell.

Becker, F., & Zarit, S.H. (1978). Training older adults as peer counselors. *Educational Gerontology*, 3, 241–250.

Bratter, B., & Freeman, E. (1990, Winter). The maturing of peer counseling. *Counseling and Therapy Generations*, 49–52.

Campbell, R. (1995). A peer counseling program for older persons. In S.L. Hatcher (Ed.), *Peer programs on the college campus: Theory, training, and voice of the peers* (pp. 161–179). San Jose, CA: Resource Publications.

Kerson, R.S., & Michelsen, R.W. (1995). Counseling homebound clients and their families. *Journal of Gerontological Social Work*, 24(3–4), 159–190.

Sebring, D.L., & Moglia, P. (1987, Spring). Amyotrophic lateral sclerosis: Psychosocial interventions for patients and their families. *Health and Social Work*, 113–120.

Young, J.M., & McNicoll, P. (1998). Against all odds: Positive life experiences of people with advanced amyotrophic lateral sclerosis. *Health and Social Work*, 23(1), 35–43.

Mediating Conflict within a Marriage

6

Lynn E. Stern
and
Berit Ingersoll-Dayton

CLIENTS' BACKGROUND

BARBARA, A HOMEMAKER IN HER EARLY 60S, WAS REFERRED FOR PSY-CHOTHERAPY BY HER PHYSICIAN. She was deeply depressed about her family relationships, particularly her relationship with her husband. She characterized her husband of 40 years, Arthur, who was in his mid-60s, as a self-centered workaholic who was unable to support her emotionally. Barbara and Arthur were financially comfortable. They immigrated from Australia more than 30 years earlier so that Arthur could have greater job opportunities. Since that time, he had devoted himself to his job as a mechanical engineer. Arthur's extended family still lived in Australia, but Barbara's widowed father had also immigrated to the United States. Over time, her father became increasingly frail and the couple invited him to live with them. Despite her caregiving efforts, Barbara felt harshly criticized by her father and was angry that her husband always sided with her father and not with her.

Arthur and Barbara had three daughters, now in their 30s, who were married and lived nearby. Barbara and Arthur very much enjoyed spending time with their five grandchildren. However, their relationships with their daughters were a source of friction. When Barbara got into a fight with one of her daughters, Arthur would side with the daughter and not with her. Barbara felt emotionally abandoned by Arthur's unwillingness to give her the support that she needed in her family relationships. In turn, Barbara refused to give Arthur the physical affection that he desired. Both believed that the other was withholding a vital part of their relationship.

83

INTERVENTION SUMMARY

I (Lynn Stern) saw Arthur and Barbara intermittently at the clinic for 5 years. We took several breaks in therapy for a number of reasons. After each of these breaks, Barbara's physician referred her for additional psychotherapy and/or the couple asked to resume treatment. Although most of our sessions included both Arthur and Barbara, I also worked with each spouse individually for several sessions. In addition, I asked a co-therapist to join us when we reached a therapeutic stalemate. Each phase of this therapy is described next.

Couples Therapy

My initial sessions were with Barbara. She had a warm smile and looked me squarely in the eye. She was forthright to the point of harshness. The world was black and white for Barbara: People were either for her or against her. Indeed, most of the world seemed to be against her. Barbara began by describing her father's cruelty toward her since childhood. Although he lived with Barbara and she cooked and cleaned for him, he was never thankful for or appreciative of any of her efforts. Her anger quickly turned toward her husband, who tended to side with his father-in-law rather than with her. Barbara began to focus on Arthur and decided that her major problems were with him. She insisted that he attend therapy with her, saying, "This is not my problem. If Arthur were a better husband, I would be fine."

We subsequently broadened the view of the problem to the marital relationship and invited Arthur to join Barbara at the next session. The contrast between Arthur and Barbara was striking. Whereas Barbara cared little about her appearance, Arthur was particularly dapper. She was solitary and critical, whereas he was popular but self-contained about his feelings. Barbara insisted on his unconditional loyalty to her when she was involved in an argument with her daughters or her father, but Arthur tended to see both sides of a dispute.

Barbara wanted togetherness, whereas Arthur wanted to live a more separate and independent life. Barbara believed that wives should devote themselves to their families. She had raised their daughters, made an attractive home, cooked, cleaned, and supported her husband throughout his career. Barbara had few independent interests or friends. Most of her relationships with friends and family were characterized by difficulties. Barbara believed that her relationship with her husband should be central to her life and that her devotion to him should be reciprocated by his emotional caring and willingness to spend time with her. Arthur, in contrast, was a self-sufficient man who enjoyed his work and was well liked by his colleagues and friends. He spent many hours alone with his projects and wished that his wife had some hobbies or activities that she found equally absorbing.

During the first marital session, Barbara listed her grievances against Arthur. She recalled a number of incidents in which she felt emotionally abandoned by her husband, such as when he conversed with others at his office parties or sided with her father or their daughters. Arthur, in turn, complained that Barbara was not interested in a sexual relationship with him and that she never acknowledged the ways in which he tried to be a good husband.

The bitterness and pain in these early marital sessions were palpable. I began by taking a very active therapeutic role and focused on the hostile marital communication. I identified ways in which they were causing each other pain and insisted that they reduce their hostile remarks toward each other during the sessions. Barbara was particularly antagonistic and would frequently say to Arthur, "You are a hypocrite," or, "I don't know why I ever married you." I explored with Barbara whether she was considering a divorce and urged her not to discuss this highly charged topic unless she was serious. When Barbara was hostile, Arthur tended to disengage from the discussion. I addressed this marital dynamic by asking Arthur how he felt when Barbara verbally attacked him. He responded initially by saying that he did not know how he felt. Later, he acknowledged that he felt unappreciated. I wondered whether a possible underlying source of Barbara's complaints was that Arthur had been involved in an extramarital affair. I addressed this issue directly by asking Arthur about this possibility. He replied, "There are no secrets in our marriage. I have never had an affair." Interestingly, when I asked Barbara whether she believed Arthur, she said that she did.

Similar to other couples in therapy, Barbara and Arthur each wanted me to agree with their complaints and to make a judgment against the other. Instead, I responded to their complaints with a request for clarification, such as, "What did that mean to you?" or, "How did you feel?" I also responded to their attempts to draw me into their arguments by asking that they talk directly in a nonblaming manner to each other during our sessions.

The next therapeutic phase focused on the specific content of their desired changes. First, we addressed Barbara's desire for more attention and affection from Arthur. I asked, "How will you know if he loves you?" Barbara responded with a list of conditions that included complimenting her in public, talking to her more at home, decreasing the amount of time he spent on work, and siding with her in family disputes. In the subsequent weeks, Arthur followed through on several of these areas of requested behavior change, such as complimenting her in public and spending more time conversing with her at home. However, Barbara remained adamant that these changes were inadequate. Arthur began to talk about his frustration when he accommodated Barbara but she neither acknowledged his attempts nor made any changes in her own behavior.

We then turned to Arthur's desire for more physical intimacy in the relationship. I gave the couple a series of progressively more intimate homework assignments that included expressing verbal affection, expressing verbal affection while hugging, kissing each other, and lying together for 10 minutes in bed while holding each other. The couple rarely followed through on any of these assignments. Barbara explained that she was not willing to be physically intimate with someone who did not appreciate her. Arthur retorted by listing all of the ways in which he had changed to accommodate her. At one particularly poignant session, Arthur eloquently described his disappointment and frustration: "I am feeling upset that I have made all these changes and you can't give me any physical intimacy. Will it ever be enough?"

At this point in therapy, I began to believe that we were not making sufficient progress. I told Arthur and Barbara that I thought that we had come to a standstill in therapy and that we needed help from an outside expert. I explained that I had become accustomed to their patterns of relating and that another therapist, who was less involved with them, might be more effective in helping them to develop new ways of relating. They agreed to meet with the new therapist, who specialized in treating couples and who worked in another agency. Arthur and Barbara saw this new therapist for a number of sessions, but neither of them established a therapeutic relationship with him because they found him aloof and not empathic.

They eventually called and asked to resume therapy with me. Instead, I referred them to Ann, another therapist in our clinic, whom I thought could add a fresh perspective. Arthur and Barbara met with Ann for a number of sessions, established a warm therapeutic relationship with her, but made little progress in relation to their marital problems. Ann also began to feel increasingly pessimistic concerning the potential for marital change. Despite her reservations and mine, we acknowledged that the couple was desperate for a change in their relationship and we agreed to try another method of therapy.

Individual Therapy

Ann and I decided to work with Arthur and Barbara individually because we reasoned that Barbara, in particular, needed to grow as an individual. We hypothesized that the conflict in their marriage might diminish if Barbara could find more creative outlets. We decided that continuity with Ann was especially important for Barbara. I agreed to work with Arthur. This new approach resulted in one of our first breakthroughs. Ironically, the breakthrough occurred for Arthur rather than for Barbara.

Arthur and I began our work together by exploring his relationships in his family of origin. This exploration led to an examination of why he was so influenced by his desire to please others. Because of this desire, Arthur was constantly responding to the feelings of others to the point that he did not know his own feelings. In addition, by attending to others (e.g., his daughters, his father-in-law), he often alienated his wife. His inability to put limits on requests for his time even in relation to volunteer activities made Barbara feel less important than his casual acquaintances.

As we discussed his early childhood experiences, Arthur began to understand that the loss of his mother when he was 8 had profoundly influenced his personality. When his mother died, Arthur began to believe that he needed to earn the love and nurturing of others. In so doing, he became an accommodating and well-liked child. Arthur was very sensitive to the feelings of others, but not to his own. During one particularly poignant session, Arthur cried as he talked about his mother's death and his desire to win the love of others. For Arthur, this was a new experience because he had never cried about her death. During these individual sessions, Arthur started experiencing a broader range of emotions and became less reserved. This change resulted in more emotional expressiveness toward Barbara. He began to express more negative as well as positive feelings toward her. He also acknowledged, for the first time, that he was lonely within their relationship.

Meanwhile, Barbara was becoming increasingly uncomfortable with individual sessions. In her mind, the purpose of therapy was not so much focused on individual growth as it was on changing the marital relationship. Arthur had made substantial individual progress and was hopeful that his growth might have a positive impact on the marital relationship. Ann and I suggested that the couple take a break from therapy to gauge whether any of the changes that Arthur had made would have a beneficial effect on their relationship.

Some months later, Barbara's physician again referred her for therapy because he believed that she was under considerable stress. Despite the changes that Arthur had made during individual therapy, their marital relationship remained acrimonious. Ann and I agreed to work collaboratively as co-therapists with the couple. We reasoned that co-therapy would address Barbara's need for connectedness within her marriage while helping us, as therapists, to maintain our neutrality in sessions that often were heated.

Couples Therapy with a Co-therapist

Initially, I was anxious about working as a co-therapist with Ann. Although I had experience working as a co-therapist in the context of a group, I thought that my skills as a therapist would be more exposed in this arena. I wondered whether Ann might feel that I was intervening too much during the sessions or, perhaps, intervening too little. In addition, Ann might think that I was not insightful or skilled as a therapist. However, because she and I had worked together for many years in the clinic, I was fairly confident that we would work well together. On the basis of hearing her discuss cases during peer supervision, I knew that we shared a similar perspective in relation to working with couples; that is, we viewed marital dysfunction as a problem between two partners rather than as individual pathology. Also, I sensed that I could work easily with Ann. She had a certain humility about her own effectiveness and did not need to be in control.

Ann and I needed to work as a team if we were going to help this couple significantly change their relationship. The sessions with Arthur and Barbara were extremely heated. Each time we saw the couple, there was a new crisis at home. There was a pull to get involved in the successive crises and to lose sight of the larger need for changes in the marital dynamic. As co-therapists, we could keep the focus on the need for broader changes without becoming overwhelmed by the details of daily problems. It took both of us to keep this couple focused on the larger marital issues because each spouse was so determined to blame the other for the most recent dispute. Working together as co-therapists gave us greater strength in the face of the couple's hostility and confusion.

Ann and I soon found that working together allowed us to play different roles during the sessions. While one of us intervened with the couple, the other observed Barbara's and Arthur's manner of speech, facial expressions, and posture. We took turns as observer and intervener, thereby supporting each other's interventions. For example, during one session, Ann said to Barbara, "You look angry." I followed up on Ann's observation by asking Barbara, "What were you thinking about during the last few minutes?" To enhance our teamwork, Ann and I looked at each other to ensure that we were in agreement and listened quietly while the other was talking. Throughout these co-therapy sessions, we were modeling to Arthur and Barbara styles of effective communication and a way of working together as a team.

During the co-therapy sessions, we focused on the couple's contrasting values and their hostile communication patterns. We tried to help each of them to be kinder to the other and to understand their differences as related in part to gender. To diffuse their mutual blaming, we provided education about patterns of gender-related communication and recommended the book *Men Are from Mars, Women Are from Venus* (Gray, 1992). This book helped the couple, especially Arthur, to view their differences as cultural rather than simply as symptomatic of their unique relationship. We asked them to read specific portions of the book at home (e.g., listening without becoming angry, providing emotional support when one spouse was upset, relinquishing the need to change the other). We suggested that Arthur and Barbara practice each of the skills at home and then discuss their progress during therapy sessions. Our work as co-therapists was interrupted when physicians discovered that Barbara had cancer and she needed treatment.

After several months of chemotherapy, Arthur called to say that Barbara's condition had improved and they wanted to work on improving their relationship. We decided to resume co-therapy with both spouses, and they returned for a final series of sessions. We immediately noted a change in the way in which Barbara and Arthur were relating. They were more thoughtful of each other's feelings and less harsh in their criticism. Barbara told us that during her treatment and rehabilitation, Arthur had cared for her with tender devotion. Barbara uncharacteristically described Arthur as "a wonderful caregiver." She used a portion of the session to enumerate the ways in which he had given his undivided attention to nurture her back to health. As therapists, we served as witnesses to her affirmation of Arthur and their marriage. Barbara could finally say that she believed in Arthur's love for her.

Barbara and Arthur were eager to make a fresh start in their relationship. They realized that their time together might be limited by her health. Arthur was content to enjoy the new changes in their relationship. He had decided to relinquish his request for a more sexual relationship because, in part, his needs were satisfied by the physical intimacy of caregiving. Barbara was thereby relieved of disappointing Arthur, but she continued to resent the ways in which Arthur had hurt her in the past. These resentments cast a shadow on their ability to move forward. We suggested that this might be an opportune time to forgive each other and move on with their relationship. We asked Barbara, "Do you want to end your life with these feelings?" She somewhat hesitantly agreed that she did not. When we posed this question to Arthur, he replied, "I have nothing to forgive her for." Therefore, we focused the forgiveness process on Barbara.

Our efforts to help Barbara let go of her resentments and forgive Arthur represented the final turning point in this marital therapy. As homework for the forgiveness session, we asked Barbara to list on paper the times when she felt most abandoned or betrayed by Arthur. At the next session, we again asked Barbara whether she was ready to begin the forgiveness process. Unlike previous sessions, Barbara seemed ready to bring an end to the marital conflict. We further supported her by stating, "You have it in your power to let the past go." The remainder of the session was particularly intense. Barbara read aloud six different events that she most resented. After reading each event, Arthur apologized. Each time we asked Barbara whether she accepted his apology, and she responded, "I do."

In our final session with Barbara and Arthur, we noted a gentleness and comfort between the spouses. The animosity that had characterized their relationship for so many years was replaced with mutual compassion. They sat close together, and their eyes were filled with warmth and tenderness when they looked at each other. They each acknowledged their love and appreciation for the other. There was also a feeling of sadness as neither Barbara nor Arthur knew how much longer they would have to enjoy their rekindled affection for each other. Indeed, Barbara died a few months after the last session. In a letter summarizing his feelings about the therapy process and his marriage, Arthur wrote, "All in all, we've had a really good marriage."

INTERVENTION ANALYSIS

This therapy involved a number of different interventions and various combinations of clients and therapists. At times, it seemed as though we were making very little progress. However, Arthur's growth during our individual sessions and Barbara's ability to forgive at the end of therapy represented two turning points that made this process worthwhile. This marital case emphasized how factors such as poor health can serve as an opportunity for growth and healing within relationships. Perhaps most important was our ability to space the phases of therapy. In so doing, Barbara and Arthur were able to assess their gains and decide how to make better use of the next phase of therapy.

Demonstration of Respect

I deeply respected both members of this couple. People generally found Arthur much more engaging than Barbara. She was accustomed to feeling that his friends did not like her. Although I very much liked Arthur, I found that I could empathize with Barbara's sense of aloneness. At the same time, I believed that it was nontherapeutic to allow Barbara to criticize Arthur viciously throughout our sessions. My active attempts to prohibit hurtful interactions stemmed from my view that they both deserved each other's respect and that I needed to model that respect for them. I first demonstrated this respect by my willingness to accept Barbara's definition of the problem—that it was her marriage that was causing her such pain. The referring physician had suggested individual therapy focusing on stress reduction. I chose, however, to follow Barbara's understanding about the source of her stress and therefore worked with the marital dyad.

I had a fundamental belief that this couple could change. I was impressed that despite their acrimonious relationship, they had sustained a long-term marriage. I noted their extraordinary intelligence and that they were capable of enjoying and appreciating each other, especially when they were on vacation and away from their normal routine. My belief in their ability to change was part of what sustained me throughout many sessions of limited progress. I also demonstrated my respect by sharing with them my clinical observations when I believed that we had come to a therapeutic impasse. When I shared my observations, I was inviting their participation in helping me to decide whether to discontinue therapy for a time.

Use of the Clients' Strengths

Barbara and Arthur had a number of individual strengths that I built on throughout therapy. One of Arthur's strengths was his motivation to try to understand and change the dysfunctional dynamics of their marriage. I could always count on Arthur to follow through on homework assignments, such as talking with Barbara for half an hour two times per week. Arthur was also hopeful that he could make the marriage better. I frequently built on this hopefulness by beginning discussions with him rather than with Barbara, who tended to be much more negative about their ability to change the marriage.

Despite her negativity, Barbara also had a number of strengths that contributed to our therapeutic work. Although she saw Arthur as self-centered and hurtful toward her, she adored him. Barbara often stated, "I don't know if I can stand this marriage," but when I delved more deeply into her feelings, she could acknowledge her love for Arthur. This affirmation of her love helped both her and Arthur maintain their motivation for change. Furthermore, Barbara believed strongly in the institution of marriage and did not want to get a divorce. I used this strength by asking her to imagine what it would be like to live alone. When Barbara actually contemplated the ramifications of being alone, she felt less negative about her present situation.

Barbara and Arthur were also intelligent and reflective. When I described patterns that persisted in their relationship, they understood and appreciated my observations. Their intelligence allowed me to make more complicated analyses than I could with many other clients. So, for example, when I pointed out that they were allowing the needs of other family members (e.g., Barbara's father) to serve as a wedge between them in caring for each other, they could perceive this pattern. Although they often returned to their old patterns of relating, we could use the subsequent therapy session to examine the recurrence of the pattern and make connections to other patterns (e.g., problematic interactions with their daughters) that were occurring in their marriage.

Blurred Boundaries

My emotional connection to Arthur and Barbara was especially strong. I think that this connection was related to a number of factors. First, they were considerably younger than many of my clients and therefore were likely to have a number of years ahead. This sense that Arthur and Barbara had a substantial future made me particularly committed to helping them to enhance their relationship.

Second, I was attracted to their strong desire for a better life. I witnessed considerable change at various points in the therapeutic process. Sometimes these changes were small, such as when Barbara and Arthur could discuss their relationship without a great deal of animosity. At other times, the changes were more dramatic, such as when Arthur recalled his early childhood pain and thereby gained more understanding about his current feelings.

Third, I was aware that both Barbara and Arthur had high regard for me. They perceived me as sensitive and insightful, and they were extremely appreciative of my help. After taking a break from therapy, they returned to ask for additional sessions. Their need for my assistance made me feel connected to them and competent.

Finally, I experienced pressure from Barbara's physician to continue therapy. Even when we had decided to discontinue therapy, her physician referred Barbara for additional therapy, which indicated that he thought that therapy was helpful.

Each of these factors contributed to my feeling that I was indispensable to this couple. My own feelings of connectedness as well as the persistence of the physician and the clients to resume therapy may have resulted in an attempt to work with them beyond the point of helpfulness. At times, I sensed that the boundary between determining what was helpful and unhelpful had become blurred. At such times, I took various steps to regain my objectivity. One tactic was to invite Ann to join me as a co-therapist. The other tactic was to suggest to Arthur and Barbara that we take a break from therapy so that they could reassess their own resources and I could reflect on the extent to which therapy was helping this couple. During the break and throughout my work with Barbara and Arthur, I took advantage of supervision to clarify my own feelings, goals, and intervention.

Changes in the Therapeutic Relationship over Time

The ongoing nature of this therapy allowed us to develop a strong therapeutic relationship. My identification with aspects of Arthur's and Barbara's personalities grew over time. Each of them had qualities that were reminiscent of my own. With Arthur, I saw that we shared a common desire to please others. Because of this similarity, I could understand the ways in which this desire helped Arthur to establish relationships as it limited his ability to understand his own needs. With Barbara, I could empathize with her sense of abandonment. The poignancy of her stories made me remember times when I had felt left out by others. These similarities in our personalities and life experiences allowed me to empathize with each spouse's feelings and to understand how their contrasting feelings could result in such polarization.

The duration of our therapeutic work allowed Barbara and Arthur to transfer feelings from the past onto me. Over time, I think that both of them saw me as a benevolent mother figure. Barbara's mother had died when she was a young adult, and Arthur had lost his mother during childhood. Both spouses remembered their mothers as warm, accepting, and nurturing. Their transference of those feelings to me enabled them to view me positively and to respond nondefensively to my therapeutic suggestions. The nature of our relationship may have been particularly important for Barbara because she encountered so many difficulties in her interactions with others. The uniquely positive quality of our relationship may have also contributed to her desire for ongoing contact.

Our ability to take breaks from therapy over time also contributed to two important therapeutic changes. First, knowing that they could return to therapy allowed Arthur and Barbara to consider discontinuing therapy. They were unsure of their ability to manage their relationship independently, but I could reassure them that the clinic would allow me to see them again if they needed assistance. I could encourage them to try to work out their conflicts independently while providing them with a safety net if they needed it. Second, this safety net approach allowed me to be available to them at a crucial juncture after Barbara's illness. Her illness and Arthur's caregiving made Barbara want to resume therapy. It was at this point that she was finally willing to make a significant change in the marriage and give up her resentment toward Arthur.

Benefits and Difficulties of the Therapeutic Relationship for the Clients and the Therapists

The therapy sessions and the relationship that developed among Arthur, Barbara, Ann, and me had a profound influence on each of us. For Barbara, the central areas of change were her ability to trust and forgive. Barbara was accustomed to being viewed by others as a "problem person." To avoid hurtful encounters, she isolated herself and became increasingly distrustful. Several times during the earlier part of therapy, Barbara was frustrated because she expected me to side with her in criticizing Arthur. During these periods of frustration, Barbara frequently suggested ending our therapy sessions, but she never followed through with this suggestion. At the same time, I tried to remain nonblaming and empathic. Slowly, I sensed that she trusted me, and, in time, she became somewhat less defensive toward Arthur. This metamorphosis may have laid the groundwork for her ability to accept Arthur's caregiving during her illness and forgive his earlier hurtful behaviors.

For Arthur, therapy was also a bittersweet experience. He was often frustrated at the lack of mutual follow-through on therapeutic assignments. In contrast to his commitment to therapy and the completion of homework assignments, Barbara rarely completed assignments because she viewed the marital problem as his failing. Ultimately, the impact of therapy was more dramatic for Arthur than for Barbara. In the beginning of therapy, he was very reserved about his feelings. Over time, Arthur came to understand the power of his own feelings. The session concerning his mother's death helped Arthur to experience the depth of his emotions. After this session, he became committed to more openness in revealing his feelings to himself and to others. In the letter that Arthur wrote to me after the end of our sessions, he discussed the relief that he felt after being "released from the prison of my emotions."

Ann and I reacted to this marital therapy with feelings of satisfaction mixed with frustration. We battled hopelessness many times during and after our sessions. Time and again, we saw new patterns of marital interaction emerge followed by a reversion to the old patterns of blame. I felt frustrated as I saw Barbara and Arthur stuck in a relationship of pain and resentment. At other times, I experienced great satisfaction as I saw the couple become able to speak about their relationship without hostility and contempt. I was pleased that I was able to avoid taking sides but that I could take an assertive role when communication between the spouses became hurtful. Overall, I was proud of the role that I had played in helping Arthur and Barbara to discover more harmony and affection in their relationship.

Words of Wisdom

As I reflect on this couple's therapy, there are some ways in which I would have handled the sessions differently. Specifically, I wish that I had encouraged the couple to be more responsible for their own change. An ideal opportunity would have been the times when Arthur and Barbara requested that we resume therapy. At these points, it would have been helpful to reflect with them on the overall process. If I could do it again, I would review where we were stuck before our last break and discuss how we could make this next phase different. A clearer description of their hopes and goals may have facilitated our progress.

There are also a number of areas in which I believe that I made good therapeutic decisions. First, with this couple it was important that I work with each of them individually and together. Working with them individually gave me the opportunity to hear their unique stories and to focus on individual issues that were impeding growth. The time during which I worked with them together gave me an opportunity to highlight contrasting values and differences in communication styles.

Second, although initially I was anxious about working with another therapist, I found the involvement of a co-therapist to be very helpful. Our ability to work well as a team involved a few important ingredients. One ingredient was a similarity in our working styles; we used a similar balance between empathy and confrontation. A second ingredient was an ability to share leadership during the sessions. Neither of us believed that we needed to be "the star therapist."

Therapists should not assume that these two ingredients naturally occur when conducting co-therapy. Instead, there is a need to discuss issues of style and approach up front as well as throughout the process of working together. I suggest that before starting co-therapy, the therapists talk about a number of issues, including how much to intervene, who will lead the sessions or how leadership will be divided, how to handle clients' attempts to divide them as co-therapists, and how they will provide feedback to each other over time. Also, I think that it is crucial to set aside some time after each session to discuss concerns that were raised during the session, issues that were not fully addressed, and ways in which you would like the other therapist to intervene differently in the future.

Third, I believe that it was extremely helpful that we took several breaks from therapy. These breaks helped the clients to assess their own capabilities and helped me to gain objectivity in thinking about our work together. The final break that occurred after Barbara's diagnosis and treatment was particularly important. That break allowed the couple to experience themselves in a new situation in which their relationship was nurtured. The final sessions that followed could build on the strengths of their relationship.

This case exemplifies the intricate relationship between what occurs inside and outside therapy sessions. Gains made within therapy sessions sometimes are not appreciated until a crisis occurs. For this couple, the crisis clearly was Barbara's illness, which allowed both Barbara and Arthur to value the progress that they had made and to build on their progress within therapy. Barbara's illness and Arthur's caregiving enabled them to cherish the relationship that they had been working on during therapy. Finally, they could appreciate the bond of love that had been hidden behind the hurt and acrimony. This experience served as a catalyst for the final step in therapy: forgiveness and reaffirmation of their marriage.

ADDITIONAL RESOURCES

There are a number of resources that are relevant to working with older couples. Practitioners who are interested in using a systems perspective when working with older people and their families may find a book chapter by Keller and Bromley (1989) to be helpful. In the chapter, the authors discussed both the principles of family therapy and specific strategies and techniques for working with older people within a family context. The unique concerns of older couples are highlighted in two other book chapters (Long & Mancini, 1990; Neidhardt & Allen, 1993). These authors examined strains that occur in long-term marriages as a result of life events such as retirement, poor health, and the loss of family and friends.

Several references are available for couples who want to improve their marriages. Two books that are written for the public are particularly helpful in work with older spouses. One of these books, Men Are from Mars, Women Are from Venus (Gray, 1992), was used with the couple described in this chapter and focuses on the communication patterns used by men and women. The author points out that men and women communicate, think, and feel differently. In this book, John Gray teaches couples how to solve problems that result from these gender differences. Another book, Fighting for Your Marriage (Markman, Stanley, & Blumberg, 1994), also presents helpful ways of enhancing marital relationships. These authors describe some of the core issues that are involved in conflict between spouses and discuss strategies for resolving such conflict. Both of these books can be offered to clients as tools for helping them to understand and resolve their differences. They provide a number of practical exercises that couples can try at home and then discuss during therapy sessions.

A variety of themes emerge when conducting therapy with older couples. In the case presented here, one of the themes was forgiveness. Facilitating the process of forgiveness may be a particularly important skill for therapists who deal with later-life marital problems. Hargrave and his colleagues (Hargrave, 1994; Hargrave & Anderson, 1992) have written extensively on this process. They developed a framework for helping therapists to understand the process of forgiveness. In their books, they provide suggestions for facilitating forgiveness and case examples illustrating its application to work with older people and their families. For a very readable book on forgiveness that is written for a general audience and that can be shared with clients, also consider *Forgive and Forget* (Smedes, 1984).

Another theme that was related to this case is countertransference. When working with older clients, therapists may experience their own unresolved feelings. An excellent book, *Countertransference and Older Clients* (Genevay & Katz, 1990), helps therapists to examine the many facets of countertransference that can arise when working with different types of aging clients, such as dealing with family members who are caring for their elders, facilitating nursing facility placement, and dealing with clients' failing health and impending death.

REFERENCES

Genevay, B., & Katz, R. (1990). *Countertransference and older clients*. Thousand Oaks, CA: Sage Publications.

Gray, J. (1992). *Men are from Mars, women are from Venus*. New York: HarperCollins.

Hargrave, T.D. (1994). *Families and forgiveness: Healing wounds in the intergenerational family*. New York: Brunner/Mazel.

Hargrave, T.D., & Anderson, W.T. (1992). *Finishing well: Aging and reparation in the intergenerational family*. New York: Brunner/Mazel.

Keller, J.F., & Bromley, M.C. (1989). Psychotherapy with the elderly: A systemic model. In G.A. Hughston, V.A. Christopherson, & M.J. Bonjean (Eds.), *Aging and family therapy: Practitioner perspectives on Golden Pond* (pp. 29–46). New York: Haworth Press.

Long, J., & Mancini, J.A. (1990). Aging couples and the family system. In T.H. Brubaker (Ed.), *Family relationships in later life* (2nd ed., pp. 29–47). Thousand Oaks, CA: Sage Publications.

Markman, H., Stanley, S., & Blumberg, S.L. (1994). *Fighting for your marriage*. San Francisco: Jossey-Bass.

Neidhardt, E.R., & Allen, J. (Eds.). (1993). *Family therapy with the elderly*. Thousand Oaks, CA: Sage Publications.

Smedes, L.B. (1984). *Forgive and forget*. New York: Harper & Row.

Working with Groups

II

The Power of Group Cognitive Therapy

7

Sally Edwards
and
Janet Fogler

CLIENTS' BACKGROUND

ROSE, A SINGLE, RETIRED SECRETARY, AGE 64, HAD EXPERIENCED LOW-LEVEL DEPRESSION THROUGHOUT HER LIFE. She was an only child raised by a highly critical mother who saw life as a constant struggle. Rose's life was one of isolation. Her parents were suspicious of outsiders and never invited anyone to their home. Although Rose got a job as a secretary after high school, she remained in her parents' home and never developed a completely independent life. Her social life consisted of the company of her parents and one or two friends from work. After Rose's retirement and her father's death, Rose's mother became more demanding of her attention. Although her mother was frail, she was able to take care of herself. Rose felt guilty when she was absent from a meal or went out with a friend in the evening. She developed severe depressive symptoms—she spent part of the day in bed, took no pleasure in previously enjoyed activities, became critical of the one or two friends who she had, and began to develop possible psychosomatic symptoms. Her self-esteem plummeted, and although she knew that she needed to get out of the house and interact with people, she was unable to make herself take part in any pleasurable activities. Rose was referred to the social work department for individual therapy by her physician, who had prescribed antidepressant medications that caused side effects that she was unwilling to tolerate. She attended five individual therapy sessions and then was encouraged to join the cognitive therapy group.

Roger, age 72, a retired professor who had no history of mood disorder, experienced severe depression upon his retirement. He developed a persistent belief that his career had been useless and second-rate and that his former colleagues were "against me." He was filled with doom. He believed that he had made some terrible mistakes in his research career. He lost confidence in his ability to do even rudimentary activities. His family was mystified and devastated by the change in him. He had always been a high achiever, who put himself through college and graduate school and became a professor at a large western university. After retirement, he moved with his wife, who was several years younger, to her new job as a research scientist for a pharmaceutical company. Roger was referred to the group by a psychiatrist who had started him on an antidepressant medication.

Mood disorders, especially depression and anxiety, are common conditions among older adults. Although mood disorders can be related to physical factors as well as psychological factors, distorted thoughts or beliefs often serve to create or maintain dysfunctional mood states. Older people have had a lifetime to develop automatic ways of thinking and responding to events. Because these thought patterns are habitual and spring so easily to the mind, the individual assumes that they are true and held universally. At the same time, when feeling depressed or anxious, people tend to find evidence that supports distorted or negative thoughts.

As therapists, we noted that many of our clients with depression or anxiety manifested cognitive distortions that were resistant to modification. For example, Roger stated that since his retirement, he was useless. He said, "There's nothing left for me in my life. My former colleagues don't respect me. I can't make connections to new people." His therapist thought that Roger would gain from participation in group cognitive therapy sessions because he would have an opportunity to follow through on a commitment, set goals in a structured setting, and test his belief that he could not connect with people.

GROUP'S BACKGROUND

Cognitive therapy was developed in the late 1950s by Aaron Beck (1972) to help people overcome depression. Since then, this therapeutic approach has become one of the most successful and widely practiced psychotherapies for a wide range of problems. This approach is a proven technique for the treatment of mood disorders and involves the process of helping people recognize what they are thinking, test the validity of their thoughts, and, when invalid, substitute more appropriate thoughts. Using cognitive therapy does not imply replacing inaccurate negative thoughts with inaccurate positive thoughts but rather describing a situation or event in accurate, realistic words.

Cognitive therapy, with its emphasis on practical techniques, is a positive approach for working with older adults. Because some older adults may be uncomfortable with psychotherapeutic interventions, an approach that uses educational methods and introduces concrete techniques for instituting change may be more acceptable to them. We call our group "New Ways to Feel Good" as encouragement to older adults who know that they want to improve the way that they feel but might be intimidated by the term "cognitive therapy." We recruit group members by sending notices to health care providers and putting press releases in newspapers, in seniors' newsletters, and on radio stations. Because our group therapy is billable to Medicare and other insurance plans, each of our participants is required to have a DSM-IV diagnosis. However, cognitive therapy can also be useful with clients who do not have a clinical diagnosis but whose distorted thoughts affect their quality of life.

We schedule an individual interview with potential group members to assess for a DSM-IV diagnosis and to introduce the idea of group cognitive therapy to them. Older adults often have little knowledge of therapeutic treatment and interventions and may be more comfortable in initial group sessions if they have previously met group leaders and are given adequate information about the group's construction and process. Basic prerequisites for participation are 1) diagnosis of a mood disorder, 2) an element of distortion in thinking, 3) absence of dementia, 4) ability to hear in the group setting, 5) acceptance of the basic premise that the way that we think can affect the way that we feel, and 6) commitment to weekly group attendance for the full 10 weeks. No attempt is made to screen for compatibility or similarity among group members, and the groups that we have offered have been varied in terms of age, educational level, functional status, and lifestyle. Some potential participants are referred to other interventions because they do not have a DSM-IV diagnosis, they do not believe that the concepts of cognitive therapy apply to them, or they do not want to reveal personal problems to a group of strangers.

Participants in our groups have ranged in age from 58 to 84. The majority of the participants have been women, which is true of many groups of older adults. Diagnoses have included depression, anxiety, bipolar disorder, and adjustment disorder, but most participants have had moderate to severe depression. Many of the participants are also being treated with medications that have been prescribed by psychiatrists or primary care physicians.

INTERVENTION SUMMARY

"New Ways to Feel Good" consisted of 10 weekly sessions of 1–2 hours each, facilitated by two clinical social workers. Group membership was limited to a maximum of 10 participants. Although the upper limit may seem larger than many therapy groups, we have discovered that with this age group, precarious health, uncertain schedules, or participation under pressure from others often contributed to the early attrition of one or more members. Group members varied greatly in age, functional status, and educational background; however, their life experiences gave them an appreciation of one another.

Group members often came to the first meeting with concerns about what would be expected of them in a therapy group. An initial goal of the group was to establish a comfortable, nonthreatening environment that would allow participants to connect to one another. Concepts of cognitive therapy were introduced in an educational mode, using tools such as lectures and reading assignments. Members were given homework assignments to enhance their understanding of the therapy and to work toward identified goals. Weekly sessions followed a similar format and consisted of several components, which are described next.

Go-Around Question

Each session began with a brief, nonthreatening "go-around question" that encouraged all group members to participate and promoted sharing. As the group progressed, the questions proceeded from innocuous ("Tell us about a favorite book, movie, or TV show") to more meaningful ("What was a core value of your family of origin?"). The question about core values provided a turning point for Rose. She had seemed very nervous in the first two sessions and had asked to pass on the first go-around question. When called on to set a goal for therapy, she was unable to be more specific than "I want to be less depressed." The first time she revealed anything personal was in the third session in response to the go-around question about values learned in one's family of origin. Other participants set the stage by discussing problematic values in their families, such as, "Boys are more important than girls," and, "Children should be seen and not heard." She recalled that her family had stressed the belief that people other than family are not to be trusted. Her family never attended social events, and no one outside the family was ever invited to their home. Another participant said, "You could be talking about my family. My family didn't mix with people outside the family either, and it's always been hard for me to be trusting and comfortable around unfamiliar people." A short lecture that followed this go-around question discussed the establishment of core beliefs and explained how family values learned in our formative years can affect our thoughts, attitudes, and behaviors throughout life. This session seemed to provide new insight for Rose, as she began to be less tense and guarded.

Short Lecture

One of the therapists gave a 10- to 20-minute lecture that presented the basic concepts of cognitive therapy. These lectures built upon each other to increase a person's knowledge of and capacity to use the techniques taught. Lecture topics included an overview of cognitive therapy; identification of automatic thoughts; cognitive distortions, such as overgeneralization, mind reading, all-or-nothing thinking, "should" statements, and labeling; goal setting; problem solving; and techniques to correct distorted thinking. Reading assignments from such texts as *Feeling Good* (Burns, 1992) or *Mind over Mood* (Padesky & Greenberger, 1995) reinforced the concepts that were presented in the lectures.

The pace of the lectures was dependent on group members' ability to demonstrate that they could understand and apply the concepts. Because participants came to the group from varied backgrounds, some with previous knowledge of cognitive techniques and experience in therapy and others with no experience in psychological ideas or group participation, the books offered the opportunity for members to supplement learning with additional reading if they chose.

Discussion of Problems

Participants often dealt with stressful situations involving relationships, physical health problems, losses, or life changes. As they discussed their problems, they made statements that seemed to illustrate distorted thinking. At those times, one of the therapists would ask, "Can we work together to see whether that thought is accurate?" The job of the therapist was not to tell participants how to think but to help them find evidence that a distorted thought was not accurate. This process was collaborative. As participants became familiar with the concepts and techniques of cognitive therapy, they were encouraged to point out distortions to fellow group members. The facilitators' goal was to enable group members to participate in the process of identifying distorted thoughts and suggesting alternative, accurate thoughts.

Although Rose knew that one of the ways to become less depressed was to have more contact with people, she could not force herself to call a friend. When group members encouraged her to call, she said, "I'm sure my friend is mad at me because I haven't returned her phone calls." We asked the group whether they could find a distortion in this statement, and a group member said, "That sounds like fortune telling to me." *Fortune telling* is a prediction about how things will turn out, usually badly, and is one of the distortions that the group learns about in the sessions. A group member suggested that Rose's friend might be worried about her and would be relieved to get a telephone call. Rose accepted the homework assignment of calling her friend to say hello. The following week, Rose reported that her friend had been worried about her and was pleased to hear from her. They made plans to go to a movie. When the other participants responded excitedly to her report, Rose seemed gratified.

Another major hurdle for Rose was dealing with the guilt that she felt whenever her mother complained about her going out for the evening. Using the survey method, one of the methods that a person can use to check for distorted thinking, the facilitators polled the group to see how many members believed that a person who lives with a parent always needs to be available to the parent. No one supported that opinion. Everyone concluded that Rose was a very faithful daughter and that she did not need to be with her mother at all times. One member said, "If I had to spend one day a month with my mother, I'd be depressed," and the group, including Rose, broke into laughter.

During the first few group sessions, Roger was guarded and humorless. He seemed uninterested in the group process and in other group members. He contributed to the group only when called on. We were surprised that session after session he continued to attend. Roger made his first voluntary contribution to the group discussion when another group member, June, described her struggle with a new computer program and an impatient boss at work. Her self-esteem was suffering and she was ready to quit, although she needed to work for a few more years until retirement.

Roger suggested that June take a class in computers at the local community college. Several group members were interested in learning more about computers, and Roger described some basic uses of a computer. Because Roger was animated and becoming involved for the first time, we allowed this discussion to continue even though it was a departure from our focus on cognition. Roger began to perceive himself as a problem solver and to feel useful in the context of the group, although he never revealed to the group the depths of his depression and rarely disclosed any personal information.

To address Roger's belief that retired people are no longer useful and contributing to society, we constructed a go-around question: "What activities have you pursued after retirement?" Roger seemed surprised by the variety of pursuits mentioned by other participants. He further questioned Sam, who volunteered at the Children's Science Museum, about his activities there. Roger also seemed to recognize more clearly his own distortions about retirement when another group member stated, "Once you've retired, there's nothing left in life," and he found that he could not totally agree.

Goal Setting and Goal Review

Periodically throughout the sessions, participants were asked to set concrete goals and report on their progress toward achieving these identified goals. Goals were routinely reviewed to assess whether they had been completed or needed to be altered. For instance, when Roger first stated a goal, he said that he wanted to feel more useful and productive. We directed him to be more specific, and he then decided that he would like to try some kind of volunteer work. His assignment for that week was to explore volunteer possibilities in the community. After a couple of weeks of his exploration, we encouraged him to make a decision about which agency to contact and make an appointment to speak with their volunteer coordinator.

Homework Assignments

Weekly homework assignments were given to the group as a whole. These assignments reinforced learning and provided opportunities to use the techniques that participants had learned. One ongoing assignment was to keep a daily record of dysfunctional thoughts. This log described a situation, the accompanying negative emotions, and the thoughts that provoked the emotions. As participants became more skilled in using cognitive techniques, they were able to substitute more rational thoughts for their automatic responses. (For an example of Rose's daily automatic thoughts log, see Table 7.1.) Individual assignments also were given to address a particular issue. Examples of individual assignments were Rose's assignment to call her friend or Roger's assignment to explore volunteer activities. During each weekly session, participants reported on homework assignments.

INTERVENTION ANALYSIS

Using cognitive therapy in a group setting offers participants the opportunity to take part in a psychotherapeutic process within a social context. Whereas some participants benefited most from learning to recognize distorted thoughts and substitute more realistic ones, others gained from the supportive relationships that they formed during the meetings. Although participants had different problems and distinct strengths, they frequently mentioned the comfort that they found in knowing that they were not alone in their feelings of depression or anxiety. As therapists, we worked to balance the needs of the individuals with the needs of the group. We strove to show respect for each individual yet remain cognizant of the diversity represented in the group.

Demonstration of Respect

We recognized that joining a group would be especially difficult for Rose, who was isolated and inexperienced in social interaction. We looked for opportunities to acknowledge that it is a challenge to attend a therapy group and to praise her for her commitment to the group. We also respected her choice to

Table 7.1.   Rose's record of automatic thoughts

Situation	Emotion	Automatic thought	Rational thought
I go out with a friend.	Guilty	I shouldn't leave.	It's okay to go out with a friend.
		I'm being irresponsible.	My mother won't like it, but she'll be fine.
My friend didn't call when expected.	Depressed	I did something wrong.	Maybe she's just busy.
I didn't understand the reading material for group.	Anxious	I'm so dumb. I'll probably say something stupid in the group.	If I don't understand something, someone else might not, too. Everyone in the group has been very supportive of me.

devote most of her time and effort to her mother, even though we believed that it might not be in her best interests.

In the initial sessions, when Roger was uncommunicative and guarded, we respected his choice to remain remote from the process. His previous experience in group settings had been in competitive, task-oriented professional groups. He was not used to sharing feelings or discussing personal problems, and we respected his need to acclimate slowly to a new kind of interaction style.

Use of the Clients' Strengths

Because of Rose's depression and inexperience in social settings, it was difficult at first to perceive her strengths. However, she conscientiously completed homework assignments and began to recognize when distorted negative thinking affected her mood. Both she and other group participants began to view her as one of the most diligent students of cognitive therapy. Because we recognized that she felt more comfortable contributing to group discussion when she was prepared, we always gave her an opportunity to present from her homework assignments. During one session, Rose made a self-deprecating comment, which was allowed to stand at the time. After the discussion had shifted to another topic, one group member broke into the discussion, saying, "I just have to say something. I have to tell you, Rose, how important you have been to me in this group. You listen so attentively, and I always feel like you understand me."

Roger's strengths, once revealed, were a high level of intelligence, a sense of humor, and a resolution to follow through on a commitment to the group. When he discussed his interest in technology, people began to ask his opinion about computers. We allowed time in the sessions for this type of interaction because it increased Roger's feelings of competence as well as provided valuable information to other participants. When we assigned Roger the task of exploring the volunteer options, he not only found a challenging volunteer position for himself but he also brought information back to the group and encouraged others to become volunteers.

Blurred Boundaries

Because Rose had been seen in individual therapy with one of the co-facilitators, an alliance that may have affected their relationship in the group had formed. Rose was accustomed to the full attention of her therapist, so she looked for ways to make a connection during breaks. The therapist felt protective of Rose's feelings and found it difficult to separate herself from Rose to give attention to others. The other therapist, having experienced a situation that was similar to Rose's with an overly demanding member of her own family, strongly identified with Rose in her relationship with her mother. She found herself wanting to advise Rose to move out and start a new life rather than allow her to come to her own solutions in her own time.

Roger never really acknowledged his severe depression and rarely shared his homework assignments with the group. Because he was a former professor and, as therapists, we were part of an academic medical community with hierarchical standards, we found it more difficult to address this nonconformity than if Roger had worked in another type of institution. If he had been a manager in a local industry, then we might not have recognized his stature and would have been more assertive about these issues.

Changes in the Therapeutic Relationship over Time

An important event occurred in Rose's life outside the therapy group and affected her progress in working toward expanding her social life and dealing with her mother's dependence on her. Unexpectedly, she received a letter from a childhood friend, Tracy, saying that she would be coming to town and would like to visit Rose. Although Rose felt anxious about this reunion, she agreed to meet for dinner. During the evening, Tracy told Rose how much her friendship had meant to her when they were children and said that she wished they lived close enough to get together frequently. Rose was surprised and gratified by the visit and Tracy's remarks. She described this event to the group self-consciously but proudly. This event was further evidence that Rose could be a valued friend and seemed to increase her confidence in the group and in further contact with her friend outside the group. Although Rose's mother felt left out when she went to dinner with her old friend, Rose discovered that she could tolerate her mother's displeasure.

Roger also experienced outside the group an event that may have influenced his improvement during the course of the 10-week group. His doctor prescribed an antidepressant 2 weeks before the start of the group. His mood and affect improved considerably after the first month of the group, and he began to participate more readily during group discussion and break periods.

Benefits and Difficulties of the Therapeutic Relationship for the Clients and the Therapists

Rose had experienced low self-esteem throughout her life. She had limited experience in social interactions and seemed to lack confidence in the initial sessions of the group. When she observed other people also struggling with depression and relationship difficulties, she perceived herself in a more positive light. She learned to discuss her family situation openly and to recognize that other people can be trustworthy. The group gave her positive feedback that increased her confidence level. She also benefited from keeping a daily record of automatic thoughts, which helped her to recognize distorted thoughts. As Rose became more trusting of the group members, she engaged in conversation before the sessions and during the break. Her affect became more animated, and her depression decreased. Although Rose was never likely to develop a large circle of friends or to leave her mother alone more than once or twice a week, she was determined to reestablish her connection to her friends and her freedom to socialize outside her home.

Participation in a therapy group seemed to be a mystifying experience for Roger. His experience of group meetings was limited to research and task-oriented work groups. He never revealed the devastation he felt that stemmed from his distorted thoughts about the worthlessness of his career. Although it is unclear whether Roger's improvements in mood and attitude were the result of his use of an antidepressant, his participation in the group, or a combination of factors, he became much more accurate and realistic in his review of his life. He seemed to have forgotten the severity of his depression and his distorted thinking. Although Roger never disclosed much personal information and rarely gave examples of the use of cognitive techniques, we began to notice a marked change in his demeanor and behavior after several sessions. He engaged other group members in conversation, displayed a quick wit, and related well to everyone, being especially supportive of the most difficult member of the group. He has since engaged in volunteer activities and has kept in contact with members of the group.

One of the striking characteristics of our cognitive therapy groups is the support that participants showed one another throughout the 10 sessions. Perhaps because they were willing to disclose their vulnerabilities, they also became more supportive of one another's strengths. As they shared the symptoms of their depression or anxiety and revealed their struggles to feel better, the participants understood each individual small step as a collective triumph.

As therapists, we have learned a lot from the experience of working within a group with a co-therapist. Sharing facilitation of the group, without the total responsibility for the flow, offered the opportunity to observe a colleague at work and to reflect on what happens in a group. We have also gained insight from our complementary and compatible styles. When one leader is more confrontational, the other might provide more reflective insight. We also believe that practicing cognitive therapy in a group has helped us in our practice of individual therapy. Observing the contrasting cognitive styles of the group participants has taught us to be more aware of how a given stimulus can trigger varied ways of thinking in different people.

We improved our ability to apply cognitive techniques to our own lives. The old adage "If you really want to know something, teach it" has proved to be true in our experience of using cognitive therapy with ourselves. As social workers, we tend to believe that we should be able to help people solve all of their problems. Cognitive therapy has helped us to be more realistic when confronted with clients who fail to make changes or who drop out of therapy. We recognize the accuracy in such statements as, "People need to take action for themselves to make changes," or, "I may not be the right therapist for every person." On a more personal level, we have tried to use cognitive techniques to address our feelings of guilt and frustration concerning our own aging relatives.

Words of Wisdom

Although both of us had considerable experience in doing both individual therapy and facilitating support groups, conducting therapy within the context of a group was a new practice endeavor for us. We found that one of the challenges in any kind of group therapy is reconciling the needs of the individual with the needs of the group. At times during the group, one facilitator or both may engage a participant in a therapeutic intervention as in individual therapy. The facilitators need to keep in mind the sensibilities of the individual with whom they are working within the group context while being aware that the group members are observers who need to feel safe when they reveal their own thoughts and struggles.

Two areas of concern present themselves. One is that the individual who is being counseled may feel awkward because there are observers of the interaction; another is that those who are observing an intervention with another group member may internalize the content or emotional expression of the intervention. For example, if a shy or overly sensitive participant observes an intervention that involves confronting the distorted thoughts of a particularly challenging participant, the shy participant may feel uncomfortable or inhibited about revealing his or her own thoughts.

An additional challenge of a cognitive therapy group such as the one described in this chapter is that the facilitators play dual roles: teachers as well as therapists. To use cognitive techniques, group members must have a basic understanding of the connection between thoughts and feelings. In the teaching role, facilitators must be aware that members come to the group from different baselines of understanding. A few group members may have had therapeutic experience using cognitive therapy techniques. Some grasp the concepts quickly and easily; others need considerable reinforcement of the basic concepts before they can absorb them. We found it a challenge to make sure that the inexperienced group members understood the concepts without losing the interest of those who had knowledge of cognitive techniques. We have also discovered that intellectual ability does not necessarily predict good recognition and understanding of distorted thinking.

The concepts of cognitive therapy seem simple, but facilitators must be aware that participants may struggle to understand and use them. For example, many participants had problems distinguishing between thoughts and feelings. When Rose tried to describe the way that she felt when she left her mother alone, she said, "I feel like I'm being an irresponsible daughter." We had to teach her and many others that this statement is a *thought* (i.e., the idea that someone who leaves his or her mother alone is acting irresponsibly). The *feeling* that is caused by this thought is guilt or depression.

Cognitive therapy implies a structured approach to effecting change. However, we have found that with older adults, flexibility is desirable. Older adults may experience health problems, losses, and changes in lifestyle that require venting, discussion, and problem solving. As the sessions progress, it is expected that participants will take a more active role in pointing out distortions and collaborating on finding more rational responses to events. Older adults may be less socialized to confront one another or to express disagreement however, so therapists must be aware of the tendency for participants to look to the leaders for answers. We continue to encourage participants to respond to one another rather than allow them always to defer to the leaders.

Although most participants in our groups have been appropriately referred to the cognitive therapy group, occasionally there are participants who are eligible according to our criteria but still may not benefit from the experience. For instance, Dorothy, age 82, was an only child who was doted on by her parents and given many opportunities to develop her artistic temperament. She prided herself on her knowledge of philosophy and psychology and enjoyed writing poetry. She even brought one of her poems to the assessment interview. We had difficulty helping her to focus on the interview questions. Because of her need to focus attention on herself, we had some reservations about her participation in the group, but we could find no definitive reason to exclude her.

From the first session, Dorothy demanded attention from both facilitators and group members. She was unable to focus on the general concepts of the lectures and often selected one small idea to expound on at great length. When the facilitators encouraged participants to keep a written record of automatic thoughts, she lectured the group on the advantages of writing poetry. Whenever anyone reported on progress toward a goal, she tried to play the role of therapist, asking questions, often off the mark. Because she made no effort to complete reading assignments or do homework, she was unable to make use of cognitive therapy techniques.

Other group members were clearly frustrated by her behavior, and the facilitators spent considerable effort trying to direct her energy toward cognitive therapy principles. Learning from our experience with Dorothy, we recommend that if there are concerns about a participant's ability to understand basic concepts, then the facilitators should begin with some individual sessions to evaluate the person's ability to grasp the ideas and function in group therapy. We also learned to seat one of the facilitators next to Dorothy at each session to use tactile reminders, such as a light touch on the arm, to cue her when she was monopolizing the group time. She became responsive to this cue and often apologized or curtailed her remarks.

After offering this 10-session group twice a year for several years, we remain convinced of the value of this mode of group therapy for older adults. Some participants clearly benefited from recognition of cognitive distortions and substitution of more rational thoughts. They learned how automatically they had been reacting to life events on the basis of negative thinking patterns that were developed in early life. They were able to apply techniques learned in the group to think more realistically and lessen their feelings of depression or anxiety. Even those participants, such as Roger, who were less inclined to expose distorted thoughts in the group learned about distorted thinking from observing others' disclosures. Other people may have profited mainly from the problem-solving discussions. They were able to consider alternative ways to cope with their problems based on the suggestions or experiences of other group members. Still others may have benefited primarily from the social support of a group of sympathetic individuals. We often hear people say, "It helps a lot to know that I'm not alone in my depression." As a result of one or a combination of these factors, most participants reported feeling better by the end of the 10 sessions.

At the end of each series, we offer group members the option to join an ongoing monthly group composed of past members of the weekly series and facilitated by the same two social workers. Approximately half of each group has chosen to continue in the group for a period of time to reinforce the concepts that they have learned. A few members have maintained membership in this monthly group for several years. We have found that providing group cognitive therapy has increased our range of interventions in treating mood disorders and has offered us interesting and challenging opportunities for growth.

ADDITIONAL RESOURCES

Students and practitioners who want a comprehensive and reader-friendly approach to the core principles and practice of cognitive therapy are referred to *Cognitive Therapy: Basics and Beyond* (Beck, 1995). The author is an established therapist and lecturer and the daughter of cognitive therapy founder, Aaron Beck. The book provides a step-by-step discussion of the theory, basic concepts, and techniques used in cognitive therapy. Clinical examples include transcripts from actual therapy sessions. This book also lists many other good resources about cognitive therapy for both therapists and their clients.

For several years, we have used *Feeling Good: The New Mood Therapy* (Burns, 1980) as a resource for group members to review basic concepts taught in the group sessions. Participants find this book a clear, commonsense approach to understanding their own thought processes. The forms and charts are useful, and the author's optimistic language encourages participants to believe that they can make positive changes in their lives and moods. The examples are practical and down-to-earth, but they apply mostly to younger people. We have found that we need to supplement this material with many examples that are applicable to the lives of older adults. Other books by Burns that may be useful to therapy groups are *The Feeling Good Handbook* (1992) and *Ten Days to Self-Esteem* (1993). Both of these books include many self-help forms and charts that can be assigned as homework.

We have also used *Mind over Mood: Change How You Feel by Changing the Way You Think* (Greenberger & Padesky, 1995) as a workbook for the group sessions. The *Clinician's Guide to Mind over Mood* (Padesky & Greenberger, 1995) accompanies the workbook with instructions for use by therapists with both individuals and groups. *Mind over Mood* provides a systematic approach for teaching the basic concepts and includes sample worksheets and blank worksheets for participants' use. Four case studies are followed throughout the book. We appreciate that one of them is an older adult who is dealing with issues of aging and loss. These books are especially useful for group work as they provide a step-by-step approach including guiding questions, hints and reminders, and worksheets in 12 chapters, which can be covered in a 10- to 12-week series. The *Clinician's Guide* has useful chapters on individualizing the workbook for clients and setting goals in therapy. The chapter on group therapy is especially relevant to the discussion of this chapter. It includes sample agendas for a 12-session group and strategies for dealing with different rates of client progress.

REFERENCES

Beck, A. (1972). *Depression: Causes and treatment*. Philadelphia: The University of Pennsylvania Press.
Beck, J.S. (1995). *Cognitive therapy: Basics and beyond*. New York: The Guilford Press.
Burns, D.D. (1980). *Feeling good: The new mood therapy*. New York: New American Library.
Burns, D.D. (1992). *The feeling good handbook*. New York: Avon Books.
Burns, D.D. (1993). *Ten days to self-esteem*. New York: William Morrow.
Greenberger, D., & Padesky, C.A. (1995). *Mind over mood: Change how you feel by changing the way you think*. New York: The Guilford Press.
Padesky, C.A., & Greenberger, D. (1995). *Clinician's guide to mind over mood*. New York: The Guilford Press.

Exploring the Meaning of Life in a Group Setting

8

Janet Fogler
and
Lynn E. Stern

CLIENTS' BACKGROUND

PAULA, A 65-YEAR-OLD WOMAN, MARRIED HER HIGH SCHOOL SWEET-HEART, BOB, AT AGE 19. Bob was an adequate provider, but he drank too much and became abusive when drunk. Paula chose to remain in this difficult marriage and cared for their three sons without much support from Bob. To supplement the family income, she worked part-time as a secretary. Her oldest son, Gene, developed leukemia when he was 12 and died after a long illness. Paula believed that she was just beginning to regain her equilibrium when disaster struck again. Her second son, Eric, was killed at age 17 in an automobile accident. Bob handled this loss by increasing his alcohol consumption, and Paula felt completely alone in her grief. She reluctantly decided that she and her youngest son, John, would be better off if she divorced Bob. She found a full-time job and devoted herself to her son.

John graduated from high school and began classes at the local community college. When he was 20, he began to show signs of paranoia and soon dropped out of college. He began hearing voices, and, at Paula's insistence, he saw a psychiatrist, who diagnosed him as having schizophrenia. Over time, it became clear that he needed more supervision than Paula could provide. His care manager placed him in a group home after his third hospitalization.

At a support group for parents of children with mental illness, Paula met Brian, who had recently become a widower. They found that they had a lot in common and enjoyed each other's company. Although she was apprehensive about a second marriage, she decided to take another chance on love. After their marriage, Paula moved into Brian's home, and they had 7 happy years before he died suddenly of a heart attack. Paula found herself again grieving a

113

devastating loss. Her many traumas compelled Paula to search for meaning in life. She began a personal search for ways to understand all that had happened and to create a better future for herself. She joined our Exploring the Meaning of Life group because she felt ready to meet some new people with whom she could talk about meaning and existence.

Ed, a 72-year-old retired pharmacist, grew up in a rural community in Kentucky. He was the sixth of 10 children. His father was a carpenter who worked as many hours as he could to support his large family. His mother was a quiet but kind woman who accepted her long days of housework without complaint. Ed described his childhood as being "lost in the shuffle" of many brothers and sisters. He grew up believing that the way to get love was to be a "people-pleaser." He found himself doing what other people wanted him to do, regardless of his own wishes. For example, he wanted to be a writer, but he went into pharmacy because his father said that he might not make it as a writer and that people would always need medicine. In looking back at his childhood, Ed recalled that strong feelings such as joy, sadness, fear, and play-fulness were not permitted. Although he knew that his parents cared about their children, they were unable to express their love.

In college, Ed met a girl, Jean, who lived with her fun-loving family while she was studying to be a teacher. He enjoyed having long dinners around their table, where everyone talked at once and the room was full of laughter. Ed and Jean married and moved to Michigan, where Ed was determined to create a happy household. He learned to show affection to his wife and children in both verbal and physical ways. After their three children entered school, Jean returned to her career as a teacher. She continued to enjoy her first-grade class-room and was active in the teachers' union. Ed had recently retired from the drugstore where he had worked for 40 years, which gave him time to try some new activities. He decided to join our Exploring the Meaning of Life group because he wanted to keep his mind and body active in retirement.

GROUP'S BACKGROUND

As clinical social workers in an outpatient geriatric medical clinic, we recognized the inclination of older adults to reflect on the meaning of their lives. We, too, had questions about finding meaning in life's experiences as we watched our clients and ourselves growing older. How is it that people who have experienced similar joys and sorrows interpret their lives in very different ways? Why do some people long to understand life's meaning, while others never ask the questions? How do people make sense of personal tragedy and global atrocities? Why do some people wish to die and others embrace life to the end? For 5 years, we tossed around the idea of creating a discussion group that would encourage par-ticipants to share the content of their lives, hear the accounts of others, and derive some personal meaning from the collective experience. We finally decided to offer a discussion group entitled "Exploring the Meaning of Life."

We wanted the emphasis of this group to be on components of life that are common to everyone regardless of race, religion, gender, marital status, class, or life experience. To discourage chronological storytelling, we chose to focus less on the details of each life than on the meaning that is derived from the experiences. We were determined to avoid a recitation of accomplishments that would promote a hierarchical comparison of the lives of participants. Our goal was to provide an arena in which people could candidly express their previously unspoken thoughts and beliefs about the meaning of life—acknowledging and validating both satisfying and painful experiences.

With these guidelines in mind, we brainstormed themes that embody core aspects of life. Many themes were generated: work, community, rituals, death, acceptance of change, humor, spirituality, family, love, marriage, sex, children, expectations of aging, childhood, creativity, values, dealing with adversity, pleasure, disappointment, being alone, relationships, and celebration. We consolidated these themes into seven discrete topics: The Self, Relationships, Work, Adversity, Earthly Delights, Death, and Spirituality. We chose not to focus individual sessions on themes that might leave some members out of the discussion, such as marriage, children, and sex. These themes and others—family, community, love, and childhood—were discussed in the session on relationships. We included the topic of humor in the session on earthly delights. Some themes were bound to surface in many sessions, such as acceptance of change, expectations of aging, and values. We added an eighth session, Celebration, as a celebration of the whole experience.

Before we planned the agenda for the sessions, we articulated a vision for each discussion topic. Our goal was that each session would be an entity unto itself, culminating at the end of the series in a deeper understanding of the meaning of life. Following is our concept of what we hoped the participants would accomplish in each session:

> The Self: Our goal for this session was for the participants to identify and appreciate the core aspects of their being that were enduring regardless of circumstances, such as age, marital status, health, vocation, and economic status.
>
> Relationships: We asked participants to review important relationships, both past and present, positive and negative. A central question of this session was "How have these relationships affected the way you look at life?"
>
> Work: We defined work in an all-encompassing way, including paid and unpaid work, as well as avocations, such as hobbies, sports, and artistic endeavors. We wanted participants to discuss the impact of work on

their lives, both satisfying and unsatisfying, without focusing on the details of their careers.

Adversity: We wanted participants to look back at adverse events in their lives with these three questions in mind: How do you cope when bad things happen? Did anything good come out of the adversity? Is there a reason for adversity, or do people create meaning out of adversity?

Earthly Delights: Our plan for this session was to help participants to identify small personal pleasures in the past and in the present, deal with lost pleasures, and look for opportunities to find pleasure in everyday life.

Death: We wanted to create a compassionate and nonjudgmental environment in which people would be free to talk about dying and death. We planned questions that would encourage expression of beliefs, fears, and hopes. Participants could also choose this opportunity to talk about decisions that they had made concerning death and its rituals.

Spirituality: Because this undoubtedly would be a group of people from different religious backgrounds, we knew that we needed to separate the idea of spirituality from the idea of religion. With the goal of learning from one another, we decided to ask participants to prepare their own definitions of spirituality.

Celebration: This session was planned to be a ritual that celebrated our 8-week journey together. The main discussion questions related to lessons learned throughout life and how to incorporate this knowledge into life in the present.

INTERVENTION SUMMARY

We have successfully offered this discussion group four times with a total of more than 40 participants. Like some of the other groups at our clinic, a fee of $35 was charged for the eight sessions. The participants in the four groups were attracted by news releases and posted fliers and did not previously know one another. They ranged in age from 60 to 84 years. Their educational backgrounds ranged from high school graduates to holding advanced degrees. Many occupations were represented, such as homemaker, teacher, artist, social worker, truck driver, engineer, and clerical worker. Some participants were well off financially; others accepted the offer of a scholarship for the series. Some were healthy and active; others had chronic or terminal illnesses. Some were actively engaged in life; others were socially isolated. Religious orientations included Christianity, Judaism, Hinduism, atheism, and new age philosophy. Common threads among the participants were their stated goals: "to keep learning," "to better understand other people and myself," "to discuss with others all of the interesting topics," "to continue to grow," and "to make sense of life."

"Exploring the Meaning of Life" consisted of eight weekly sessions of 2 hours each, which we facilitated. Each session covered one of our chosen themes, and the series culminated in a celebration. We limited the size of the group to 10–12 members to ensure that everyone would have the opportunity to share his or her point of view. In an initial telephone call, we advised potential members that they would be expected to participate in discussion and that no lectures would be given on the meaning of life. At the first session, ground rules were explained: Facilitators do not have the answers. There are no right or wrong answers. People are expected to listen to views that are different from their own without criticism or judgment. Confidentiality and trust are essential to open discussion.

One of our primary tasks in creating this group was to develop materials that facilitate discussion. We chose four tools that would stimulate introspection and provoke meaningful discussion: readings, homework assignments, in-class exercises, and questions for discussion.

> _Readings_: We chose brief, intriguing, and occasionally controversial readings to stimulate thinking about the theme of each session. These readings were distributed a week in advance of the discussion. The brevity was purposeful because we did not want to exclude people who might be reluctant to read lengthy articles.
>
> _Homework Assignments_: Homework questions and exercises required participants to consider thoughtfully the following week's topic, which enabled each member to be prepared for the session.
>
> _In-Class Exercises_: The exercises were intended to provide a format in which each participant would be expected to respond. The questions were designed to be answered easily whether people were highly verbal extroverts or shy people of few words. The exercises encouraged people to explore and share inner feelings.
>
> _Questions for Discussion_: The success of each session was dependent on having penetrating yet easily understood questions to stimulate discussion. Considering that group members were from diverse backgrounds and had very different life experiences, the facilitators prepared a variety of questions.

Before each session, we constructed an agenda that would fill a 2-hour period in an interesting way (see Table 8.1 for an example). Each session had at least one in-class exercise in which everyone was expected to participate. Other questions for discussion were presented as stimuli for group debate in which members might choose to participate or not. We always asked members

Table 8.1.   Sample session

The following describes the agenda and materials of the session on relationships:

In-class exercise: Pass around a manila folder that contains a list of words prepared in advance. (These words will trigger a thought or memory from each participant's life. Some examples are music, travel, nature, failure, change, childhood, time, and mother.) As the folder is passed, ask each member to scan the list and choose one word that has meaning to him or her and explain to the group why he or she chose that word.

Assigned reading that was distributed at the previous session:

"Strange is our situation here upon Earth. Each of us comes for a short visit, not knowing why. ... From the standpoint of daily life, however, there is one thing we do know ... that people are here for the sake of other people ... for the countless unknown souls with whose fate we are connected by a bond of sympathy. Many times a day I realize how much my own outer and inner life is built upon the labors of my fellow men [and women], both living and dead, and how earnestly I must exert myself in order to give in return as much as I have received and am still receiving."

—Albert Einstein

Class discussion of assigned reading.

Previous session's homework assignment: Make a list of significant relationships during:

Childhood   Middle age
Young adulthood   Older adulthood

What did you learn from doing the homework? Did anything surprise you?

10- to 15-minute break. Coffee and cookies provided.

Hand out the following list of questions about relationships. In a go-around format, ask each member to choose one question to answer:

1.   Who among the people in your life influenced your feelings or thoughts about the meaning of life?

2.   Tell the group about a loving relationship.

3.   What role has love played in your outlook on life?

4.   Relationships are often conflicted or disappointing. Describe a conflicted or disappointing relationship.

5.   Who has influenced your life?

6.   How have you influenced the life of someone else?

7.   Tell us about a relationship that changed over time and how it changed.

8.   Do you have another question about relationships you would like to answer?

Give reading and homework assignment for next week's session.

Ask for feedback about today's session.

to comment on the readings. At the end of each session, we asked for feedback about the group.

Session by session, we worked our way to greater understanding of ourselves and one another. Before the first session on The Self, we sent a letter to participants asking them to read the introductory material and write a short paragraph about themselves. We purposefully made the instructions vague, and we were intrigued by the various ways in which people defined themselves. Some made lists of achievements: family, work, and education. Some defined themselves in terms of present situations: recently retired, a new grandmother. Some used spiritual terms, such as a child of God, or described an emotional state, such as excited, exhilarated, anxious, or fearful.

Clearly, Paula had given a lot of thought to her paragraph and wrote it in poetic terms: "Even though I am a 65-year-old woman, I am first and foremost a child of God. Presently I find myself on the edges of the life that swirls around me. ... I would like to find freedom for my spirit to learn how to dance and sing and celebrate life." Conversely, Ed described himself in very factual terms: "I am 72 years old, the sixth of 10 children. I have been a pharmacist for most of my life. I have three children and two grandchildren." We realized that Ed's upbringing in a large family was a defining aspect of his self because he mentioned his large family in his first sentence. He was the only participant who described himself in terms of his position within his family of origin.

When discussing Relationships, participants revealed more than we had anticipated. Many people talked about painful and abusive marriages or problems with their adult children. Both positive and negative relationships with parents had a major impact on participants' lives. The homework assignment in preparation for this session asked participants to make a list of significant relationships during various stages of their life. It was during this session that we learned about the tragedies that Paula had endured. She spoke candidly about her abusive first marriage and the deaths of her two children. She also revealed her current struggle when her son John called to ask whether he could live with her. Although she knew from past experience that she would be unable to manage his care, she longed for a closer relationship with her remaining child. Her decision to refuse his request had intensified her feelings of guilt and sadness.

Ed responded to one of the questions listed on an in-class worksheet designed to elicit information about relationships, both positive and negative. He chose to discuss a conflicted relationship. Ed described his father in humorous yet cynical terms. He made us laugh, but we could tell that there was deep sadness underlying his words. Ed said that the only person in his family who was allowed to express emotion was his father, whose sole emotion was anger. In Ed's words, "Feelings were unacceptable." Ed further revealed that he had not seen any of his nine siblings in many years and had no desire to see any of them again.

In the session on Work, participants discussed the impact of work on their lives. In the responses to a question about advice to young people about work, two themes appeared: "Work isn't everything. Find other outlets for creativity and pleasure," and, "Find a job you really enjoy and engage yourself in it, continuing to learn." Ed was a proponent of the first theme. Although he was a successful pharmacist and provided well for his family, Ed never found his work meaningful and did not miss it when he retired. For Paula, both housework and her secretarial work had been necessary only to keep the family together. She had not derived meaning from either of these endeavors. Since the death of her second husband, however, she had become a representative for a national cosmetic line that was sold in the home or in small gatherings. She discovered that she was good at working with people and at selling products in which she believed. Her advice to the next generation was to find meaningful work that provided opportunity for growth.

In our discussion in the session on Adversity, participants revealed or elaborated on terrible, traumatic events. Nearly one third of the participants had lost a child or had a child who had developmental disabilities or mental illness. Group members were prepared to talk about and listen to the sad and painful episodes of life. People were free to describe the experience and the aftereffects. Group members left this session feeling trusted and trusting. Although Paula had talked about the tragedies of her life during the session on Relationships, it was in this session that she described their impact on her life. The pain that she had experienced was evident, as was the strength with which she had dealt with her adversity. Her lifelong philosophy was that life is a learning process. She said, "Growth and maturing and change begin at conception and continue for a lifetime—that's what makes life exciting and interesting." Her positive attitude about life and her enthusiasm for the future were inspiring to the group. Because Paula did not feel sorry for herself, other group members felt free to discuss their own experiences with adversity even though they did not compare in severity to Paula's. Ed, surprisingly, had very little to say in this session. Group leaders had anticipated that he might discuss his severed relationships with his siblings, but he evidently did not think of these estrangements as an adversity. Another participant, Duane, was a charming and well-educated 84-year-old. He had spent his life in teaching and administration, culminating in a position as a school superintendent. In this session, he revealed that his only child had died at 2 years of age in a tragic accident. He also told us that he had been advised by his doctor that he was showing signs of Alzheimer's disease. He was forthright in talking about his fears about the future.

Earthly Delights was originally titled Pleasures, but we found that this title directed many group members into discussions of children and grandchildren, which tended to be boring to other participants and left out some people. Earthly Delights led to the discussion of small, personal delights of the past and present, such as hearing birds in the morning, listening to the sound of church bells, enjoying the feel of velvet, laughing really hard, petting a dog, observing fall foliage, and enjoying food and music. This session provided a break from the intensity of previous and later sessions. Games, drama, joke telling, and music have been included as opportunities for laughter and fun.

In the week before our session on Death, we asked participants to describe their level of interest and comfort on a scale of 1–10 (1 = "I put it out of my mind" and 10 = "I'm very interested and want to explore the meaning of death"). Most people expressed a high level of both interest and comfort. The participants represented a wide range of beliefs about life after death, from a belief in the Judeo-Christian concept of heaven, to reincarnation, to the belief that "when you're dead, you're dead." Most agreed that they were more afraid of the dying process than of death itself. Group participants talked about their fears of pain, being alone, and having life prolonged by medical professionals. This session did not seem of particular interest to Ed. He stated that he believed that life ended when the body shut down. Paula, conversely, believed that the soul lived on with further opportunities for growth in future lives.

In the session on Spirituality, we encouraged people to look inside themselves for what made them live the way that they did. For people who were drawn to a discussion group on exploring the meaning of life, this topic was a natural final theme. Paula and Ed demonstrated two polar extremes within this group. Paula said, "I experience spirituality as unconditional love and seek it through faith and hope and ... contemplation." Ed, however, did not believe in anything that he could not see and explain.

Our last session, the Celebration, was planned to be a festive occasion. Group members suggested having a potluck luncheon. The main discussion questions dealt with lessons learned throughout life and how to incorporate this knowledge into life in the present. People put considerable thought into presenting strong, concise, positive pieces of wisdom to share with the group. Messages reflected a balance between following their inner voices and contributing to the welfare of others. The following examples are group members' responses to the question "What advice would you give to a young adult?":

> Live fully, joyfully, productively.
>
> Life is change. Learn how to be flexible.
>
> You never have to stop learning, growing, and developing.
>
> Take full responsibility for your life. You have a right to choose your own destiny.
>
> You don't have to meet your perception of other people's expectations.
>
> Live until you die.

INTERVENTION ANALYSIS

Although we were not conducting group therapy, group members found these sessions therapeutic. During our preparation for each session, participants' individual needs were less central to the planning than were the needs of the group. There were no stated objectives about change, and participants were not asked to set goals. Distortions and contradictions were not necessarily addressed. Participants were not asked to reflect on their emotional states during the past week or at the moment. They might choose to discuss a recent event or feeling, but facilitators did not create a specific opportunity for this type of disclosure. The sessions were opened with an introduction to the topic of the day, and the discussion stayed focused on that topic. These sessions were designed to be exploratory journeys, not group therapy.

Demonstration of Respect

The number and quality of adverse events in Paula's life dismayed both group leaders and participants. Group members were amazed at her ability to cope with extreme adversity while maintaining her sense of optimism. We showed our respect for her by giving her the opportunity to talk about her personal adversities and by letting her set the pace of disclosure. We were supportive and interested, without making her uncomfortable with excessive commiseration. Paula was a sensitive person and would have limited her discussion of these events had she believed that she was bringing down the group or exceeding her allotted time.

One of the groups included a participant, Mary, age 65, who had never married and had a limited income, living most of her life in rented rooms supported by her work as a companion for older people. She took great pride in her work and believed that she had contributed to the lives of her clients and to society as a whole. At the same time, she developed few personal relationships or social skills. Because of Mary's limited experience in social situations, she kept herself on the periphery of the discussion. She never contributed a comment unless called on by one of the leaders. She rarely completed homework assignments and at times seemed to be unaware of the proceedings. Other participants never directed comments or questions to her, perhaps for fear of putting her on the spot. We showed respect for Mary by making sure that the in-class exercises were accessible to her. We demonstrated an interest in her life, even when her remarks were off the topic. Group participants were able to follow our lead and accept Mary as she was. Our ability to make Mary comfortable in the group was evidenced by her perfect attendance.

Use of the Clients' Strengths

Every person who signed up for this group demonstrated a willingness to tackle the daunting subject of the meaning of life. They understood that there were to be no lectures or answers from the leaders, and the group members themselves were the explorers. By nature, they were inquisitive, thoughtful, revelatory, and interested in other people. Almost without exception, they were committed to the group process, completed homework assignments, and attended regularly.

Ed's strengths were intelligence, humor, and insight into himself and his relationships. He worked hard at creating a meaningful life after retirement. He was active as a volunteer at Motor Meals, he picked up his granddaughter from school when her mother was busy, and he cared for the home because his wife was still employed. We counted on Ed to bring humor to every session. We felt free to ask him to provide transportation for another group member.

Paula amazed everyone with her openness and ability to tell the truth about her life and herself. She did not expect undue sympathy because of her life's trials. She served as a model of candor and good humor. We commended her for her openness and honesty, and we believe that group members revealed more because of her example.

Duane, the 84-year-old with a preliminary diagnosis of Alzheimer's disease, was an inspiring example of a person in late life. He took a risk in signing up for "Exploring the Meaning of Life" with a group of strangers, some of whom were considerably younger than he. Perhaps Duane revealed his early-stage Alzheimer's disease because he was unsure of how he would come across to the group and wanted people to know why he might be a bit forgetful. As group leaders, we appreciated his trust in us and were prepared to acknowledge his illness and make him a full participant in the group. Despite his cognitive deficits, Duane always came prepared to discuss the readings and had completed his homework thoughtfully. He was interested in other people and asked good questions about their lives. He described himself as having great curiosity and a love of learning, and this was evident to everyone in the group.

Blurred Boundaries

Occasionally, a member of a group was seen by one of us in individual therapy. Andrew, a 74-year-old married man with two supportive children, was a retired schoolteacher. He had recently been diagnosed with multiple myeloma. He knew that he would die in 1–5 years from this disease. He joined the group because he liked the adventure of something new and the topics intrigued him. He stated, "Life has handed me a due date and I'm not coping well. This might help me pull it all together." Andrew's wife had always been somewhat antisocial, but in recent years she had refused to allow anyone in the home and severely limited their social life outside the home. Thus, Andrew was struggling in a lonely marriage with few supports. Because of the therapeutic relationship with one of the facilitators, Andrew's history and current situation were well known to the facilitator. It was frustrating to listen to the portions of his life that he was willing to share with the group, knowing that there were some inaccuracies being presented. In a group such as this, we were dealing only with the pieces of each participant's life that he or she chose to present, but in this case, the discrepancy between the stories was uncomfortable for the therapist. The boundaries between the roles of therapist and discussion group facilitator became blurred. The therapist knew that Andrew would have benefited from being more honest in the group, but the group format prohibited any allusion to the unstated history. Although this issue could be addressed in individual sessions, the therapist had to collude with Andrew's fabricated portrayal of a more satisfying life in the group sessions. As therapists, we were tempted to delve more deeply when personal problems were presented, but we recognized that in our roles as facilitators of a discussion group, we could not indulge this temptation.

Changes in the Therapeutic Relationship over Time

Paula arrived at the fifth session of the group and announced that she had great news. She was excited but afraid that others would think that she was bragging when she announced that she had won an award for the greatest increase in sales in her territory. When group members responded with enthusiasm, Paula seemed to become more comfortable talking about her positive achievements and attributes. Over the next few sessions, Paula became more likely to agree with comments from group members about her strengths.

During one of the middle sessions of the group, Ed reported that his daughter had given birth to a child with breathing problems. Clearly, he was worried and upset. Group members responded with concern and solicitations. Ed seemed to be moved by their support and was gratified by their relief when his grandson was out of danger. We noticed that he became less likely to use humor to deflect emotional content in later sessions. For example, during the session on Death, Ed revealed the depths of his worries about the possibility that his grandson might not have survived.

Benefits and Difficulties of the
Therapeutic Relationship for the Clients and the Therapists

Ed joined the group because he wanted to keep his mind and body active. In the early sessions of the group, he seemed to be a little self-conscious, perhaps because he had not anticipated as much personal revelation from other group members. He was quick to inject humor when things got too serious. Group members enjoyed and appreciated him but could not get beneath his jovial exterior. As time went by, he seemed to be more comfortable with the revelatory nature of the group. We believe that hearing the intimate details of the lives of others freed him to open up about his early years and the repercussions on his present life. He expressed sadness about his life as a child and wondered how it may have affected his ability to be emotionally available to his wife. Ed continued his custom of pleasing the crowd with humor and lighthearted banter, but as he revealed more about his life, Ed seemed more genuine to the other group members.

We noticed that Paula seemed to be strengthened by the power of the group discussion and to gain confidence in her ability to interact with interesting people. In a note of thanks to the facilitators, Paula wrote, "The opportunity to focus and discuss various aspects of my life was beneficial, and to share the experience with such a diverse and empathic group was rare indeed."

Mary, who seldom had an opportunity for social interchange, seemed to enjoy being with a kind and generous group of people led by trained facilitators. For people like Mary, who are inexperienced in social interaction, a venture into an unstructured group setting often leads to rejection. Mary benefited from the facilitators' commitment to ensuring that she was included and respected.

For Duane, the group provided mental stimulation at a time when he needed to believe that his mind was still able to learn. He especially benefited from preparing the homework assignments as he tried to put his own experiences into the context of exploring the meaning of life. Group members obviously appreciated his contributions and showed him affection and respect.

Because of the "due date" on his life, Andrew was looking for answers that he did not find in the group and was particularly intolerant of anything that he considered a waste of his time. He entered the group with the objective of learning more about the meaning of life as it related to his own situation. At this stage of his life, he was not interested in the experiences and life stories of other participants. He did appreciate being able to review his life through the assignments and exercises, but he did not feel as though he got answers from other group members or the facilitators about life's meaning.

As in all groups, time and shared intimacy created a sense of closeness and knowledge among group members. The readings, exercises, and discussion questions allowed us to know ourselves and one another on a deeper level as time went by. As the group facilitators, we learned to listen to and appreciate other people who had very different views on life.

Words of Wisdom

Because the concept of exploring the meaning of life is so daunting, it is important to carefully plan the structure for the exploration. We spent considerable time and energy creating the tools to stimulate thoughtful preparation and interesting discussion. We developed readings and homework that we expected people to use as groundwork for the week's session. We devised explicit yet diversified in-class exercises and questions for discussion to provoke an invigorating exchange of ideas during the sessions (see Table 8.2 for examples of questions asked in each session). We believe that without the expectation that participants should take responsibility for being prepared, the discussion could

Table 8.2.   Sample questions

The following are some sample questions from each session's topic:

The Self

   What are the essential parts of yourself that have stayed the same over your
      lifetime, and what parts have changed?
   How has aging affected who you are?

Relationships

   Who among the people in your life have influenced your feelings or thoughts
      about the meaning of life?
   What role has love played in your outlook on life?
   Relationships are often conflicted or disappointing. Describe a conflicted or
      disappointing relationship.

Vocation

   Are you satisfied with the choices you are making regarding your vocation? If
      not, how could you change things?
   If you were not limited by your skills or your age, what would you like to do?

Adversity

   From the perspective of what you know now, did times of adversity teach you
      something?
   Do you think that there is meaning in adversity?

Earthly Delights

   What object symbolizes or demonstrates an earthly delight for you?
   What were your family's values about pleasure? Do you still maintain these
      values?

Death

   How would you prefer to die?
   Do you have fears about death?
   What are your beliefs about death?

Spirituality

   What does spirituality mean to you?
   How do you incorporate spirituality into your life?

Celebration

   What do you know about life now that you wish you had known when you were
      younger?
   What can you share about your current life and your future that would teach
      younger people about growing older?

be shallower and might falter. We also believe strongly that if leaders do not
keep the sessions focused, then the topics could be overwhelming.

   Because this group is a journey that participants take together, we decided
that members had to commit to attend all of the sessions and to call ahead of
time if an emergency prevented them from coming. We asked people who
would miss more than one session to postpone their participation until the

next offered group. Even so, there were people whose attendance was interrupted because of illness or emergencies, and we noticed that they were less integrated into the group.

As previously stated, we knew that we wanted to ask questions that would include everyone regardless of marital status, work experience, financial status, and educational background. We believe that this decision was vital to group cohesion. We did not plan a session or ask questions that were based on marriage and children or college days. For example, we would not ask, "What did you teach your children about adversity?" but rather, "What were you taught in your family about adversity?" We also would not ask a question such as, "What did you do on your first date?" We also avoided questions that might invite comparisons or exclude people, such as, "Where did you take your last vacation?"

When we offered our first group, there were some topics that we thought required outside speakers, such as death, humor, and spirituality. We chose people in the community whom we knew had special expertise in these areas. Although they clearly knew their field, they also came prepared to impart knowledge, which was incompatible with our basic philosophy that this was an exploration, not a lecture series. After the first series, participants told us that they preferred our facilitated discussions rather than the outside speakers.

Our professional training taught us to avoid the topic of religion in a group discussion because of its potential for divisiveness among group members. Thus, we had concerns about the topic of spirituality. We felt committed to a discussion that included people of all faiths or no faith. We have been surprised and gratified that people have been respectful of one another and have avoided religious dogma. We still recognize that this is an area of great sensitivity and may require vigilance and guidance on the part of the facilitators.

"Exploring the Meaning of Life" is a work in progress. We are always on the lookout for interesting reading and new exercises. Each time we offer the group, we try something new; and at this point, we are willing to risk a small failure or two to keep the group evolving and our interest alive. As facilitators, we feel privileged to witness the disclosure of experiences and philosophies. During each session, we get a renewed opportunity to think through our own lives and respond to philosophical questions in a different way. As we observe the widely varied ways in which participants cope with later life, we have learned that there is no one way to give meaning to life. For some people, contributing to society remains preeminent; for others, it is a time to seek pleasure. Some focus on their families; others are still working on finding themselves. Some people find it essential to remain active and busy; others see this as a time of life to cut back on activity. As we age, we want to give ourselves permission to follow our own inner voices in our search for meaning.

ADDITIONAL RESOURCES

As described previously in this chapter, we developed materials that are designed to be used for an eight-session group (Fogler & Stern, 2000). The materials for each session include readings, homework assignments, in-class exercises, and questions for discussion. By using this concise packet of materials, professionals will be able to offer a similar group. However, this packet does not include the theory behind the exploration or information on group process. Some of this theory can be found in the writing of others. For example, in *Autumn Wisdom: Finding Meaning in Life's Later Years*, by clergyman and grief counselor James Miller (1995), poems and readings celebrate the later years in life. We especially like the many introspective exercises that help the reader to reflect on the meaning of their life experiences and relationships.

Mueller's book (1996) centers on four questions that help us to examine and understand the meaning of daily lives: Who am I? What do I love? How shall I live, knowing I will die? What is my gift to the family of the Earth? The author used real-life stories of people who have found fulfillment in the midst of hardship and provocative quotations as a method for analyzing meaning. He created 12 practices that could be used as homework assignments or in-class exercises.

Most public libraries and bookstores have a large section of books on spirituality. Browsing these sections may give facilitators ideas for readings and exercises. We have found that there are many good resources for inspiration, not the least of which are group members themselves.

REFERENCES

Fogler, J., & Stern, L. (2000). *Exploring the meaning of life: A handbook*. Ann Arbor, MI: Turner Geriatric Clinic.

Miller, J.E. (1995). *Autumn wisdom: Finding meaning in life's later years*. Minneapolis, MN: Augsburg Press.

Mueller, W. (1996). *How, then, shall we live?* New York: Bantam Books.

Re-creating Family Through a Writing Group

9

Ruth Campbell

CLIENTS' BACKGROUND

PAUL SCHNEIDER, A LEAN, SOMEWHAT STOOPED MAN IN HIS LATE 80s, CAME TO ANN ARBOR, MICHIGAN, from Philadelphia, where he had lived since immigrating from Europe at the beginning of World War II. He had been a promising scientific scholar, but when he arrived in the United States he could not get the kind of highly skilled job for which he was trained. Paul had a successful career as a high school teacher and had been married for 60 years to Edna, who was also a public school teacher. They came to Ann Arbor to live near their only son and his children when the struggle of living alone in a large city became too difficult for them.

My first encounter with Paul was in the clinic, where I conducted the psychosocial assessment that we do with every new client. He spoke about all of the activities that he had left behind. He had taught science to older adults in the local senior center, where he also produced a newsletter and wrote about complex scientific advances. He felt lost in this city, especially when he tried to talk to people in his new retirement home about these issues but received little response. He seemed highly nervous, talkative, and fidgety; he got up and down several times while we talked. His wife, talking to me privately, was very concerned. In the few weeks they had lived here, he had gone outside on long walks and buttonholed people about his ideas for the future. People in their building were avoiding him because he was always going on at length on topics that they did not understand. When the team of doctor, nurse, and social worker discussed his case, it was clear that despite several physical problems, it was likely that he was experiencing a bipolar disorder episode. An appointment was made with the psychiatrist. He also agreed to attend the writing group that I led, which sounded like the kind of activity that he was used to in Philadelphia.

Marianne Greene, a woman in her early 60s, was one of the younger members of the group. A retired speech therapist who took early retirement because of back problems, she was introduced by another group member who belonged to the same church. Marianne was bitter about the political changes in her hospital that made it increasingly difficult for her to enjoy her work. Marianne's history, as she related it, was not an especially happy one. Her childhood in a working-class St. Louis neighborhood was not nurturing. She was married for just a few years, then divorced. She had a daughter who, like Marianne, experienced recurrent episodes of depression. Her daughter, who lived in another state, was a constant source of stress for her. Their relationship was not an easy one, and she often felt helpless to relieve her daughter's problems.

A great source of comfort to Marianne was her cat, the subject of many poems and essays. She had a generally critical, angry stance on many issues and critiqued members' writings more directly than was the custom. She could be sarcastic, but at the same time, she clearly had a zest for life, which was reflected in her love of nature and long hikes and the singing lessons that she took weekly. Although she criticized others for talking too long and frequently scowled as she glanced repeatedly at the clock, she was prone to lecturing either during her time to read or in response to other members' writings. She carried with her to each group a backrest that she placed on her chair, a non-verbal affirmation of her physical discomfort. She also gradually became the group's photographer, taking pictures at the monthly birthday parties, holiday parties, and other celebrations.

GROUP'S BACKGROUND

In the current environment in social work of cost containment, in which short-term therapy is favored, the impact of a long-term writing group in providing a safety net for its members as they cope with the changes of aging cannot be underestimated. Although the group discussed here has been facilitated by an experienced social worker, the therapeutic outcomes are largely derived from the group interactions, and the model is adaptable to volunteer leadership and other types of settings.

The Monday writing group began in March 1978 after a press release appeared in the local media and newsletters of senior organizations, asking people older than age 60, "Do you want to write a book?" When about 15 people responded, the Monday group began. Requests to join the group increased, and in September 1978, the Friday writing group was formed under volunteer leadership. Since then, both groups have been meeting continuously every week. I have been the leader for the Monday group since its beginning, with coverage from other social workers for periods of up to a year when I have been on leave. The Friday writing group has had about five different facilitators since the beginning, all volunteers, including several graduate students, but primarily older adults who are interested in writing. The current facilitator was a group member who took over leadership when the previous facilitator, also a group member, died.

Because I have been leading the Monday group for more than 20 years, there is a strong sense of continuity and history. Several of the members joined because of a burning desire to write; others came because they were depressed or isolated and a social worker or a physician believed that this ongoing group would be helpful. As one of the group members wrote, "The present Monday group continues to embrace the variety of personalities, education, and interests that have existed in the group for 23 years." Educational backgrounds have ranged from high school graduates to professors with doctoral degrees. Professions have included: housewife, musician, auto worker, shop owner, businessperson, attorney, graphic artist, engineer, physician, nurse, teacher, and social worker. Group members often say, "We are a group of people who would never meet under ordinary, everyday circumstances."

Over the years, new members have been added as others leave, usually when they become too ill to attend. One woman has been in the group since it began, several for more than 15 years, and the most recent member has been coming for 3 months. Their ages range from 59 to 93. Currently, five men and eight women come each week, with absences for illness or vacations. They range from people who are healthy and active to those who have more severe physical limitations. One man, a retired engineer who has had a major stroke, is paralyzed on one side and requires a wheelchair. One woman is legally blind but still lives alone. Several have had strokes, cardiac problems, arthritis flare-ups, hip fractures, cancer, and other chronic conditions that become acute from time to time. About half of the group members are taking medication for depression, and one man has had in-patient treatment for alcoholism but is now sober. Three members are married; the others are widowed or divorced or have never married. Over the past 23 years, 60 older adults have participated in the group.

The Monday writing group is loosely structured. During the first 15 or 20 minutes, members are encouraged to talk about what is going on in their lives or anything that is on their minds. During these discussions, births of grandchildren and great-grandchildren, deaths of family members, the current world crisis, and local community issues may be discussed. After this, members begin reading what they have written at home, and the group proceeds in order around the table. Members who have not written during the past week will usually relate a story that explains why they have not written or share an oral offering instead of writing. It is common for people who have not written to tell jokes. The most published author in the group, Laura, a 93-year-old woman who is legally blind, is greatly appreciated for her joke-telling ability. One member records programs or songs that he likes and then brings his tape recorder in to share these with the group.

One of the key questions that emerge in the group from time to time is, "Is this therapy, or is this just a writing group?" In fact, one of the advantages of a writing group is that members do identify themselves as writers, not as people who need therapy, even though most of them recognize and praise the therapeutic value of this approach. The most accurate answer may be that the writing group lies somewhere in between and perhaps is best described as a surrogate family. Members go in and come out of the hospital, have various crises, and return to the group. Birthdays are celebrated, members visit one another when they are ill, and when real family members come to town they are usually brought in to meet the group. When a member of the writing group dies, most of the group members attend the memorial service and mourn with the family. Frequently, poetry or essays that the person has written are read as part of the memorial service. One of the original members joined the group because her own family was not interested in hearing about her family history. She thought that if she began writing, they would gradually understand its significance. This process has been repeated many times. Family members express gratitude for the writings, whether family reminiscence, fiction, or poetry, both during the lifetime of the member and then after, as a living legacy of their relative.

Writing reveals often-intimate matters, so members of the group may know more about one another's lives than do members of their own families. Although reminiscence certainly is a part of what they write, the group is anchored in the present. During the conversations at the beginning of each week, people argue, commiserate, or applaud one another as they report on illnesses, children's visits, a class reunion, a political scandal, or the Super Bowl. During the readings, each member is on stage, presenting his or her personal thoughts and feelings and receiving the kind of focused attention that happens infrequently in daily life. It takes a kind of bravery, rooted in trust, for a person to expose deep feelings to a group. It is this process of self-disclosure as well as the poem, mystery story, or reminiscence produced that makes writing groups such a vital part of people's lives. I have seen this process repeated in other writing groups that have started as 10-session groups and then, with the urging of group members, go on and on. At the Turner Clinic, there are two other writing groups that are more than 5 years old, each led by a volunteer retired English professor, and there are other examples of writing groups in senior centers and other meeting places in the community. Whether it is "therapy" or "writing," it is a dynamic type of intervention.

INTERVENTION SUMMARY

To illustrate the dynamics of the Monday writing group, I examine the involvement of two members, Paul and Marianne, and provide a summary of one group session.

Paul Schneider

Paul talked incessantly at his first session. When I asked him to stop, he would, but he tended to forget and launch into his ideas for the future, which involved complicated technological concepts. His foreign accent was also a disadvantage—group members reacted to it negatively, as if every word uttered were incomprehensible. However, two other European intellectuals were in the group and had been accepted and were loved and admired. They helped to ease Paul's acceptance, and he was asked to come back and bring his writings. At the second session, he brought poems that he had written to his wife, which were simple and lovely and very well received by the group. However, he clearly was nervous, trembling constantly. In the following week, his behavior became more erratic. The psychiatrist believed that he needed immediate admission to the psychiatric unit. He refused, struck out at the psychiatrist, and was taken in handcuffs by the police to the hospital, where he was admitted involuntarily.

The tragedy for Paul was that from his perspective, he had escaped the Nazis in Europe and was now being forced by the police into what he saw as imprisonment. "This is worse than the Nazis," he said in tears when I visited him shortly after he was admitted. He was "preparing my defense" for the commitment hearing. He asked me to read what he had written—a carefully formulated essay on why he should not be hospitalized and a moving poem about his longing to see his wife:

> "Home"[1]
> Dear Wife,
> Home is
> Where you are ...
> I searched for you
> In many places!
> I found you,
> Married you,
> And "never let you go."
> Now temporarily "homeless,"
> But not "wifeless,"
> I hope
> We shall be together again
> At home together
> Where we belong!

When he presented this poem to the probate court judge, the judge was sympathetic but recognized the need for treatment. He gave Paul the choice of three hospitals. Paul chose one, and that he was given some control helped

---

[1]Printed with permission of the author's estate.

him to accept the treatment. He formed an alliance with his new psychiatrist, improved with medication, and came home after about 3 weeks.

Shortly after hospitalization, he returned to the group. I was nervous about whether the group members would accept him again. With his permission, I told the group about his hospitalization, and although nothing was mentioned in the group, he received a warm, if not effusive, welcome. With most new members and particularly with Paul, I am supportive and encouraging, playing a much more active role than usual in allying myself with him and trying to ease his acceptance into the group. Paul was quite different than he had been initially, subdued and quiet. He read pieces that he had written in Philadelphia in his senior center newsletter. I asked him to read some of the poems that he had written in the hospital:

> "You and I"[2]
> You see things
> You say, "Why?"
> I dream of things.
> I say, "Why not?"
> You see ...
> I dream ...

Group members were so moved by these poems that even Laura, who especially did not like foreign accents (her low vision caused by macular degeneration probably made adapting to one more challenge difficult) and had previously said that she could not understand him, praised his poetry. In bestowing her infrequent praise on Paul, she guaranteed his legitimacy as a group member.

Paul did not want to see another psychiatrist after he left the hospital but agreed to have his medications monitored by his primary care physician. He said that he would attend the writing group as his therapy. He wrote every week. For the first year or so, most of his pieces explained some kind of scientific issue. Some members liked these pieces; others were not interested. But Paul's manner, which was gentle and courtly, his obvious intelligence, and his quiet sense of humor endeared him to the group. He became the scientific expert, and all questions that were remotely related to science were referred to him. He greatly appreciated Laura's wit, which was quick and biting, and they engaged in gentle teasing in which others were happy to join.

Paul's big breakthrough in the group came when he began writing stories about his childhood, his family and education, and later his escape from Nazi-occupied Europe and his early days in the United States. He wrote of his mother and father, of family members who had died in concentration camps, of happy family vacations in Europe, and of individuals whom he admired and respected. These were wonderful stories, and they were written at the encouragement of

---

[2]Printed with permission of the author's estate.

the group. Each time he said, "This isn't very interesting." They would protest, "Yes, it is!" Paul managed to convey a world that most of us did not know—the lack of food during World War I, families moving furtively from one place to another. Some of the stories were difficult for him to read without crying, and he would ask me or another group member to read them for him. His stories about his mother, who died during the war, were especially hard for him, yet these were the stories that were the most praised and encouraged by the group.

He never lost his awe of science, and one of his greatest joys in the group was to explain some recent development, bringing the newspaper clippings with him. He experienced a recurrence of bipolar disorder when his medication was changed, and he became quite agitated. This was resolved through outpatient treatment, and he was absent from the group for just a few weeks. Paul did not like to discuss his illness, and he continued to refuse ongoing therapy. He had several individual sessions with me but worried so about taking up my time, despite his obvious pleasure in talking about his life, that we met only when he was feeling especially worried about something, such as his wife's health. He insisted that all he needed was the group. He did stay on the medication and was followed closely by his internist.

Paul's wife, Edna, came to the group from time to time, but she clearly regarded it as his territory. She attended all of the parties along with other spouses. After about 6 years, Paul's physical condition—he had two types of cancer and other health problems—forced him in and out of the hospital. Edna had pulmonary problems and needed portable oxygen. Paul believed that he could not leave her and stopped coming to the group, despite his wife's protests to the contrary. He was, however, quite weak, and when he did attend the group, it was clearly difficult for him to sit in a chair that long. Group members visited and called Paul and his wife. When Paul died, everyone went to his memorial service. His poems and photographs of his life were printed in the program. In addition, his writings were on display. He is still referred to from time to time in the group: "Did you see that story about the space mission? Paul would have liked that." Laura says, "Paul was a real gentleman," and those of us who knew him nod in agreement.

For Paul Schneider, the writing group was an effective therapy because it reaffirmed his identity as a scientist, and it helped him to review his life and to come to terms with traumatic circumstances such as the death of his parents and other family members. More than that, it gave him a community in which he had a clearly defined role and brought him friendships that reached across his own personal history and allowed him to continue to learn, which, besides his love for his family, probably was the enduring theme in his life.

Marianne Greene

In the 5 years that Marianne was a group member, she experienced several personal crises: the death of her cat, her daughter's psychiatric hospitalization, legal separation from her husband, and, most significant, the diagnosis she received of ovarian cancer. She wrote about the death of her cat and her own illness but could talk about her daughter only hesitantly. She was not able to write about their relationship and felt tremendous guilt about her inability to help her daughter. Marianne was in individual therapy and discussed these issues intensively there.

Marianne wrote about nature well, both in poetry and in prose. One favorite poem of the group's was about the death of an old tree: "For 18 years the tree was my companion. ... " But it was her recounting of her work history that really gave the group insight into her life. She wrote a series of work stories beginning with the part-time jobs she had during the school year, to waiting tables at summer resorts, to her first real jobs and subsequent career changes. These were both funny and sad stories; many of the jobs did not turn out well, but Marianne's outspoken courage and resilience were evident. As she wrote faithfully each week, she became less critical of others, noticeably softening her remarks. From time to time, she would get up and say, "I just want to show off my new outfit. Doesn't it look good?" Everyone admired her spontaneity and could only say, "It looks great!" She would also sing for us in a clear soprano voice occasionally, as a special treat.

Marianne formed friendships in the group that extended beyond Monday afternoons. She became very close to Susan, a retired nurse, who had similar feelings about the changes in health care and who had endured the death of her husband and two young children in an automobile accident early in her married life. They were about the same age and enjoyed socializing outside the group. Her most intimate attachment was with Mark, whose wife had died of cancer a short time before. Mark had been an attentive caregiver for his wife and was absent frequently from the group during her illness. He and Marianne began dating without mentioning it explicitly in the group. Gradually, snippets of, "Mark and I saw such and such over the weekend," or, "Marianne took a marvelous picture of the changing leaves up north," crept into the conversation. "It looks like we have a romance budding here," Laura remarked in the superior knowledge of one who cannot see but knows nonetheless. That announcement seemed to expose the secret, and the relationship was acknowledged and accepted. If Mark came in late, then room was made for him to sit next to Marianne, for example. It seemed a natural development, although it was the first romance to bloom in the group. Although Mark's personality remained the same, affable and friendly, a popular member of the group, Marianne's demeanor changed noticeably. She was much more open and relaxed and seemed for the first time since she had entered the group to be visibly happy.

What gave their relationship added poignancy was that soon after it began, Marianne was diagnosed as having ovarian cancer. She continued to show off her new wigs and her new clothes, but she weakened visibly throughout the treatments and whether she came to the group depended on the timing of her chemotherapy. When she was able to come to the group, she reported on the various medications that were available and on the progress of her illness. Susan and Mark provided transportation to appointments and other concrete help. Mark and Marianne decided to go ahead with plans that they had made for a trip to the Caribbean. The trip was discussed in the group, and while they were gone, we all worried about how it might be going. When Mark returned, he brought pictures that showed Marianne in bed with a scarf around her head, looking out the window at the beach. Besides one difficult episode on the airplane when she became quite ill, the trip went well and the achievement of doing it seemed to be a highlight for Marianne. Shortly after the trip, she began hospice care and returned to the group only once or twice.

During the last months of her life, her younger brother, Steven, came from the East Coast to take care of her along with the hospice team and Mark. Because Marianne could not attend the group, Steven did. He came every Monday for about 3 months. At first, he gave "the Marianne report," but gradually, at the group's insistence, he began to write about his life and his sister's. "You know her as Marianne; I know her as Polly, my big sister. ..." He became a member on his own account. When Marianne's daughter joined him to care for her mother, she also attended but did not participate as a writer the way that Steven did. After Marianne's death, Steven continued to come as he took care of all of the details of clearing out her apartment and settling her accounts. His departure was sad for the group, mingling the loss of Marianne, a long-time member, with this short-term but intense relationship with her brother. Several group members continue correspondence with him and with Marianne's daughter. After Marianne's death, several people wrote of their feelings for her and their grief at her early death.

No one could have anticipated that Marianne, one of the youngest and most vital members, would have died before many of the older and more frail writers, but during her time in the group, she wrote so much about her life and spoke so openly of her thoughts and feelings that it felt as though we had gone through her entire life with her during that period. For Marianne, the group provided an outlet for her creativity and a cushion to deal with the difficult circumstances of her life. It seemed to spark her more positive emotions, and, in the way in which she conducted her final months, the sense of joy in her life was even more evident. The bonding of her biological family with this created family seemed both natural and affirming.

Notes from a Typical Writing Group Session

Sarah, who was 87 years old, came back to the group after an absence of more than a month as a result of a stroke and her subsequent hospitalization and rehabilitation in a nursing facility. She brought her home care aide with her. Sarah now had to use a walker, and although she had recovered much of her normal speech with therapy, she still slurred words and often became discouraged by the thickness of her speech. She introduced the aide to the group, and there was a general discussion about Sarah's illness as well as an update on Charlotte, the only remaining member of the original group, who had just undergone hip surgery. After a brief conversation, the group settled down to read. I began with the ritual question, "Who would like to start?" Sarah immediately said that she would, at which point the group broke into laughter and not-too-subtle glances at one another. Sarah always wanted to go first, and in her absence, this had been both noted and not missed. Sarah, who was adept at ignoring these cues, read her poem on how she was struggling to cope with age and loss. Her husband died more than a year before, her sons lived in distant western states, and she was frequently struck with bouts of loneliness and depression exacerbated by the frightening experience of the stroke. She expressed all of this in her poem.

Susan then read about her visit to the doctor that week when he said he could not do the knee replacement that she had counted on because her other medical problems put her at too much risk. She ended in tears. There were many questions and sympathetic comments from the group. We had been following Susan's painful medical problems closely.

Next, Richard talked about the family reunion he had with 45 members of his wife's family gathered in a building that he and his wife own and rent out to the community for gatherings such as this. He had been too busy that week to write. Barbara read Laura's short story. (Laura cannot read because she has been blind for the past 15 years but types her own stories and has them edited and sometimes published in magazines and newspapers as feature stories.) The story was a rewrite of one she had read before, and she asked the group whether she should keep in the addition, which she wrote at the suggestion of the group the last time she read it. Everyone said in a chorus, "Keep it in." At that point, the center receptionist came into the room to announce that Tom called and could not come to the group. He has been having chemotherapy and felt too ill to come. Susan, Sarah, and Charles all said that they would call him and encourage him to come next week.

Charles, who was next, apologized to the group. "This is the first time I haven't written [he had been in the group for about a year]. I thought maybe I shouldn't show my face, but I decided to come anyway." Sarah shouted, "That's okay. We'll forgive you, but you better write next week!" Others gently chided him but told him that he should always come, whether he has written anything or not. "We'd miss you," Susan said. It was now Barbara's turn to read her own story about her high school reunion in Cleveland. At the dinner, she met a former classmate who told her that he had had "an enormous crush" on her while they were in high school. He asked his wife for permission to take Barbara out for dinner. "His wife said, 'Sure,'" Barbara said triumphantly. "So we went out to dinner and had a wonderful evening." As Barbara read her story, she seemed to glow with the brightness of that high school senior who had a secret admirer.

Gloria, the newest group member who lived in the same senior citizens' building as Sarah, read her poem in tribute to Sarah for rejoining the group after her stroke. Sarah was delighted. Everyone applauded Gloria's poem. Marianne read a short tribute to her cat, a rewrite of a poem that she had read earlier. Mark said that he had not written this week because he was illustrating his poems called "Letters to God" and that had taken up all of his time. The group had heard and debated each of these poems, mainly critical of organized religion and its spiritual failures. Barbara encouraged him to finish the book.

Paul talked about the discovery of a new gene that he had just heard about on the radio and what it could mean to the cure of a chronic disease. A heated discussion on the use of genetics began among Marianne, Richard, and Sidney, who also did not write that week but participated with fervor in this discussion, which he viewed as an ethical crisis.

In the break in the middle of the 2-hour group, several people spoke individually to Susan to offer advice and help. Some people used the extra time produced by this week's "nonwriters" to tell jokes or expand on Mark's religious poems and Sidney's ethical philosophy. The use of humor in this group is very important. It is almost as though people feel the need to leaven with a light-hearted tone the heavy emotional tone that can pervade. At the end of this session, Charles said, "What a good session, and we didn't even talk about politics once! I love this group."

INTERVENTION ANALYSIS

The role of the leader in this well-established group is low key but important. In concrete terms, I act as the timekeeper, making sure no one goes on too long. I am responsible for ensuring that each member will have enough time to read or talk. If I am derelict in my duties, someone usually says, "We're running behind. We better move on or everyone won't have a chance to read." In addition, I am responsible for announcing the break halfway through and getting people back from their individual conversations during the break. I also talk to members privately; in this session, for example, I spoke to Susan, suggesting that she get a second opinion about her knee replacement and offering help to find a physician for her. Besides maintaining the flow, the leader promotes interaction and models tolerance.

The group is rarely openly critical, but certain people are easily targeted. Sarah, for instance, is criticized because she often violates group norms by interrupting when others are speaking, rustling her papers and telling long, irrelevant stories in the guise of helping someone. My function as leader includes imposing limits on Sarah and modeling appropriate ways of dealing with this disruptive behavior. In this group, leadership has been assumed by various members during my absences, primarily Barbara and Charlotte, both retired social workers. Whoever takes the leadership role, it exists as a kind of protection for group members so that the group will operate under certain norms, such as ensuring each person time to read or talk and paying attention to each person when he or she is "on stage." It also lets the group relax, knowing that someone is in charge.

The therapy comes from recognition and reinforcement of people's strengths. Richard, for example, who spoke about his family reunion, is in a wheelchair as a result of a stroke that affected his mobility but not his mind, with its encyclopedic grasp of local and family history and wide-ranging knowledge on many topics. He is perceived in the group as an expert and is frequently called on to furnish factual information. From his own library, he brought in an old University of Michigan yearbook in which one of the classmates pictured was Charles's mother. Charles, who is 86, was thrilled to see this book for the first time, proof of his mother's achievements at a time when not many women went to college. The therapy also comes from the ability to process for oneself through writing about unpleasant things, such as Susan's dismissal by the doctor, and then, by reading it to the group, find sympathy and encouragement. Perhaps most important, as seen in Charles's final comment on the session, the therapy comes from the sense of belonging, a family-like acceptance ("family—the place where when you go there they have to take you in"), which the group engenders.

Demonstration of Respect

Members of the group are expected to say something each week, whether they have written or not. The ritual of going around the table from one person to another with the goal of including each member by the time the 2-hour session ends is set in stone. Each member's contribution is respected, and the norm is to show appreciation and interest even if the member has not written anything for a while. In Paul's case, the respect for his past and his knowledge was critical to his participation in the group. That his illness, erratic behavior, and hospitalizations were never mentioned in the group represented an understanding of his strong feelings that these be kept private. He was accepted as a person with exceptional expertise, which was essential to his sense of pride and dignity. He was viewed the way he wished to be, and this acceptance helped him to reestablish his identity after relocation and a traumatic illness.

Marianne was shown respect throughout her illness by members' visiting her, taking her brother and daughter into the group as members, and participating in her memorial service. Before her illness, respect was paid to her lifelong struggles in earning a living. Perhaps most meaningful to her was the understanding and empathy of many group members when her cat died. Others talked about their own relationships with animals, commiserated, and listened at length to her memories of her pet.

Respect can at times be a barrier in this group. There are always a few people at any given time who really want criticism in order to improve their writing. This happens sporadically, but it is clear that the group is more comfortable in giving praise than criticism. Silence or very little reaction seems to be as much criticism as most will allow themselves. A few people over the years have left the group because they were interested in publishing and improving their writing. Others stayed but joined more focused courses or seminars to accomplish this purpose. Some members obviously are not interested in any criticism of what they have written. One of our most gifted writers, a woman with little formal education and a childhood in the Appalachian Mountains, would state firmly at even the slightest hint that something could be changed, "I don't lie. That's how it happened."

Use of the Clients' Strengths

The process of writing enhances the strengths of each participant. The routine of writing at home each week and then reading in front of the group builds confidence and self-esteem. It is risky and takes a certain amount of bravery to expose personal feelings and experiences to a group of 10 or so people who listen to you closely as you speak. The group process also requires paying attention most of the time to what someone else is saying. Listening with full attention is an exercise that most of us practice infrequently, but doing so is energizing and stimulating.

Both Paul and Marianne demonstrated strength in the way in which they persevered despite the challenges that they faced. What is probably unique in this kind of group is that the old struggles, the personal history, come alive and are then joined with current struggles so that Paul and Marianne can be appreciated not just in the way they met death and illness but also in the way they triumphed over their early history.

The particular strength of a writing group is the way that it ignites creativity, not just in writing but also in a certain attitude toward life. The group members become great appreciators—of nature, of food, and of gifts brought in from time to time, such as books, photographs, and mementos. Talents are recognized and praised whether it is Mark's skill at drawing (he drew the cover of an anthology of the group's writings), Marianne's photographic skills, or Charlotte's wonderful cakes brought to celebrate each person's birthday. The need to create remains and may even be stronger as people age, but for most of us, creativity needs an audience, which this kind of group provides.

The other strength of any well-functioning long-term group is that it exists as a refuge and source of ongoing support. Just that it meets every week is at times a strength. There is someplace to go where others are expecting you. This kind of group, which invites but does not insist on revelation, becomes a place to go to talk about things that cannot easily be discussed elsewhere. The various personalities in this group and the acceptance of widely varying beliefs and personal eccentricities are beneficial in two ways: The person whose eccentricities are accepted receives affirmation, and those who tolerate these eccentricities can congratulate themselves on their patience and flexibility. Colleagues who have led the group during my absence frequently say, "What a strange assortment of personalities are in that group!" Perhaps it is our identity as writers that leads us to prefer and encourage colorful and unusual behaviors.

Blurred Boundaries

Over the years, I have met with several group members in individual therapy sessions. Some have moved from individual therapy to the group as part of their treatment. As needed, I coordinate services, such as home care or hospice care (in Paul's and Marianne's cases), and provide other social work services. Laura periodically needs me to provide transportation, send in her handicapped parking form, or look up something for her. In payment for these services, she gives me a treat, such as a ripe pear or a bunch of grapes. In Sarah's case, especially, I am in frequent contact with her sons to provide updates on her health and to add or subtract services.

An advantage to leading a group as part of a clinic program such as ours is that the leader can move easily among the roles of group leader, care manager, and counselor. In Paul's case, I assumed all three roles. Especially during his illness, I met frequently with the family, intervened with the court system, and consulted his psychiatrist. I visited him at the psychiatric hospital and maintained contact with his family throughout this process. I interacted frequently with his internist concerning his medications and increasing health problems. As his condition worsened, I arranged for hospice services and even worked with his family after his death concerning emotional and financial issues. Group members continue to call Paul's wife, and she is invited to all group social activities, such as our annual Christmas party.

In Marianne's case, I provided care management services, particularly in the last stages of her illness, such as coordinating with hospice care and consulting with her physician. I also helped her to find mental health services for her daughter in another state when Marianne believed that her daughter's care was inadequate. Another clinic social worker saw Marianne for individual therapy, which she preferred to keep separate and confidential from the group activity.

At one time or another, I have performed various care management services for all of the group members: referring them for counseling, getting home care services and house cleaning services for some, referring to other physicians when they needed a second opinion, crisis intervention (e.g., I was called first when one group member was found on the floor of her apartment when she had a stroke), and brief consultation and counseling before or after group sessions. I know many of the participants' family members and am in telephone contact with those who live far away. The group has become an entry point for services and a natural place to look for help for those who are reluctant to use the formal system. I see no conflict between these roles as long as confidentiality is respected and personal issues are not brought up within the group unless the group member chooses to do so.

For the group members themselves, blurred boundaries might be perceived in the social activities that become a ritual of being a member. Richard and his wife invite the group to their home twice each year to enjoy their screened-in porch and wildflower garden with tadpoles in the spring. We also go to their property in the woods once a year to view trillium in season. Barbara has a Christmas party at her home every year, and others invite group members to special occasions. One of our members invited us to attend a Sikh religious ceremony at her brother's house, and on another occasion, several group members joined Tom as he became a member of the Catholic church. The hospital visits, the participation in memorial services, the birthday parties, and get-well messages are no longer blurred boundaries but an essential part of the group experience.

Changes in the Therapeutic Relationship over Time

The process of being accepted in the group is not easy and must be heavily supported by the facilitator. Bringing a new person into a cohesive group is, to extend the family analogy, like bringing in a new child and saying to her brother, "We like having you so much that we wanted to have another child." It is a mixed message at best. (The response to such a statement could be, "If you like me so much, then why do you need anyone else?") There are small but visible changes as new members emerge from the leader's protection and are accepted by group members. In Paul's case, Laura's approval hastened his acceptance. Gradually, people became used to his accent and differentiated him from the other two European men who were part of the group. Also, Paul's good nature and courtesy won over many who were put off by his initial excesses. First tolerated because I brought him into the group, he eventually won acceptance on his own, forming alliances with Marianne, Charlotte, and Richard as he read various pieces that he believed met each of their special interests. At first reluctant to share any personal history, he was more comfortable in the role of a teacher, clarifying science concepts. Once he felt established in this niche, he could venture into more personal—and often painful—history. This took several years and massive amounts of encouragement but was clearly a big step forward for him when he could write about these difficult and rewarding times from his past.

Marianne changed from a critical, acerbic person to a warm, gentle, even joyful person, especially as her friendship with Mark progressed and her health declined. The group, of course, was not totally responsible for this softening and relaxing of her previous combative stance toward life, but I think that the group represented an opportunity for her to reveal the parts of her life that she was most proud of and to underplay what gave her the most guilt and frustration. Even though she had spoken very little, if ever, about her brother, his emergence when she needed him and his absorption in the group was positive for her, perhaps allowing her to see herself less as a person with an unsatisfactory family life than as someone surrounded by people who deeply cared for her.

I think that my most important function in this group is to support and advocate for group members at crucial stages, especially when they enter the group, when they are absent because of illness or other problems, and when they feel attacked or unappreciated by another group member. Because I am often the person who brings a new member into the group (although I always ask the group ahead of time for their approval) and because the person whom I bring frequently is someone who is depressed, withdrawn, or has not been accepted in another group, I believe that I have a responsibility both to demonstrate tolerance and to be open to criticism or resentment among other group members at this intrusion. I have learned through the years that everyone eventually is accepted. In one case, a group member left because she could not tolerate Sarah's frequent interruptions, but that has been the only negative outcome of this kind of open-door policy.

Benefits and Difficulties of the Therapeutic Relationship for the Clients and the Therapist

This group has worked as a safety net for people who may not fit into other kinds of activities. Some, of course, are attracted by the writing and come for that purpose. Others come for the friendship and the routine of a weekly obligation. Simply being able to observe members on a weekly basis allows the leader to notice small changes in behavior and cognition and to intervene at an earlier stage than is possible without frequent contact. The relationship established also engenders trust and a feeling that anyone can come to me with a problem when it occurs. When Laura's brother, for example, came to town determined that she should move to a safer place, she brought him to me to discuss other options. In the group, I could see Paul's behavior changing and could question his physician about the effects of his medication. This kind of coordination may be unusual in the care of older adults but clearly is beneficial and provides a more seamless way of delivering services.

Older people frequently are reluctant to go into therapy, even under extreme circumstances. The writing group presents an acceptable way of dealing with personal problems that is not immediately identifiable as "mental health treatment." For some, it is self-selective. Those group members have always wanted to write, and aging presents a kind of deadline—do it now or never. Others have been referred to the group by other helping professionals not because they have expressed any interest in writing but because it seemed a safe milieu for them to be involved in a long-term commitment. One member of our group, for example, almost never wrote, but he contributed by bringing in photographs or tapes. He might have done just as well in another kind of ongoing group, although this was the only one that he agreed to attend. Each time he did write, it was received with great enthusiasm and he talked each time about what he was working on, promising to bring it in soon. After he died, his family found bits of stories that he had indeed been working on at home but never finished. Even the illusion of being a writer has the power of bestowing a kind of status that is not possible in other kinds of therapy groups.

Words of Wisdom

For the therapist, the writing group is both humbling and stimulating. No amount of proselytizing about the wisdom of older adults, the need to "empower" them, can convey the force of being part of a group like this, in which the wisdom flows like water and group members contradict you, ride over you, and just plain take charge. To be in a group in which ideas are tossed back and forth, in which personal histories weave in and out of current events, philosophy, and mundane matters of living, is an exhilarating kind of experience. I know of nothing that can refresh me, renew my enthusiasm, or restore my energy for working with older adults more than attending a session of the Monday writing group. My only suggestion for other practitioners is that they take the selfish route and try it.

I feel especially privileged to have been able to work with this group for so many years. I realize that it is not feasible in many settings to allow a worker to spend 2 hours a week every week for 23 years with the same group. Since 1978, there have been 60 members of the writing group. Most have been in the group at least 5 years, with just a few people staying in less than a year. If I had to justify the group according to strict cost-effective guidelines, it might be difficult to make a good case, but taking a wider view of the impact that this group has had on the clinic and its programs and on a much larger number of older people strengthens the argument that it is in reality quite cost-effective.

This group has led to five other ongoing writing groups in our clinic, all of which have been successful from the participants' point of view and all led by volunteers. It has also served as a model for six-session writing groups that social work staff and interns facilitate in 11 local nursing facilities for residents with depression, anxiety, and dementia under a grant from the local community mental health program as well as a short-term group for African American older adults in a senior center. Components of the writing group have been incorporated into other discussion and "neighbor-to-neighbor" groups.

Several anthologies have been published by the groups, and various group members have produced their own collections of writings. The two anthologies, one published in 1984 (Kaminsky, 1984) and the second in 1991 (Brown & Campbell, 1991), were funded by grants from the University of Michigan Hospital and the Friends of University Hospital, a volunteer group that operates the gift shop and pursues other fundraising activities. Book sales also help to finance these publications as well as other clinic educational materials and resource guides. Books are sold in local bookstores, through direct mail brochures, and through advertising in local and national publications. Book signings and readings are held in the community, and feature stories appear in local media. The publicity generated from these publications is invaluable in terms of public relations and the increase in visibility and support for the clinic in general.

It is sometimes difficult because of my modest role as a facilitator to identify this role as a social work function. However, looking at the impact that this group has made on the lives of the participants and the sheer joy of being associated with it, I cannot help but believe that more social workers should be doing this kind of work. Especially as a way to reach people who otherwise would avoid involvement in a social services setting, the writing group is an effective approach.

This type of activity can and should be held in all types of settings: senior centers, churches, senior housing, and clinics. It is inexpensive and can be led by trained volunteers. There is also a cadre of retired professionals in every community who look for stimulating volunteer jobs and often have difficulty finding them. This kind of activity is well suited to retired teachers and other professionals. Whether led by professional staff or volunteers, it is a relatively inexpensive activity and can be justified to administrators on the economic grounds of serving a group of people in 2-hour weekly sessions. The specific advantage of a writing group is that there are products to display, books to publish, and readings to organize for the public, which bring publicity and create a positive view of aging that might be particularly appealing to administrators in institutional settings for older adults.

The minimum number of sessions for such a group is 8–10. It takes time for people to become comfortable and to get to know one another. Short-term groups are effective for many people, and perhaps most would be interested in a time-limited group, especially older people who would like to start writing their memoirs. In my experience, several short-term groups have started and then met on their own at members' homes once they established a warm relationship and became reluctant to give it up. Also, the pressure of a deadline each week is helpful to a writer, and some cannot write independently without that pressure.

I am not a writer, and I do not think that teaching writing or grammar is a purpose of this group. The leader, however, should have a love of writing and reading and a respect for the written word. The opportunity to create a family-like atmosphere starts with sharing personal histories but can flower into group sharing of rituals at each member's birthday, opening the group to family and friends of the members, meeting occasionally in members' houses, keeping in close contact during illnesses, and encouraging friendships outside the group, even arranging that those with cars bring those who do not have transportation. In the Monday writing group, birthdays are celebrated each month; a cake is brought by one member, and a card is circulated among all to be signed. This is always arranged by the group members without the leader's assistance.

Receiving invitations to read what they have written to other community groups also gives members a feeling of being special.

Finally, after doing this for so many years, I feel a missionary zeal for expanding this kind of activity and a disappointment that it is not more widely available to others. What activity could be more age-appropriate? The distillation of years of living needs to be expressed and disseminated to family, friends, and all those who could learn from the experiences of older people. It provides closure and understanding to the writer; a glimpse of an unknown world to younger readers; and an appreciation of the complexity, richness, and resilience of the human spirit.

ADDITIONAL RESOURCES

Writing groups for older adults have been well documented in the literature. The therapeutic effect of writing has been examined by DeSalvo (1999) in *Writing as a Way of Healing*. She explored the work of such widely known authors as Alice Walker, Henry Miller, and Isabel Allende to demonstrate how their writing helped them to survive difficult times in their lives.

In his book I *Never Told Anybody: Teaching Poetry Writing in a Nursing Home*, Koch (1977) described the impact of poets' teaching poetry to frail older people. His description of "poetry ideas," which he uses to inspire individual and group poems, is helpful to those who want to replicate these activities. One of his ideas, for example, is to "write a poem about the quietest times, or the quietest things you can think of." Kaminsky's (1984) edited volume *The Uses of Reminiscence: New Ways of Working with Older Adults* presents various short-term writing groups that have grown out of the Artists and Elders Project in New York City held in senior centers, libraries, nursing facilities, and union halls.

Writing has proved to be an effective and creative strategy for working with older adults in the community and in residential settings. Inspired by Butler's (1963) seminal work on life review and incorporating the concepts of life review and reminiscence, Myerhoff's (1978) wonderful book *Number Our Days* evokes the power of the living history groups that she organized in a Jewish community center in Venice, California. Although these groups largely were oral, not written, reminiscence, the group interaction and the stories that emerged are similar to the experiences of most writing groups.

Birren and Deutchman wrote in their book *Guiding Autobiography Groups for Older Adults: Exploring the Fabric of Life*, "Writing about one's life and sharing it with others is a high point of human experience that should be encouraged by those who can take the initiative and provide the time and energy to guide the process" (1991, p. ix). They discussed in depth how to lead such a group and gave a detailed outline of each week's theme and sensitizing questions.

Research demonstrates the effectiveness of writing groups. A study by Smyth, Stone, Hurewitz, and Kaell (1999) found that participants in a randomized study who were assigned to write about emotionally traumatic experiences in their lives showed improvements in their medical conditions, health care, and well-being, whereas control group patients showed no change. Supiano, Ozminkowski, Campbell, and Lapidos (1989) described a controlled study of poetry writing groups in six nursing facilities. This study demonstrated that participation in writing groups promoted positive changes in nursing facility residents, especially among those who were depressed and had cognitive impairments.

A qualitative description of the experiences of two frail older adults in a journal writing group illustrates how writing can be used to enhance meaning at the end of life. Supiano (1991) discussed how a group organized around the metaphor of life as a patchwork quilt helped two older women to express their sense of completion shortly before they died.

REFERENCES

Birren, J.E., & Deutchman, D.P. (1991). *Guiding autobiography groups for older adults: Exploring the fabric of life.* Baltimore: The Johns Hopkins University Press.

Brown, L., & Campbell, R. (Eds.). (1991). *Never say never, II.* Ann Arbor: Turner Geriatric Services, University of Michigan Hospitals.

Butler, R. (1963). The life review: An interpretation of reminiscence in the aged. *Psychiatry, 26,* 65–76.

DeSalvo, L. (1999). *Writing as a way of healing.* New York: HarperCollins.

Kaminsky, M. (Ed.). (1984). *The uses of reminiscence: New ways of working with older adults.* New York: The Haworth Press.

Koch, K. (1977). *I never told anybody: Teaching poetry writing in a nursing home.* New York: (Ed.). Random House.

Myerhoff, B. (1978). *Number our days.* New York: E.P. Dutton.

Smyth, J.J., Stone, A.A., Hurewitz, A., & Kaell, A. (1999). Effects of writing about stressful experiences on symptom reduction in patients with asthma or rheumatoid arthritis. *Journal of the American Medical Association, 281*(14), 1304–1309.

Supiano, K.P. (1991). Writing at life's closure. *Clinical Gerontologist, 11*(2), 43–46.

Supiano, K.P., Ozminkowski, R.J., Campbell, R., & Lapidos, C. (1989). Effectiveness of writing groups in nursing homes. *Journal of Applied Gerontology, 8*(3), 382–400.

Intergenerational Group Work in the Nursing Facility

10

Mary Rumman

CLIENTS' BACKGROUND

JANE BROWN, A RETIRED MEDICAL SOCIAL WORKER, WAS AN 80-YEAR-OLD WIDOW WITH TWO DAUGHTERS. Her husband had died some years earlier from Alzheimer's disease. Jane had athetosis, a rare movement disorder that resulted from a stroke and that caused spontaneous and involuntary jerking movements of her arms, hands, and head, frequently leaving her exhausted. She also had difficulty swallowing, experienced some mild dementia, and required oxygen 24 hours a day. She spent most of her time in a wheelchair. Because of her need for ongoing care, her daughter Laurie suggested a move across the country to the nursing facility where Laurie volunteered and where I was the nursing facility social worker. Jane enjoyed people but was very weak and needed assistance with activities. Laurie talked with me concerning her guilt about moving her mother such a distance, especially because her mother could not remember where she was and why she had moved. Laurie also said that it was hard to get her mother into activities because of the assistance that she needed to get to the activity as well as during the activity.

Another resident in the nursing facility, Mabel Schindler, was an 85-year-old widow whose daughter, Gladys, and son, Ron, lived nearby. She had lived most of her life on a farm on the outskirts of the town until she moved to the nursing facility 5 years earlier. She had enjoyed music most of her life and had played piano for sing-alongs at church. She had been diagnosed with Alzheimer's disease 8 years earlier and since coming to the nursing facility spent most of her time in her room. She had arthritis, and she was beginning to experience contractures in her arms and legs. Mabel often appeared angry, and she frequently yelled at staff who cared for her. This was partly because of her pain and partly because she had adopted a gruff manner of relating since she developed Alzheimer's disease. I visited Mabel on a regular basis and found that once I could break through her gruff exterior, she would talk with me about her past, especially about farming. Her daughter tried to visit regularly but told me that it was hard because she did not know what to say and her mother did not always recognize her.

GROUP'S BACKGROUND

During the time that this group met, I was a nursing facility social worker. I led family caregiving groups as well as various resident groups. Cheryl, a colleague and a social worker at the clinic, had been coming to our nursing facility to lead enrichment groups. These groups were funded through a grant from the State of Michigan Office of Services to the Aging. The purpose of the groups was to enrich residents' lives through reminiscence and creative outlets to increase feelings of self-worth. The grant provided funding for Cheryl to go into all of the nursing facilities in the county to conduct these groups. One of the groups focused on memory improvement. Cheryl told me that a daughter of one of the male residents in another nursing facility had visited a memory improvement group. Until that point, the male resident had hardly spoken during the sessions, but the daughter was able to trigger some very distinct memories for him. Cheryl was considering forming an intergenerational group that included the older nursing facility residents and their children. I shared my concerns about the struggles of family members concerning what to talk about. I mentioned some of the issues voiced by Mabel's and Jane's daughters. I also talked with her about how hard it was for some residents to fit into regular group activities without more personal attention. Jointly we developed an intergenerational memory group to address our combined goals: to enhance residents' ability to trigger memories that they could enjoy with family and to model for family members ways to interact with their older loved ones in the nursing facility. After the first group, we discovered that the benefits of an intergenerational group for residents and family members far exceeded our initial goals.

We intended that in this group, family members and residents would participate together. In a few group sessions, the resident came alone but this was not as effective. In the case of Mabel's family, her son and daughter alternated attending the sessions. Having family members attend also helped with transporting residents to the group, an often-cumbersome task for nursing facility staff. Most of our group sessions were with residents and their adult children, but a few other family members also came, including nieces and spouses.

The group's members were recruited by invitation. I handpicked the residents for the group on the basis of certain criteria. The first criterion was that the resident had dementia and the ability to get to the activity by walking or wheelchair. The second was that the resident did not normally attend any of the regular activities at the facility. The third was that family members were available and interested in enhancing their interactions with their older relative who was a resident. I then wrote a letter to the family members of the residents who fit these criteria and invited them to attend the group together. The letter briefly outlined the kinds of activities that we planned and the overall goals of the group. The letter stated that family members were being invited because I wanted them to know that I believed that the resident was appropriate for the group and that it was designed especially for him or her. This note was important because some families were unsure that their relative was really capable of participating in such an activity.

Invitations were sent to 20–30 family members (our nursing facility had more than 200 residents), and reservations were taken. We limited each group to six to eight pairs. We did not turn away anyone. After this first group, I, for future groups, contacted those who had not initially chosen to participate. The groups met in the late afternoon for 1-hour sessions. This time was chosen because it was the easiest time to reserve room space, it is normally a low point in a resident's day, and family members who worked were more likely to be able to come late in the day than in the middle of the day.

INTERVENTION SUMMARY

The group consisted of eight 1-hour sessions. The exercises in these sessions were based on the memory groups that Cheryl had facilitated in many other nursing facilities. The original exercises used known techniques for memory improvement, for example, eliciting a memory using the first letter of the word. We modified the exercises so that they would fit with an intergenerational group and added some exercises that I previously had used. Cheryl and I shared group leadership by each facilitating a portion of the exercises during each session on the basis of our preferences and experience with them. Sessions began by reviewing everyone's names using the memory techniques that we learned in the first session.

Most of the residents came to the group fairly easily. It was helpful that they were with someone whom they knew (or recognized) and that they had one-to-one attention during the sessions. Although some were uncomfortable, especially at the beginning of the sessions, most were able to relax once the session began.

Our first session began with a name-association game in which the group members were asked to tell their names along with an adjective that described them and started with the first letter of their name. At our first session, Jane was unable to think of an adjective that described her. At this point, group members were encouraged to help her out, and family members suggested various words. Jane picked "Joyful Jane" for herself. Mabel described herself as

"Moody Mabel." At that point in the group, she was not smiling and her gruff demeanor was evident. Her fists were clenched and her eyes were downcast.

Later, the group was asked to complete proverbs and nursery rhymes that they learned when they were younger. The group facilitators would begin a nursery rhyme and then, usually as a group, others would respond. Some members could remember these rhymes better than others. Mabel was able to complete them all quickly. The group members praised her for her memory, and by the end of the session, she was sitting up in her chair and occasionally would smile.

Our second session involved visual memory in which group members were asked to close their eyes and visualize a family member who was close to them, perhaps a parent or grandparent. They were then asked to talk about that person. They were also asked to relate the story behind their names. Some were able to do this better than others. Later, they were asked to think about the house in which they grew up and what rooms were in the house. They then talked about a favorite room or place in their house. Jane's daughter, Ann, who was visiting from out of state, attended this meeting along with Laurie. Jane was particularly weak that day with a bad cough but came anyway. Laurie told us after the meeting that the interaction in that group helped confirm for Ann that they had made a good decision to move her mother to this nursing facility. Consequently, this helped Laurie deal with some of the guilt that she had been feeling.

In the third session, The World's Fair, group members were given cards with a letter of the alphabet on them and began a pretend trip to the World's Fair. Each member was asked what they might bring on the trip that began with the letter that they were given (e.g., M for money). The group rehearsed these items. Later in the session, people were asked to share memories of traveling to a World's Fair and other places.

It was during this session that Jane suddenly remembered a train trip that she had taken many times from her hometown across the state to visit her cousin Margaret. Her memory sparked Laurie to tell the group how as a young woman, her mother had taken a courageous trip across the country by train for 5 days and nights with her elderly parents to bring them to live with her. Laurie then elaborated that this journey had inspired Laurie to bring her own mother, Jane, to live near her just a few months before. This sharing seemed to enhance the mother–daughter bond and show Jane's strength and courage, which was a much different image than she usually presented at the nursing facility. Later, Laurie told us that after this session, she had made another meaningful connection when she shared Jane's memories of her train trips with her mother's 92-year-old cousin Margaret.

In the fourth session, The Reminiscence Box, memories were stimulated through all of the senses. Group members were asked to respond to each item in the box (e.g., Hershey's kisses, baby powder, cow bell, cinnamon, crocheted doilies, fresh flowers, old pictures) and share the memories that the items evoked. One of the items was a cow bell, and we asked group members to close their eyes, listen, and tell what the sound reminded them of. The responses were many, including a school bell, cow bell, and, of course, dinner bell. These initial responses led to members' sharing other memories. During this session, Mabel especially responded to the chocolate kiss. After eating it, she talked about a candy store in town that she used to frequent. With some coaching, she was able to elaborate on the cost of the candy and her favorite kinds.

Music and the use of auditory memory were the focus of the fifth session. The nursing facility had been given an Autoharp the year before, after a family member had seen one used in a group that I supervised. We decided to use the Autoharp in the music session. It is a simple instrument that is played by pushing a button for the appropriate chord and then strumming the strings with a pick. I fashioned a larger pick for residents who could not hold the smaller one. I demonstrated how to strum and helped them by pushing the buttons for the appropriate chords and, if necessary, holding their hands while they strummed. (With time, residents usually can learn to push the buttons themselves if the chords are not too complicated.) After encouraging the group members to remember words to songs from their youth, we had a sing-along with various group members accompanying.

Mabel had grown up with music in her life and mastered the Autoharp quickly. Despite her arthritis, she strummed it well and the group members were impressed by how well she played. This was another shining moment for Mabel, and she smiled frequently during this session. The music session was a fun one, and the group members sang many of the songs easily. For many older people with dementia and word-finding problems, singing along with a familiar song often stimulates the flow of words in a way that does not occur when words are spoken.

The sixth session, a memory movement session, proved to be a dramatic one for Jane. In this session, we introduced an exercise in which each person remembered a movement based on a role that had been important during his or her life and demonstrated it for the group (e.g., kneading dough). The movements were given a name (e.g., "the kneader") and then rehearsed by the whole group. In this session, Jane modeled for us how she used to serve a tennis ball. In the words of her daughter Laurie, she "slammed a tennis ball across the court so hard she practically threw herself out of her wheelchair." We all sat up and took notice. In that instant, everyone's perception of Jane changed. Jane then led the rest of us through the motion of serving tennis balls and told us how she used to play on the court of a friend whose family was wealthier than hers. This was a magnificent moment. We could see Jane's strength and skill as she showed us how to serve on her "tennis court."

The seventh session featured a circus and ice cream parlor theme. We used a large felt board with various circus-related felt pieces. We began by placing three circus rings on the board. Group members suggested which characters to place on the board. After they were taken off, the members were asked to recall what was there. A storytelling technique was used for the ice cream parlor; we used the felt board to tell a story about a mother and son going to the ice cream parlor. The group members were asked to recall the story. However, remembering the recently told story proved to be difficult for many older members, as their short-term recall was impaired.

The final session was a combination of reminiscence and show and tell. During this session, the family member–resident pairs were asked to discuss certain questions and then share their responses with the group. Some questions were purely reminiscence (e.g., What do you remember about your school?), and some were geared to advice giving (e.g., What is the best way to discipline a child?). This paired exercise provided a good opportunity for one-to-one sharing. One mother–daughter pair shared that they had attended the same school growing up. Another pair requested more time to talk during an especially engrossing topic concerning the hometown in which they lived. At the memory movement session 2 weeks before, Mabel had demonstrated for us how to plant a garden. During the advice portion of this session, she was asked to give us some advice about planting and protecting crops. She told a story about how she used to tie tin cans together out in the field to keep raccoons away. When asked, she also shared how she used onion skins to make dye for Easter eggs.

In the second half of this session, we staged a show-and-tell in which family members brought from home mementos that were precious to the residents or illustrated an aspect of their lives. Many brought pictures, but others brought collections. One resident's daughter brought a tea set that her mother had used for entertaining. There was a richness of experience and personality that came through during this session.

INTERVENTION ANALYSIS

There were many benefits to offering a group that combined residents and family members. We found that the group provided a much richer experience for all than would have been possible if these two groups had met separately. The opportunity for us to model for family members and for families to model for one another a variety of ways of relating to their relatives who were residents was an invaluable way of helping in a nonjudgmental way. The strong bond that resulted among the family members far exceeded our expectations. In addition, the relationships between residents and their family members were strengthened.

Demonstration of Respect

Our intergenerational group demonstrated respect in many ways. First, we used the names that the residents and family members preferred. As facilitators, we modeled a number of ground rules, which the group followed well. We provided a positive, safe environment in which risk taking was encouraged. For example, all responses that group members made were accepted, including negative emotions, such as when Mabel gruffly referred to herself as "moody" in the first session. We encouraged group members to help one another. As an example, we did this at the beginning by suggesting adjectives for Jane to use to describe herself.

Second, we tried to treat everyone in the group as equals. The family members were expected to participate equally with the residents. We treated everyone as a whole person, taking into account his or her entire life, with a history (through reminiscence) and a future (through families' carrying on their traditions and values). We also tried to reinforce the residents' roles as their children's parents. To do this, we frequently tried to solicit the advice or expertise of the residents during the sessions, as when we asked Mabel about gardening.

Use of the Clients' Strengths

Each resident had different strengths that became apparent at various times in the group sessions. Once we were aware of them, we capitalized on residents' strengths by highlighting and affirming them. For example, Mabel played the Autoharp well and demonstrated musical talent. She also had an excellent memory for nursery rhymes. Group members felt free about giving and accepting praise in these situations. As a result, Mabel seemed happier and less tense.

Areas in which the residents had achieved a level of mastery in their lives were highlighted. For example, one group member was a fine baker. Her daughter bragged a little for her mother about some of the fine wedding cakes that she had made, and the group responded positively to this resident's accomplishments. As noted by Laurie after her mother slammed the tennis ball, evoking these strengths and accomplishments changed others' perceptions of the residents in the group. After the memory group session, Laurie often heard the comment, "I really like your mother," which she believed to be in response to both the person she had been and the person she was in the group.

Blurred Boundaries

I knew all of the residents in the group before it started and previously had multiple encounters with most of them, which gave me some insight into their background, family, and personality. My roles as a nursing facility social worker and as a group facilitator were consistent in that I was trying to help the residents to maintain the highest level of psychosocial functioning possible and to reinforce their worth as people. Having worked in this nursing facility for many years, I found that I grew attached to many of the residents, and there was an "extended family" feeling among the employees, residents, and families. In this group situation, the roles of the group members were well defined, unlike many other situations in nursing facilities. The structure of the group reinforced the importance of the residents as "parents," the family members as "children," and the leaders as "facilitators." Family members were valued because they knew their relative the best and could help to stimulate key memories. Sometimes in a nursing facility setting, the importance of adult children as caregivers is undervalued in light of others' taking on the actual day-to-day caregiving role. This group reinforced their worth and the important parent–child roles. In my role as a facilitator, it was easy to reinforce this natural family unit with no blurring of boundaries.

Although the primary clients were the nursing facility residents, the secondary clients were the family members. We had to accommodate our style to two sets of clients. For the most part, this was not a problem, but at times, the family members were looking for something different from the group than we had intended. For example, one daughter wished that the group would provide more exercise opportunities for her mother, who was immobile. Another daughter was struggling with so much guilt about the decision to place her mother in the nursing facility that she was not fully able to enjoy the sessions and really needed more of an opportunity than the group allowed to seek support from other family members. Usually, these needs did not interfere with the group process and I was able to give additional support to the family members outside the sessions. We welcomed feedback from family members and over time modified the group sessions to incorporate their suggestions. For example, we gradually included more reminiscence opportunities because these times proved to be so enjoyable for both the residents and their families.

Changes in the Therapeutic Relationship over Time

Over time, the family members became the group leaders, especially when it came to eliciting responses from their own relative who was a resident. They were the experts in their older relative's history. I never would have known that Jane was such a good tennis player without Laurie's ability to elicit that memory. My cofacilitator and I began to take more secondary roles with respect to group leadership. Instead, our role was focused on modeling for family members how to ask questions and how to improve communication. We were able to model acceptance of what a person said even when it was confusing or a distortion of reality. I knew that it was hard for Mabel's son to cope with his mother's gruffness both on individual visits and in the group. By allowing Mabel to describe herself as "Moody Mabel" even though this description was not particularly flattering, we showed Ron that his mother could express unhappy and negative thoughts and that we would still accept her. In a similar way, we were able to model the acceptance of the older group member as a historian by asking questions, such as the one posed to Mabel about how she colored Easter eggs using onion skins as dyes.

On occasion, a family member was unable to come to a session. This created a difficult dynamic because the resident did not have someone special to accompany him or her. To compensate for the potential loneliness, Cheryl and I would trade off sitting with that person in the group session. However, because we did not know the person's history well, we could not elicit as much from him or her as the family member could. Sometimes family members would trade off attending, as in the case of Gladys and Ron. This proved to be more enriching than detrimental, except at the beginning when the new family member had to become acquainted with the other group members.

One of the unexpected positive outcomes of this group was the genuine interest in and caring of family members about the other residents. Laurie noted after the group sessions how wonderful it was that more people (i.e., the family members and residents from the group) really knew her mother as a person rather than as a frail, sick, older person in a nursing facility. Jane also began to recognize some of the other family members.

At the beginning of the intergenerational group, I was the only other person whom most of the family members knew. A defining and somewhat unexpected way in which this relationship changed was that, eventually, the family members began to seek support from one another, rather than just me, and a network evolved. Laurie noted that they often talked with each other to solve problems and share ideas and experiences in relating to their parents in positive ways. One example of this was when Gladys and Ron both were out of town for a week and various other group family members volunteered to visit Mabel during that time so that she would have visitors. Knowing other residents broadened the horizons of family members. When they came to see their own family member, they sometimes took them to visit other residents. Because of their dementia, many of the residents did not remember one another, but their family members were able to pave the way for brief conversations.

An indication of the success of the group was the request by family members to have reunion groups after the intergenerational group came to an end. The families organized these reunions. For example, one of the family members organized a birthday party for her mother after the group sessions had ended, to which she invited all of the group members. Even though her mother did not know who all of the people were, it did not make any difference. The excitement in the room from the honored guest as well as the participants was contagious. In essence, this group provided for many of the participants a natural support network within the nursing facility.

Benefits and Difficulties of the Therapeutic Relationship for Residents, Families, and Facilitators

For the residents, the intergenerational group affirmed their worth as human beings. They received praise from other group members for their past accomplishments as well as their current abilities. During the group sessions, residents were frequently looked to as teachers. This respect resulted in their increased pride, confidence, and happiness during the group sessions. As noted, it was especially thrilling to see Mabel smile when she was appreciated for her gardening ability. Jane grew to enjoy the sessions and was able to verbalize to me that she looked forward to Laurie's coming so that they could attend the group together. The friendship network was especially good for Jane because she was new to the area and did not know anyone nearby. Laurie observed that the way in which group members related together "affirmed who Mother was, not just in her current condition but as an energetic, courageous person with a lifetime of experience."

Many family members had previously noted how hard it was to visit their relative who was a resident because they no longer had anything to say. The group allowed them to spend some enjoyable time with their loved one without the pressure of constant one-to-one conversations. The family members learned ways to visit that included interactions with other residents. Gladys told me how thankful she was to be able to take her mother to visit some other residents instead of spending all of her time visiting alone. Another benefit for Gladys was that she could once again view her mother in a positive light because the other family members had done so. It helped to ease the embarrassment that she felt when Mabel responded to others in a gruff manner.

From my perspective as a leader, this group proved to be a successful intervention because it highlighted the unique strengths of the older participants while drawing on the special knowledge of family members. In a practical way, the group made it possible for me to document progress firsthand in resident charts in terms of responsiveness and mood. It was rewarding to be able to intervene on multiple levels with families and residents at the same time, not to mention that the group format was efficient. In a 1-hour session, we were able to provide socialization and affirmation to many isolated residents while at the same time providing support to their family members.

The nonthreatening structure of the group allowed us to intervene easily with family members who otherwise might not have sought help or advice. For example, it was helpful to model for Gladys and Ron that it was acceptable that their mother expressed negative thoughts without needing to address their embarrassment directly. Because the family members became their own support network, the group assumed some of the responsibility that I felt for being the sole support for certain family members.

Another benefit was that I learned about the residents' many qualities that could be used in my future work with them and could be described to other nursing facility staff to facilitate their interactions. For example, I learned that one resident really responded to music and I encouraged staff to play tapes for her. Also, after discovering that Mabel knew a great deal about gardening and enjoyed giving advice, I encouraged the staff to ask her questions during bathing and dressing to help divert her attention from what was often a difficult time for her.

For me, the negative aspects of the group were minor. I was required to evaluate each resident for his or her appropriateness for the group and to send a letter to each family. These tasks required an extra time commitment. Another negative aspect of the group was that because this group was targeted to a specific group of residents, others were left out. In addition, the group was not available to distant family members or to those who had inflexible work schedules. However, in my opinion, the benefits outweighed the difficulties.

Words of Wisdom

The group far surpassed our initial goals. We had hoped to improve residents' memory skills and to model another way for families to visit with them. We were not prepared for the strong community and support network that evolved. Not only were group members extremely supportive of one another but this support extended well beyond the actual group itself. Including both residents and their families greatly strengthened the benefits for all.

We have made a number of modifications to the group sessions over time, based on feedback from participants. The first session in which we introduced ourselves by using a word beginning with the same first letter as our name ("Joyful Jane") was fun. It set the tone for everyone to cooperate. We also used these names in the go-around question at the beginning of each session. In evaluations given to the family members, most were unanimous in their belief that the memory movement session and the music session were their favorites. Many family members commented on how all could participate in the singing as well as the movements of familiar tasks. I have used the memory movement session in other nursing facilities as well, and it almost always receives a positive response. We received mixed reactions to the reminiscence box session that used sensory skills because not all of the group members had the use of all of their senses. Using their sense of smell was the most difficult for many residents. In subsequent groups, we expanded on the session involving memories of home by asking residents to bring pictures of their families. In so doing, another layer of memories was added to this session. The least favorite session was the circus and ice cream parlor session. It proved to be the most difficult for the residents because it required more short-term memory than most of these residents were capable of and did not lead to as many personal memories for them. In subsequent groups, I omitted this session.

Group work with families can be rewarding. This particular group format helped me as a nursing facility social worker to get to know families on a more personal level than in the normal day-to-day encounters that I had at other times. Sometimes when family members do not know the staff, they harbor concerns and bring them up when they are too large to handle or in such a way that the encounter is confrontational at the outset. Establishing this more casual relationship with family members created a friendly bond between them and me. It allowed us to deal with future problems on the basis of a feeling of camaraderie; we could work as a team to help their relative. This improved relationship also encouraged families to come to me sooner than later when a problem arose.

Despite offering this group to both men and women, most of the participants were mothers and daughters. This may have been because many of the daughters did not work outside the home and had more flexibility to attend the meetings. It also could be that the format was more conducive to women's interests, although when I have used these exercises in mixed-gender groups they have been successful. Whatever the reason, it may require more effort to seek out more men. An alternative way to conduct this group is to design it especially for spouses. Instead of focusing on childhood memories, the focus could be on topics such as marriage, personalities, and interests. This kind of group might have particular value for spouses when one is living in the nursing facility and the other is not. Such couples have few places to go where they both are accepted equally and their relationships are honored.

Finally, the value of group work in general in the nursing facility cannot be ignored. Many groups that I have facilitated in the nursing facility have developed out of a particular need. A newcomers' group was designed for new residents who needed orientation to the nursing facility and an opportunity to express their feelings about the transition from their homes; family support groups were designed for similar reasons. A welcoming committee group was developed for the primary reason of finding ways for current residents to feel needed by helping others and the secondary reason of finding ways for new residents to feel welcomed. A wing activity group developed after the restructuring of a hallway eliminated a sitting area for residents and required those with dementia to become accustomed to a new area to congregate and socialize. A reminiscence group developed from a need for depressed residents to increase self-worth by affirming their histories. The needs in one nursing facility may be different from the needs in another. The main point is that nursing facilities lend themselves easily to conducting group work, and it behooves the practitioner to develop these groups. The value of the socialization and affirmation received by the resident through interaction in a group is immeasurable.

ADDITIONAL RESOURCES

The literature contains much material about reminiscence groups. In a chapter by Burnside (1994), she discussed reminiscence group therapy and mentioned how it can be used with confused older adults. Her resource list provides many suggestions about resources that can be used in such groups. Orten, Allen, and Cook (1989) discovered that having a skilled therapist conduct reminiscence therapy is important to the outcome. Tabourne (1995) found that structured reminiscence helps decrease disorientation, increase social interaction, and enhance life review for frail older people. Finally, an article by Woods and

McKiernan (1995) reviewed the literature about reminiscence with people with dementia and concluded that even those with severe dementia can be stimulated by reminiscence work. They also gave some practical suggestions on how to lead such a group.

One method that we used to trigger memories was music. To learn more about the ways in which music can be used with older people with dementia, consider a chapter by Clair (1996) called "Music as a Therapeutic Approach with People with Dementia," which makes reference to multiple studies on music therapy with older people, including caregivers. There are many books of "oldies" music that work well when group singing is being encouraged.

In most of our group sessions, we used established memory techniques to help residents learn and remember (Fogler & Stern, 1994). For example, to learn names we chose words to describe ourselves beginning with the same letter of our first names. This association technique of using the same letter can be helpful with recall. These memory techniques provided a strong basis for structuring the group sessions.

Although there is little in the literature that discusses family members' being involved in groups such as the one that we conducted, an auxiliary article describes a Family Stories Workshop (Hepburn et al., 1997) in which family members participated in a 6-week workshop to develop stories of their relatives' lives. They presented these stories, sometimes in audiovisual format, to the staff. Although the task was project oriented and did not involve resident participation, staff members found that the family members' views of their residents usually improved as they moved away from a disease-related picture to seeing them again through their life span, in much the same way that our group's family members did. These family members also began to bond with one another, providing an informal support network that we also witnessed in our group.

Finally, an enjoyable resource for the nursing facility social worker that gives suggestions on group ideas in the nursing facility is a manual by Smith (1993). Her creative approaches to group work provide a good basis for planning a nursing facility group.

REFERENCES

Burnside, I. (1994). Reminiscence group therapy. In I. Burnside & M.G. Schmidt (Eds.), *Working with older adults: Group process and techniques* (pp. 163–178). Boston: Jones & Bartlett.

Clair, A.A. (1996). Music as a therapeutic approach with people with dementia. In *Therapeutic uses of music with older adults* (pp. 63–90). Baltimore: Health Professions Press.

Fogler, J., & Stern, L. (1994). *Improving memory: How to remember what you're starting to forget.* Baltimore: The Johns Hopkins University Press.

Hepburn, K., Caron, W., Luptak, M., Ostwald, S., Grant, L., & Keenan, J. (1997). The family stories workshop: Stories for those who cannot remember. *Gerontologist, 37*(6), 827–832.

Orten, J., Allen, M., & Cook, J. (1989). Reminiscence groups with confused nursing center residents: An experimental study. *Social Work in Health Care*, 14(1), 73–86.

Smith, J. (1993). *Resident support groups: A resource manual*. Escondido, CA: Legal Beagle Press.

Tabourne, C. (1995). The effects of a life review program on disorientation, social interaction and self-esteem of nursing home residents. *International Journal of Aging and Human Development*, 4(3), 251–266.

Woods, B., & McKiernan, F. (1995). Evaluating the impact of reminiscence on older people with dementia. In B.K. Haight & J.D. Webster (Eds.), *The art and science of reminiscing* (pp. 233–242). Washington, DC: Taylor & Francis.

Working with Families and Systems

III

Breaking Generational Family Patterns

Janet Fogler

CLIENT'S BACKGROUND

BETTY O'BRIEN, AGE 61, WAS FIRST SEEN IN THE GERIATRIC CLINIC WHEN SHE ACCOMPANIED HER 71-YEAR-OLD HUSBAND, Mike, to his medical appointment. Mike was a recovering alcoholic who had received a diagnosis of Alzheimer's disease. Mike's doctor, who was concerned about Betty's symptoms of severe depression and anxiety, referred her to me for counseling. In addition to these emotional problems, Betty had asthma, osteoporosis, and lupus. She had recently undergone a total hip replacement and was on a powerful combination of medications—steroids, antidepressants, and pain medications.

Betty was the oldest of two children and was raised in a home with her parents and her paternal grandmother, all of whom were alcoholics. She recalled receiving little supervision or nurturing from her parents; she had slept on the couch in the living room because she had never had a room of her own. Her mother tried to take care of the children, but there was often too much work and too little money. Betty described an argument with her father in which, under the influence of alcohol, he threatened to kill her. She became passive ("I never talked back again") and escaped from the constant battles in her family by going to the nearby public library. Her parents never seemed to notice when she came home late at night even as a young child. Betty had done well in elementary school, but as she grew older, she lost interest in school. She was ashamed to bring friends to her home and became more and more of a loner. After high school, she got a job at a drugstore near her home and longed to escape her unhappy home environment.

Betty continued to live with her parents for several years until she met Mike, who was 10 years older than she. Mike, who delivered products to the drugstore, was divorced and had three children who lived with his ex-wife. Although there were many warning signs of problems in the relationship, Betty was eager to leave her difficult environment and have a home of her own. When Mike asked her to marry him, she jumped at the chance. She said, "I needed someone to love me. I needed to get away from the problems at home." Mike and Betty had one child, a son, Grant.

Betty loved Grant very much, and she did her best to give him a good upbringing while continuing to work at the drugstore until she retired on disability at age 50. Mike was often abusive and threatening, especially when he was drinking. She left him for short periods on several occasions during the early years of the marriage, but she always came back because she did not believe that she could make it financially without him. After Betty retired, Mike invited her father, Harry, to move in with them to help with the finances. Betty found herself back in a home with her alcoholic father, as well as an alcoholic husband and a son who was struggling with problems of his own.

Mike had recently become delusional and threatening. Betty was afraid of him and found her situation intolerable, but she could not afford to leave him as she had no money or health insurance of her own. Continual conflict with her father also increased Betty's depression and anxiety. Harry was angry and demanding, and he never expressed any appreciation for Betty's efforts. Harry was actually in better health than either Betty or Mike, but he did not acknowledge or show any sympathy for their problems. Grant was also a source of anxiety. He was using drugs and had dropped out of high school. He had attended a drug rehabilitation center and completed work toward a high school diploma. Although Grant was working in construction and attending a community college part time, Betty said, "He's always busy doing nothing. He won't help out at home." The conflict and chaos in the home were beginning to reach the level of the turmoil in her childhood home.

INTERVENTION SUMMARY

At our first session, Betty presented as a thin woman who moved painfully with a cane and appeared to be older than her age. She was tearful and tremulous and described herself as extremely depressed, anxious, and overwhelmed with her family responsibilities and her own health problems. She reported having frequent crying spells and sleepless nights. Betty thought that she would be better off dead and admitted that she had fantasized about jumping off a bridge. She did, however, state that her religious beliefs and the impact on her son kept her from acting on this impulse. She described a nightmarish period over the previous 6 months in which Mike verbally abused everyone in the family; accused her of being unfaithful; refused to shave, bathe, or change clothes; and aggressively demanded sex. The diagnosis of Alzheimer's disease was a possible explanation for his delusional thinking, but Betty was unacquainted with the effects of dementia on thinking and behavior. Betty had no one to call on for support outside the family. Even though there was a history of conflict within the family, they remained almost totally dependent on each other. For example, Betty's father moved into his daughter's home, although family dynamics guaranteed that this would be a disastrous situation.

My first goal of the therapy was to make a connection with Betty, who described herself as a loner and had little experience in a trusting relationship. She had no experience in a relationship in which someone really listened to her and respected her point of view. She desperately needed the support of someone who did not require anything in return. I listened attentively to her descriptions of a difficult life and her complaints about her husband, father, and son. I was able to affirm that her burdens were great and her feelings of depression and anxiety were not unusual for someone in her situation. I was also concerned about both the number and the dosages of Betty's medications. She saw several doctors, who prescribed medications for her various conditions. Her rheumatologist not only managed her lupus but also prescribed medications for her depression and anxiety. I set up an appointment for her with one of the clinic's geropsychiatrists to assess her depression and to review her medications. The psychiatrist disagreed with the choice of Betty's psychotropic medications and recommended a reduction in the dosages and number of medications.

Betty stated two goals for therapy in the initial stage of our work. The first was to change or learn to cope with the recent difficult behaviors of her husband, specifically the paranoia, aggressive sexual demands, and refusal to take care of personal hygiene. Because of the history of the relationship, she found it most difficult to deal with his aggressive sexual demands. I encouraged Betty to speak to Mike's doctor, who was able to prescribe a medication that proved to be useful in controlling some of Mike's aggressive tendencies. I also began to educate Betty about dementia and how it affected not only memory but also judgment and reason. She learned that Mike's behaviors were not uncommon in someone with dementia, even in a marriage that had not endured the difficulties of her own. I gave Betty materials to read and suggested that she attend a caregiver's support group. She declined to attend the group because she said that she was so overwhelmed by her situation that she could not take on a new activity and she did not want to hear about other people's problems.

Betty was somewhat skeptical about seeing her husband's difficult behaviors as part of an illness because he had always been difficult to deal with, but over time she began to gain some understanding about how dementia can affect memory, reasoning, judgment, and behavior. She began to apply some of the behavioral techniques that we had talked about. She learned to use distraction rather than argument or harangue when he became sexually aggressive. She was able to tell Mike that she would talk about his request for sex when she was finished with what she was doing. By then, Mike would not remember the discussion. This, of course, did not keep him from requesting sex again before too long, but it was more effective than arguing and not as stressful for Betty. When Mike accused her of being unfaithful, she learned to make a brief, calm statement about her faithfulness and then move on to something else. She began to see that arguing or trying to reason with Mike resulted in his increased agitation and stress.

Betty was able to improve her communication with Mike about his hygiene by speaking in short, simple sentences and limiting the content to one idea at a time. For example, instead of ordering him to shave and get dressed in the morning, she tried to instruct him step by step in the process of shaving and dressing. She also began to realize that getting him to shave every day was neither necessary nor worth the effort that it required.

The second goal of therapy identified by Betty was to think about plans for the future. The family survived on a limited income with no external social support. As Betty stated, "I have no support. I shouldn't have to put up with this— him, Dad, Grant. I don't think I can stand it." Betty wanted to move from their home, which was in a small town and required too much effort to maintain. She thought that she might be able to manage herself and Mike if they moved to a smaller place and if Harry and Grant got their own apartments. Even though she was often disappointed and angry with her son, Betty also really wanted to be of assistance to Grant and to encourage him to finish college. To sell the home, Betty needed to petition the probate court for guardianship because Mike was no longer competent to make decisions. I suggested that Betty and Mike, as well as Harry, might be eligible for low-cost senior housing and referred Betty to the Housing Bureau for Seniors to determine eligibility and availability. Betty got Grant to take Harry to visit two available options for one-bedroom apartments, and his name was added to a waiting list.

Over the next year, Betty showed amazing fortitude. She rallied her internal resources and enlisted Grant's aid to make major changes. She got guardianship over Mike and signed up for a two-bedroom senior subsidized apartment. Grant helped her to get the house ready for sale. Despite her disabilities and continuous battle with pain, depression, and anxiety, Betty was able to carry her plans through to completion. The family home was sold, Mike and Betty moved to a two-bedroom apartment in low-cost senior housing, and Harry moved to a one-bedroom apartment in another building. Grant moved into an apartment with a friend.

During this period, my functions were more closely associated with care management than psychotherapy. In a complicated situation such as this, however, in which deteriorating health, an unsuitable living situation, and limited finances require concrete solutions, there is a great advantage in not defining the role of therapist too narrowly. Betty talked to me about housing options and financial plans. I assisted her in working with Social Security and the Department of Social Services to facilitate a division of assets between Betty and Mike. In so doing, Mike could become eligible for Medicaid if he needed nursing facility care without totally depleting Betty's assets. My knowledge and understanding of Betty's physical and emotional health problems, plus my well-established relationship with her, allowed me to monitor both her progress toward her concrete goals and the effects of these activities on her health.

After this period of activity and change, accompanied by feelings of accomplishment, Betty settled into the task of daily living with Mike's dementia and her own illnesses. She alternated between feelings of resentment and guilt about Mike's condition and the care that she needed to provide him. Lupus and osteoporosis continued to take their toll. Betty was now more disabled—she needed a walker to ambulate and had to give up driving. She required stronger medications for pain management, and overuse of medications again became a problem. When her doctor tried to cut back on some of her medications, she became more anxious, began smoking after a long period of abstinence, and talked of wanting to use alcohol. Betty became more depressed, asking, "Why am I living? I wish I would die."

As Mike's condition deteriorated rapidly, he became weaker and more confused but less belligerent and aggressive. He also began to require more physical care. He fell frequently, and Betty was unable to help him up. Although Harry actually made a good adjustment to his apartment, he refused to acknowledge that his needs were well cared for and badgered both Betty and Grant for additional help. Betty, Mike, and Harry all began to rely more heavily on Grant. Still in young adulthood, he was called on to provide care for three older, disabled people, in addition to working full time and attending classes part time. He was asked to run errands, grocery shop, and take his relatives to doctors' appointments. He provided as much help as he could, although somewhat erratically, but he had little time for socializing and commiserating. Because she had no social contacts outside the family, Betty resented that when Grant dropped off groceries, he would not sit down and talk for a while. I encouraged her to take advantage of community services for her concrete needs and reserve Grant for social support. However, in the family tradition, Betty refused outside help, such as Motor Meals or a local agency that could provide transportation and grocery shopping.

As Mike's condition continued to deteriorate, he required full-time nursing care. The slow pace of a governmental agency in authorizing Medicaid for Mike made Betty extremely anxious, as she had little faith in the system. While assuring her that Mike would be eligible for Medicaid services, I called Social Services to check on the status of the application. When approval was received, both of us felt relieved. Once Betty placed her husband in a nursing facility, she began to concentrate more on her own health conditions, but her depression did not abate. She experienced a combination of feelings that are common among caregivers—relief that she was no longer burdened with the responsibility for Mike's care and guilt for feeling this relief. Whenever she visited Mike in the nursing facility, her guilt increased, along with her depression. She found no pleasure in life and sometimes thought of suicide. She expressed a lot of anger toward her father, whom she felt had always demanded too much from her, and toward

Grant, whom she felt did not help her enough. Given his demanding schedule, Grant was actually very supportive of his parents and grandfather. He visited his father in the nursing facility and monitored his care, because Betty was unable to get there frequently. However, Grant had a pattern of ignoring his parents' situation when things were under control, dropping everything to help when a crisis arose, and then feeling angry and overwhelmed. Although Betty felt angry about her father's lack of understanding of her burden, she, in turn, had problems recognizing the burdens of her son, who was overwhelmed with his responsibilities. Betty had received almost no nurturing or appreciation from her own parents and, in turn, found it difficult to put the needs of her child above her own. At this time in therapy, I tried to help Betty to understand these inconsistencies in her expectations. I expressed my admiration for the faithfulness of her son and my sympathy for the many demands on his life.

Betty continued to rely on medications for controlling her pain, depression, and anxiety. I noticed an increase in her trembling, and she complained of terrible fatigue. I consulted with her primary care physician; he reported that Betty was asking for an increase in her dosages of medications, and he was concerned that she might not be following explicit instructions. After our discussion, Betty's primary care physician, with her permission, contacted the specialists that Betty was seeing and asked that they allow him to manage all of her medications. They agreed to this request. The doctor also ordered a visiting nurse, a home health aide, and a physical therapist to provide in-home services. Betty liked all of these providers, especially the home health aide, who was authorized by Medicare to provide homemaking services such as meal preparation, laundry, and light housekeeping, as long as a skilled care provider such as a nurse or a physical therapist was ordered by the doctor. Betty began to understand that it was helpful to receive some services from outside the family.

At a point in the therapy when Betty complained about her son's lack of help, I received a telephone call from Grant, who was overwhelmed and exhausted. I asked Betty whether I could meet with her and Grant together. Betty and I talked ahead of time about what we could accomplish at this meeting. I encouraged Betty to state her appreciation of Grant's help as well as enumerate her needs and Mike's and Harry's. In the meeting, Grant was also able to tell Betty ways in which he appreciated her before describing the limitations of his abilities to provide help to three aging relatives, given his obligations to school and work. I encouraged Grant to set limits on what he could do and then to be reliable in following through on his commitments to the family. I encouraged both Betty and Grant to consider using community resources to supplement the family's resources. This experience in problem solving as a family was a learning experience for everyone, and I believe that all of us felt that a better basis for dealing with the future had been established.

I also encouraged Betty to look outside the family for social support. Her description of herself as a loner and her belief that she did not want to or could not make friends were, I believed, a function of her low self-esteem and her inexperience in social situations. I found her to be kind, engaging, and warm when she became trusting and comfortable in a relationship. I asked her to consider accepting a peer counselor, one of a group of older volunteers at our clinic who provide friendly visiting, social support, and occasional transportation to isolated older adults. She was uninterested until she found out that the peer counselor might be able to take her to some of her appointments. The peer counselor, Joan, was a no-nonsense kind of person who had a good sense of humor and was not easily discouraged. As she got to know Joan and develop trust in her, Betty began to see herself as a person who could develop a friendship and benefit from interaction with others. Joan became fond of Betty, and this was apparent to Betty and made her feel like a worthwhile person.

Shortly after Joan entered Betty's life, her home health aide discovered that Betty had stashes of pills all over the apartment, including some that her doctor did not know she was taking. The visiting nurse and the primary care physician were able to confront her with this information and prevail upon her to enter an in-patient program for substance abuse. With encouragement and support from her professional providers, Grant, and Joan, Betty was able to take this step. She spent a few weeks in an in-patient unit for substance abuse in older adults, followed by several months in a day treatment program. Joan was especially helpful to Betty during this period. Joan called her almost every day and provided some transportation to the day treatment program, in which Betty learned a lot about addiction, and this helped her to understand herself and other members of her family better. She enjoyed the support of the people in her treatment group, and she learned that people liked and respected her. She was proud of her ability to learn new information and enjoyed being in a classroom setting.

I kept in touch with Betty by telephone during the time that she was in treatment for substance abuse. I also was contacted by Grant to help plan a strategy for supporting Betty after her discharge from the day treatment program. This process demonstrated the power of the team approach to health care. The physician, social worker, visiting nurse, home health aide, peer counselor, and family member were able to work together to accomplish a major initiative in Betty's progress toward better health. I do not believe that any one of us would have had access to all of the information about Betty's situation or could have provided the wide-ranging support that was necessary to achieve this goal. I was surprised to receive a note of appreciation from Betty after her discharge from the program. This action was out of character for her and beyond her ability when she was depressed, anxious, and under the influence of addictive medication. When we met again in person, I was amazed not only by the improvement in her mood but also by the clarity of her thinking.

To build on the education and socialization gains that Betty made in the day treatment program, I encouraged Betty to take part in an Al-Anon group offered in a church setting located not far from her apartment. She was nervous about this prospect but took it seriously. She attended every session and learned a lot about the affect of alcohol on families. She still felt insecure and uncomfortable in a group, but the participants were sympathetic to her situation and provided support for her to stand up to unreasonable demands from her father. When Betty presented the problem of her father, who demanded that Betty or Grant pick up his medications from the drugstore even though the store made regular deliveries to his apartment building, the group members were able to point out the irrationality in this demand and support Betty in her refusal. Betty reported that she felt less guilty about not complying with her father's demands because the group had supported her.

Betty's health improved greatly after her recovery from drug dependence, but she continued to struggle with depression and guilt about her husband's nursing facility placement and her father's complaints about not fulfilling all of his needs. She sometimes still felt abandoned by her son. In our sessions, we began to explore the relationship between Betty and Grant. I noted many situations in which Betty had provided good care for her son and also noted his accomplishments as he continued to work toward a college degree. When I repeatedly pointed out to Betty these accomplishments and gave her credit for making important changes in family dynamics, she felt better about herself. She began to recognize her own strengths as a survivor of a harrowing childhood and a difficult marriage. She also began to acknowledge Grant's strengths in dealing with the difficulties in his life. When she recalled that the children from Mike's previous marriage led much less functional lives, she could see the influence that she must have had on her own son. Betty's ability to mother her adult child improved with her self-esteem. She was more understanding when his responsibilities to work and school took precedence over some of her needs. She was less critical of the decisions that he made. She began to talk about visits with Grant that were not connected to providing concrete help. After she was invited to a gathering for a barbecue at Grant's apartment, Betty told me, "It was the most wonderful day. I was so proud of him."

Almost a year later, Mike died, and Harry's death followed within the next year. It is sad but true that relief from these two conflicted relationships contributed to the continued improvement in Betty's mood. Even so, Betty struggled with guilt about her lack of grief after Mike's death. As we talked about the long course of his illness, she was able to accept that much of her grieving had occurred before he died.

The concluding phase of our therapy took place as we examined all that had happened since we had met 5 years before. We reviewed the difficult tasks that she had accomplished—moving into a more manageable living situation, assisting her father to find housing, managing Mike's care as long as she could, finding Mike an affordable nursing facility that would provide him good care, obtaining Medicaid coverage for his long-term care while preserving some assets for herself, addressing her issues of substance abuse and going through a long and difficult rehabilitation process, and developing a better relationship with Grant.

In so many ways, Betty's life was better now than when we first met. She said that she no longer had the desire to drink alcohol or take more medications. Her pain actually had decreased even though she was on much less pain medication. Betty expressed great appreciation for her primary care physician and all of those who had helped her through the past years. She stated, "I feel more confident than I have in a long time." She was determined to continue to build a better relationship with her son and wanted to support him in ways in which she had never felt supported by her parents.

Betty will probably remain on antidepressants for the rest of her life, but she has terminated regular psychotherapy sessions with me. After a year had gone by since our last meeting, I saw Betty at the clinic and was struck by the changes in her. She had driven herself to her appointment and was walking with only a cane for support. She had a new short haircut, and she looked happy and relaxed. She told me that Grant was still extremely busy and had the usual problems of too little money and too much work. He still did not have as much time for her as she would like, but she took pride in the fact that she could be helpful to him on occasion. She asked about Joan and expressed her admiration for and appreciation of her, but she had made no effort to keep in touch with Joan since Mike's death. Betty will always be somewhat of a loner, but I believe that she has gained some confidence in her ability to interact with people. The family will always be her main social support, and the family seems to be functioning much better.

INTERVENTION ANALYSIS

Betty's therapy took place over a period of 5 years, during which many events occurred. She had little experience with or confidence in her ability to have associations outside the family. Thus, the establishment of a dependable therapeutic relationship was crucial to the outcome of this therapy. Our relationship developed over time and changed as the situation changed. At times, my role as a therapist broadened to include roles as a care manager, resource finder, and advocate. My capacity to function in a flexible manner allowed me to accommodate my client's needs over a lengthy period of many changes.

Demonstration of Respect

Because Betty had little experience in a trusting relationship, I knew that I had to be absolutely reliable in our relationship. Given the fragile nature of her self-esteem, I looked for ways to compliment her on her management of an event before exploring ways to make positive changes. For example, I might say, "I really admire you for your patience and loyalty," before making suggestions about how to manage better her husband's aggression. I did not hesitate to show Betty that I liked her very much, as she had so little confidence in her ability to make friends. I let Betty set the timetable for our sessions. When things were going better, I met with her less frequently. When crises occurred, I made myself available for more sessions. When she was unable to get to the clinic because of illness, I kept in touch by telephone. On a few occasions, I visited her at her home. Because our ages were not so different and she needed to experience a friendly relationship, I treated her like a contemporary. I respected Betty's innate intelligence and never talked down to her. I believed that she could make positive changes in her life, and she knew that I believed in her.

Use of the Client's Strengths

Betty had survived a difficult life. Although she had often spoken of wishing to die, she had no intention of taking her own life because she recognized how painful that would be to her son. Betty had dealt not only with a barren and abusive childhood and a difficult marriage but also with her own severe and painful medical conditions. When she was not hampered by depression or anger, she was likable and showed the ability to reach out to others. Betty's love for her son was steadfast. She would at times be disappointed and angry with him, but at other times, her pride and love for him shone in her eyes. Although she had reason to resent her father and her husband and she benefited from opportunities to vent her anger in therapy, she also was remarkably fair-minded when presented with any evidence of their support and love. Her loyalty to her family withstood many difficult tests. Because my respect and admiration for Betty were genuine, I was able to draw Betty's attention to her many strengths. Although she had trouble recognizing her own value, she was able to listen and benefit from hearing someone else enumerate her strengths and express admiration for her.

Blurred Boundaries

Because Betty was nearer to my own age than many of my clients, I had a tendency to compare my life to hers and feel more compassion for the difficulties of her life. I had to be careful not to overextend my assistance to her and in that way make her too dependent on me. Sometimes, because her burdens were so great, I wanted to do things for her that she could do for herself; however, I also knew that each time she accomplished something on her own, she gained confidence in her abilities. She had such severe financial difficulties that I once considered offering her some money, but I knew that this act would definitely blur the boundaries.

At the same time that I felt such compassion for Betty's situation, I also felt great empathy for Grant. During this period, my own parents were dealing with declining health and eventual death. As I struggled with the demands on my time and emotions, I could not help reflecting on the more severe demands on Grant at a time in his life that seemed much too soon for such strenuous caregiving tasks. I found myself advocating for him while also supporting Betty.

The last time Betty called me for help was after her father's death, when she was feeling angry about his care at the hospital and guilty about their unresolved relationship. Because our sessions had ebbed and flowed depending on Betty's need, I did not recognize this as a closing session. I believe that her silence since then is a sign of Betty's strength and health, and I hope that it lasts for many years. Even so, she was a part of my life for a long time, and I miss seeing her.

Changes in the Therapeutic Relationship over Time

During the 5 years that I worked with Betty, there were several stages of therapy. When we first met, she was feeling helpless and desperate. She had no experience with a therapeutic relationship, and I needed to be directive in helping her to set and work toward goals. Wishes for death were never far from Betty's mind. When she arrived for a session, she would be trembling and tearful and would often say, "Oh, I really need you today." More than almost any other client I have had, she seemed to gain strength during the sessions. She would invariably leave the session visibly better than when she arrived. I think that she felt so alone in her difficult situation, especially in the early years when Grant was immersed in his own problems, having someone who listened, cared, and helped to solve problems was life sustaining.

During the period when Betty was establishing guardianship, selling her home, and moving, she gained confidence and was less dependent on our relationship. Grant was very helpful to her then, and they worked together to accomplish a lot. Betty's depression seemed to lessen during this time when she knew what she needed to do and worked toward concrete goals. When Mike was admitted to the nursing facility, Betty became depressed again and began to talk more about perceiving no meaning in her life. She became more disabled and had to give up driving, which was a blow to her sense of independence. She was in a lot of pain and was becoming addicted to a variety of medications. Her physical health problems dominated her life, and she used our therapy primarily in times of crisis. She began to depend on medications to dull both her physical and her mental anguish. She was less open and less goal oriented. Betty's treatment for substance abuse was a real turning point. She learned a lot about herself and her family; she began to address how she wanted to manage her life and to make efforts to work toward positive goals. This was also a time of learning to trust and depend on other people, both in the day treatment program and in the Al-Anon group.

After the deaths of her husband and her father, Betty could consider how she wanted to live the rest of her life and could work on improving her relationship with her son. This was a time for her to reflect on all that she had been through and to acknowledge her own strengths. I served as a witness to her struggles and her gains. I could remind her of what she had accomplished and how much better she felt than when we first met.

Benefits and Difficulties of the Therapeutic Relationship for the Client and the Therapist

Betty benefited from therapy in several ways: fundamental support for her position, which had been almost totally lacking in her life; problem-solving strategies for dealing with her husband's illness, the financial arrangements, and the move to low-cost senior apartment buildings; advocacy with doctors, home health care providers, psychiatrist, nursing facilities, and other community agencies; introduction to other social support, through peer counselor and Al-Anon group; the model of a reliable relationship; and her increase in self-esteem and confidence to handle her life.

The first stage of the therapy was crucial to all of the rest. This case is a good example of how important it is to establish a supportive therapeutic relationship. Betty felt so worthless and so overwhelmed when we first met that any statement that might be interpreted as judgmental or critical could have ended the therapy. Betty responded appreciatively to kindness and concern, but she could be stubborn toward and unforgiving of those whom she believed slighted her in some way. Because she did learn to trust me, I could encourage her to persevere in her dealings with other essential providers, even when they were less sensitive to her emotional needs. The other vital ingredient in this successful therapy was the structure of the team. Because the medical clinic provided the doctor, social worker, psychiatrist, peer counselor, and referral to the home care providers, we were able to discuss this case frequently and conveniently, with easy access to medical records. Betty and her son were also considered part of the team. Members of the team had different perspectives on the situation, each of which was essential in forming a complete picture of the situation.

The final stage of the therapy was also significant. After the deaths of Mike and Harry, Betty was able to concentrate on her own health and on her relationship with her son. The therapy consisted of a review of all that had happened, authenticating Betty's burdens, and recognizing the strengths required to cope with such burdens. Relieved of the guilt and resentment that had consumed her during the previous few years, she was able to see herself for the resilient person that she was. She was also able to lessen the pressure on her son, allowing him to appreciate her more.

This therapy also had a strong impact on me. I learned how resilient the human spirit can be—how even with little nurturing, an individual can develop strengths to survive difficult situations. I learned how certain situations can be resolved only by the death of others. I also saw how family function could be improved, even if not totally changed. Betty learned to empathize with and understand her son's difficulties, whereas Betty's parents were never able to recognize hers.

Words of Wisdom

Betty's therapy illustrates a case in which psychotherapy is combined with care management. I believe that this amalgamation of roles is appropriate in treating older adults. As a therapist, I had the luxury of spending considerable time getting to know my client, which put me in a better position to coordinate services than a care manager whose only contact might be an assessment visit and coordination of care. Likewise, the contact that I had with other providers as a care manager gave me information and insight that I would not have gained in a therapy session. As a care manager, I was approached by a family member, whom I was then able to incorporate into a therapy session. This blending of roles increased my knowledge of the client and her situation and allowed for greater resolution of a complex case.

Another great advantage to me in this case was access to the other health care providers. Betty often had questions regarding her medications or health care, which I was then able to clarify through contact with her doctor. Easy access to Mike's psychiatrist allowed me to consult him regarding Mike's aggressive behavior. The home health care aide's discovery of Betty's stashes of pills and the visiting nurse's discussion with her about substance abuse treatment reached Betty in a way that none of the rest of us did. The other team members were then able to provide support to Betty to follow through on this treatment.

An intervention that is often crucial to the treatment of older adults is contact with family members. In the treatment of younger adults, therapists rarely have contact with family members unless they are involved in family therapy. In this case, my contact with Grant was useful, both to me in terms of understanding the family dynamics and to Betty and Grant in being provided a structured setting in which to air points of view. Because I was present at the family conference, I was able to keep Betty from feeling criticized by statements that were meant to be informative and to promote problem solving. I believe that without the presence of a therapist, such a problem-solving session can dredge up feelings of blame and resentment. Of course, I was careful to be fair-minded in such a session, and Betty always knew that she was the client.

The last point provided by this multifaceted case is the length and breadth of therapy with older adults. This case demonstrates how therapy can span several years, changing focus as failing health, financial strains, caregiving issues, and death affect older adults and their families. It further illustrates how family patterns can pass from one generation to the next, until the occurrence of some crisis that may bring one member of the family into treatment. The provision of psychotherapy in a medical clinic with a team care approach allowed

Betty to obtain an intervention that saw her through several difficult years to a period of relative wellness and peace.

ADDITIONAL RESOURCES

A booklet from the U.S. Department of Health, *Substance Abuse Among Older Adults* (Blow, 1998), discusses the relationship between aging and substance abuse and offers guidance on identifying, screening, and assessing not only substance abuse but also disorders such as dementia and delirium that can mask or mimic a drinking or prescription drug problem. Practical accommodations to treatment for older adults and a discussion of how to assess outcomes and intervene within a managed care context round out the document.

An article on intergenerational ambivalence (Luescher & Pillemer, 1998) provides a good structure for considering the relationships between older adults and their adult children. Rather than interpret intergenerational relationships within opposite and limited frameworks of generational solidarity or conflict, the authors propose that ambivalence is a more useful concept for understanding relationships between older adults and their children. Luescher and Pillemer's theory is helpful in understanding families that have many elements of solidarity, such as mutual reciprocity, but also include substantial elements of conflict and dissatisfaction.

Two excellent resources for aiding families that are dealing with the difficult behaviors of relatives with Alzheimer's disease are *The 36-Hour Day* (Mace, Rabins, & McHugh, 1999) and *Understanding Difficult Behaviors* (Robinson, Spencer, & White, 1991). *The 36-Hour Day* is a comprehensive book that covers the latest information on resources for patients and families, recent trends on research and drug treatments, advice on the day-to-day problems of caregiving, and recommendations about long-term care. *Understanding Difficult Behaviors* is organized according to 11 behavior problems, such as incontinence, problems with bathing, or problems with wandering. The authors discuss possible causes and coping strategies. The many helpful suggestions are written in accessible and sensitive language.

Alzheimer's Disease and Marriage (Wright, 1993), which is based on caregiving research and personal data on individual relationships, discusses the effects of Alzheimer's disease on marriage. The author explores marital dimensions such as household tasks, companionship, affection and sexuality, and commitment. She provides details on how to approach and interact with a spouse who has Alzheimer's disease.

REFERENCES

Blow, F. (1998). *Substance abuse among older adults. Treatment Improved Protocol* (TIP) *Series* (*Publication No.* |SMA| 98-3179). Washington, DC: U.S. Department of Health and Human Services, Center for Substance Abuse Treatment.

Luescher, K., & Pillemer, K. (1998). Intergenerational ambivalence: A new approach to the study of parent–child relations in later life. *Journal of Marriage and the Family, 60,* 413–425.

Mace, N.L., Rabins, P.V., & McHugh, P.R. (1999). *The 36-hour day: A guide to caring for persons with Alzheimer's disease, related dementing illnesses and memory loss in later life* (3rd ed.). Baltimore: The Johns Hopkins University Press.

Robinson, A., Spencer, B., & White, L. (1991). *Understanding difficult behaviors: Some practical suggestions for coping with Alzheimer's disease and related illnesses.* Ypsilanti: Eastern Michigan University.

Wright, L.K. (1993). *Alzheimer's disease and marriage.* Thousand Oaks, CA: Sage Publications.

Forming Relationships— The Key to Creative Care Management

12

Katherine P. Supiano

CLIENT'S BACKGROUND

MISS CLARK WAS A 69-YEAR-OLD SINGLE, AFRICAN AMERICAN WOMAN WHO WAS REFERRED BY A COMMUNITY PHYSICIAN who was acquainted with the Turner Geriatric Clinic's Care Management Program. This evaluation was arranged by the patient's nephew and niece and agreed to by Miss Clark. The evaluation was conducted in Miss Clark's home; her niece and nephew attended, but I spent most of the interview alone with Miss Clark while they waited outside. Her physician provided me with Miss Clark's medical chart, and I reviewed it before the visit. Miss Clark was prescribed medications for controlling her hypertension and cholesterol. Medical concerns included a cognitive deficit of approximately 24 months' duration, increasing paranoia, and poor appetite as evidenced by a loss of 15 pounds in the past year. Neuropsychometric testing conducted 2 months earlier revealed a Mini-Mental State Evaluation score of 18 of 30, a score suggesting cognitive decline and supporting the family's and the physician's concerns about Miss Clark's driving ability.

Through conversations with Miss Clark's physician and family members before the home visit, I learned that she had held a responsible, professional administrative position at a university and was considered a pioneer in the local African American community. She was the first woman in her family to obtain a postsecondary education. She was an only child and had cared for her parents in their home until their deaths in advanced age. Her family described her long-standing personality as "strong-willed and determined." She had never accepted help from other family members in caring for her parents, was viewed as an authority figure in her church, and was approached by others for financial advice. Although not especially close to her niece and nephew, she respected their educational accomplishments and professional status. Miss Clark had been receiving primary medical care from her physician for the past 12 years and was essentially compliant with medical advice.

INTERVENTION SUMMARY

As requests for care management services increased from community physicians not associated with the clinic and others providing services for older adults, the clinic's social work department developed a fee-for-service care management program called "Living Well." Referrals could come from anyone in the community, including, as in this case, the client's relatives who were referred by the client's physician. The first step, after the intake telephone call, is a home visit whereby a comprehensive assessment is conducted by a social worker. When possible, information from relatives and a physician's report are reviewed by the social worker before the home visit. After the initial visit, a care plan is set up with the client and the family and subsequent visits are made on the basis of the requirements of each client. The care plan is adjusted and modified as the client's needs change.

Initial Interview

Before visiting the home, I telephoned Miss Clark's niece and nephew and informed them that my goal for this first interview was to hear her story and that it might seem that I was aligning myself with her at their expense. I contacted Miss Clark on the morning of our appointment to introduce myself and explain her doctor's wishes. Miss Clark arrived home 15 minutes late for our appointment, having gone grocery shopping and having presumably forgotten our planned meeting. Her nephew was able to enter the home with the assistance of an older neighbor, as neither he nor Miss Clark's niece had a key because of her distrust of them. Upon her arrival, Miss Clark was nonplussed to find us in her home. She was defensive about our intentions, presumably sensing that our concerns might force a change in her situation. Throughout our interview, her every sentence concluded with an assertion that neither her family nor the interviewer were going to move her out of her house. Miss Clark was cooperative through the interview, responding favorably to our assertions that our goal was to support her desire to remain independent. Her speech was tangential and occasionally circumstantial. She was able to retain a conversational idea for approximately 90 seconds and then returned to the concrete assertion that she was not going to move. She could return to the conversational idea with a simple prompt. Her cognitive ability showed intact and rich long-term memory, judgment mildly impaired with intact concrete decision-making skills, poor insight into personal circumstances, significant paranoia directed at family members, and moderately impaired short-term and immediate recall. To allay her suspicions, I encouraged Miss Clark to show me her home without her family's accompaniment, and I followed her direction and timing. Throughout the tour, Miss Clark paced and seemed agitated. She was unable to sit for more than a few moments, and she checked and rechecked doors and windows to confirm that they were locked.

My relationship with Miss Clark began with the home assessment. During the assessment process, I emphasized her personal strengths and existing supports and attempted to join with her concerning areas that she perceived as important. For Miss Clark, I quickly perceived her pride in her home and praised her care of it. The assessment included the following factors: personal strengths, such as attitude about independence, coping strategies, endurance, faith, and spiritual values; family supports, including perceptions of responsibility and attitudes toward outside care; and financial resources, including ability and attitudes toward paying for care.

My assessment indicated that Miss Clark was eating adequately. Her kitchen showed no evidence of food spoilage and was adequately stocked. The kitchen showed little evidence of actual cooking taking place, and it seemed that Miss Clark "grazed" on snack foods and fruit. She appeared physically robust, though slender. She denied smoking and alcohol consumption. Miss Clark showed me her medicine for her hypertension and cholesterol. She was unaware that she was out of her medication. I was able to perform only a cursory pill count in her presence, not wishing to provoke her, and it seemed that she was taking roughly $1^1/_2$ times her dose, perhaps double dosing every other day. She kept her empty pill bottles, which cluttered the kitchen counter.

An assessment of her activities of daily living revealed complete independence in personal care; she was appropriately dressed and groomed. Miss Clark was independent in all mobility areas: She climbed stairs without exertion, showed no evidence of balance problems, performed her own home cleaning, and mowed her own lawn. Her judgment interfered with task execution; for example, she incorrectly bagged her trash but otherwise compensated very well. She correctly used a telephone. Miss Clark denied having any difficulty with managing her personal finances, but her family had expressed concern that she had overlooked some bills. Her family did not perform financial duties, but Miss Clark had intermittently agreed to and then refused an attorney's involvement in these matters.

Home Safety Evaluation

An evaluation of the safety of the client's home is an essential component of comprehensive care management, as it provides information that is needed for making environmental modifications. For our purposes, it also provides a comfortable foundation for beginning a relationship of trust with a client, as the focus is on the environment rather than on real or imagined problems with the client.

Miss Clark lived in what had once been her parents' house. She described their house renovations in detail and took great pride in her home. The house was structurally well maintained and was ideal for an aging individual. Bedroom, bathroom, and laundry were all located on the main floor. The bathroom was fully accessible with a walk-in shower and grab bars, although she needed none of these. The kitchen had an accessible layout. The stove was gas, potentially more dangerous than electric because of an open flame and difficulties with pilot lights. The kitchen curtains were a fire hazard, as they draped near the range. The house had no smoke detectors. There was no evidence of hazardous wires or outlets. The house had clear access paths without throw rugs and was functionally uncluttered. There was sufficient available lighting, although the curtains in the rear of the home were drawn and it was dark. The telephone was functional. The home was wired with a security system and was prominently labeled. The basement windows were secured, and windows and doors had working locks. The house was located in a safe neighborhood. Miss Clark knew and was known by her neighbors.

On the basis of my initial evaluation, I made several recommendations. First, I asked Miss Clark's doctor to consider a medication to address her paranoia. Paranoid symptoms are common in dementing illnesses and can lead to clients' rejecting support when they need it most. Management of her paranoia would allow Miss Clark's positive personality attributes and her determination to emerge. Medications needed to be given in small doses initially and increased gradually, so it would take some time before the desired effect was achieved. During this time, Miss Clark needed to be behaviorally monitored for compliance and medication efficacy; this could be accomplished by a combination of my home visits and physician appointments at shorter intervals. Once-a-day dosing would be ideal, as it is easier for patients to remember and requires only a once-a-day prompt.

I did not discuss compliance issues with Miss Clark at the time of the evaluation, pending the physician's decision on her medication. Miss Clark's medications lent themselves to a simple once-daily dispensing system, which I arranged by removing old bottles and using a calendar and an alarm prompt. If these prompts proved insufficient, then my next step would be to arrange a daily reassurance telephone call through Salvation Army Service or a neighbor. I also left Miss Clark with printed explanations of the medications that she was taking.

The doctor indicated that he had informed Miss Clark and her family that she should not be driving. At the time of our interview, Miss Clark either did not recall or denied having had this conversation. The family made the initial contact with the Secretary of State to terminate her license. If the termination of her license was not a sufficient incentive to stop driving, then I knew that I would need to help arrange for the car to be removed and identify adequate alternative transportation, such as a city bus or cab and/or Neighborhood Senior Services Medical Transport Service.

There did not seem to be problems with impulsive buying or vulnerability to con artists, but Miss Clark's finances needed to be secured while retaining her maximum independence. At the very least, all of her ongoing bills needed to be directly paid by her bank. On the basis of this assessment, I made a note to determine whether financial power-of-attorney could be given to her niece or nephew or to her attorney to allow for monitoring and ongoing attention in the event of illness or additional decline. If Miss Clark did not wish to use these individuals, then a payee through the probate court could be arranged.

To make Miss Clark's home safer, I suggested that the kitchen curtains be adjusted promptly, as they posed an immediate hazard. Two smoke detectors needed to be installed immediately: one in the back kitchen entry and one near the bedroom. The locks on exterior doors were functional but needed to be modified to allow easier exit in case of fire. Miss Clark needed to demonstrate her ability to use the home security system at a future date.

Clearly, Miss Clark needed to discuss with her doctor advance directives and execute the paperwork fairly soon. I suggested a discussion at her next appointment with follow-up encouragement predicated on a medication trial. Assuming acceptance of the medication trial, I proposed visiting her at home weekly for 8 weeks to monitor these changes. During this time, a medication dispensing system could be implemented, home safety modifications could be arranged, and paranoid symptoms could be monitored. I would also provide emotional support while she adjusted to the loss of driving and assistance in arranging alternative transportation. Miss Clark's memory loss was compensated for by her familiarity with her surroundings and routine. This and her stated desire to remain independent in her home, as well as her family's support of this effort, made maintaining her independence a worthy goal.

Growing a Relationship

Miss Clark and her family agreed to my making weekly visits. On my home visits, I continued to attend to the development of our relationship throughout the period of goal setting, emphasizing Miss Clark's expressed goals and prioritizing our mutual goals. I attempted to use a client-centered approach in goal setting and care plan modification that addressed the specific problems of memory loss, impaired judgment, paranoia, and dependency. Such a "strengths-focused" approach extended to defining problem areas and involved reframing qualities such as stubbornness or tenacity in a way that the client could accept. I supported Miss Clark in some areas that her family found most troublesome. For example, I praised her carefulness in screening unknown visitors and encouraged her to ensure that a trusted individual was available when she had visitors. I further supported her plan to discuss with her doctor any recommendations I made before heeding them.

Of all of the concerns identified in the initial interview, Miss Clark was able to acknowledge only the difficulty with taking medication, as she remembered her doctor's strong statements about cardiac health. During a follow-up call 2 days after our initial visit, Miss Clark was unable to recall who I was but responded to the prompt that I was her "doctor's social worker." To gain entry into her house at the second visit, I built on her established relationship with her physician. Specifically, I arranged for her doctor to telephone her as I arrived. He informed her that I was coming and would be at the door shortly; Miss Clark reluctantly let me in while she was on the telephone with the doctor. She allowed me to assist in setting out her medicine but would not allow me to remove empty bottles or make any other changes. I arranged for the Salvation Army volunteers to call and suggested that they describe their call as a "reminder from your doctor." Miss Clark responded slowly but positively to the newly prescribed medication. She remained distrustful but became calmer when instructions were written out for her. She still paced through the house, but the behavior lost its frantic edge.

In the first month of service, Miss Clark allowed me to do nothing but check her pillbox "for the doctor." On the fourth visit, I suggested that she let me bring smoke detectors "since you have invested so much in the house already." She agreed but forgot by the next visit and was hostile to the idea. Later in the visit, she agreed to try them but insisted on installing them herself. She allowed me to hold the ladder and read directions to her. During this long visit, she seemed to identify me as nonthreatening help. I asked whether there was anything that I could do, "as long as I am coming next week," and she said that she needed her front shrubs removed. I arranged for the removal, but unfortunately, the workers arrived before their appointment and she chased them off her property with a rake. I was able to call them to return and stayed with Miss Clark during their work, repeatedly explaining that they were not stealing the bushes. As we stood in the yard during this visit, I was able to raise other concerns with Miss Clark, such as my observation that she was not eating well, that I sometimes found perishable food out when I came, and that she seemed worried about her safety in the house. She challenged me on each stated concern but remained engaged in dialogue, despite tangential conversation. Our talk remained "an aside" to watching the workers and was much less threatening to her than a seated, sustained conversation. As I addressed Miss Clark's goals, medicine, and home maintenance, I also addressed my care management goals for Miss Clark.

Establishing a Therapeutic Relationship

Relationship building in care management is a process similar to forming a therapeutic alliance in psychotherapy by coming alongside the client and developing trust. Relationships with care management clients are differentiated from psychotherapeutic relationships because of clients' reduced capacity for insight, increased dependency, and their perception of being "forced" into receiving assistance. Taking time in relationship formation, thoughtfully considering the client's perspective, and evaluating the emotional content of the client's position is critical in ensuring continued care delivery. My relationship with Miss Clark developed as I joined rather than confronted her. I let her converse naturally about her concerns, and I responded to the emotional tone of her comments. I was also willing to listen to her mistaken perceptions ("They are stealing my bushes") and respond to the feeling behind it ("I am not safe here"). In cases of paranoid reasoning, it is essential to respond to the false beliefs by addressing the existing feelings of fear. In addition, I was slowly becoming part of Miss Clark's world. I began each visit by reminding her of what we had done the last time I was in her house, building on the success of each previous encounter to increase her trust and awareness of my presence.

Finally, I used a good deal of conversational distraction to keep her engaged. In the lengthy visit involving shrub removal, I let her talk, but I raised related topics, such as her roses, when she became agitated about the workmen. Socially isolated older adults often hunger for relationships and willingly engage in banter that outsiders find adversarial. It is noteworthy that during our entire relationship, Miss Clark never welcomed me or expressed any appreciation for what I had done for her. Her acceptance was begrudging at best, yet she gradually allowed me to assume a greater role in providing services.

Reframing Goals with the Client

Miss Clark had a clear goal in her mind: "I want to stay in my house!" It is important to recognize how threatening change is to people who have compromised cognitive ability. Over time, I was able to help her expand her goal to include discussion of what it would take to stay safely in the house. In this process, a gradual shift from independence to interdependence took place. I said to her, "You want to stay and think you can stay. What will it take to stay here, and how will you know when it's time to go?"

Introducing Services in a Timely Manner

The success of care management interventions is reflected in the "fit" of services for the client's stated goals in his or her home environment. Providing too many services can foster dependency, provoke anger, and waste resources. Providing insufficient services places the client at risk and undermines trust. Creatively incorporating services in ways that allow people to save face gradually encourages clients to accept needed care. For example, Miss Clark needed a medication reminder. Constructing that reminder as though it came from her doctor made it more acceptable to her. Timing of suggestions for services is crucial: Introducing the medication reminder in a later visit made it less likely that she would refuse the service.

Growing a Support System

Clients' relationships with their family members are critical. Frequently families are exhausted or preoccupied by their own needs and require attention from the care manager. Proactive family communication that retains and improves family involvement is important, with the care manager assuming responsibility for initiating communication. The effective care manager views "crisis events" as opportunities to address family roles, caregiving patterns, and boundaries and to potentially resolve family conflict.

Miss Clark's niece and nephew were immediately relieved by my involvement in her care. In some families, there are mixed or mistaken feelings about a care manager's involvement. Very often, families are seeking an immediate solution to the situation, and these high expectations can lead to disappointment and eventually undermine the strategy of care. I am careful to describe the initial care plan as being built on "shifting sand"; continual reevaluation and readjustment of changing care needs is part of the plan. I told Miss Clark's family that I would introduce services slowly and seek their input on priorities for care.

In many families, there are feelings of guilt about relying on outside help. I work with families to redefine their roles, transferring to the care manager some of the instrumental duties that they find burdensome, and retaining their primary role as niece or nephew, son or daughter. It is important that this shift takes place in those areas that the family finds burdensome or inappropriate for their involvement; the care manager should never make assumptions about those roles or tasks. In Miss Clark's situation, this role modification proved to be helpful, as she began to view her niece and nephew with less hostility as they "stopped telling me what to do."

After 6 months of service, Miss Clark's nutritional status began to worsen as she became cognitively less able to follow the steps that are necessary to prepare a meal. She refused home-delivered meals, as she would not allow "strangers" on her property. I suggested to her nephew that he become involved in her meal delivery. For a week, he picked up the meal and brought it to her house himself. Miss Clark accepted this approach, as her nephew often brought food to the house. In the next week, he accompanied the Motor Meal volunteer to her house, and by the third week, she accepted the volunteer alone.

A balance between professional service and family support in another area of care was also needed for Miss Clark. In her cognitive decline, she became too disorganized to manage her finances. She had significant assets and was at risk for exploitation. Neither her nephew nor her niece was able or willing to assume this responsibility because of their own health issues and strong feelings about Miss Clark's previous accusations about their intentions. On the basis of the suggestion of her niece, I located a cousin whom Miss Clark trusted. This cousin had a son with developmental disabilities, and Miss Clark understood that her cousin had made financial arrangements for him. She accepted him as a "bill payer," and the cousin was able to coordinate his efforts with Miss Clark's attorney. Shared responsibility between family and outside service providers frequently is the most palatable solution for clients with paranoia and is most manageable for families. It is also important to attempt to address other needs that families may have and that have an impact on their ability to remain involved. For example, I referred Miss Clark's family to our Caring for Aging Relatives lecture series and an early memory loss support group to educate them about dementia. Other families may benefit from assistance in obtaining resources in child care, bill paying and insurance advocacy, family leave benefits, and encouragement to use respite services.

The support system for care management clients may also include an array of community services. In establishing initial services, the care manager is often the bridge between the service provider and the client, making the service less threatening to the client and the client more cooperative with the agency. Miss Clark would not have accepted chore assistance, meal delivery, or financial support without my increased involvement during service introduction. In this early phase of service provision, the care manager must be on-site to coach the client through the process. Reminder telephone calls, detailed information for service providers, and written instructions for the client are important to successful service delivery.

Proactive discussion and establishment of clear communication pathways with other professionals and caregivers are essential components of care management. Confidentiality issues are best resolved at the onset of care. I strongly recommend open communication among caregivers and set that as a standard for clients. I keep in confidence concerns that would be privileged in counseling relationships, might be embarrassing to the client, or are unnecessary for ensuring complete care. In Miss Clark's situation, I carefully informed her niece and nephew of her situation but saw no reason to convey Miss Clark's disparaging comments about them. With other clients, it is not uncommon for the care manager to learn of family grudges and conflicts, and there is no need to transmit these opinions.

As the care manager, I am involved typically because the client is unable to self-advocate effectively. I must be willing to mediate between service providers with their own needs and service criteria and the client to obtain services that are suitable to the client's individual needs. Resistant clients often burn bridges in service delivery, firing caregivers and alienating professional workers. Often, the care manager must advocate for the client with frustrated service providers. Using this approach, I tried to identify what would make each service provider's job easier and acknowledged their efforts on Miss Clark's behalf. I also attempted to convey accurately the difficulties that they might face with Miss Clark's accusatory approach and forgetfulness while presenting Miss Clark's better qualities. I also shared what had worked for me. For example, Miss Clark's mother had been an accomplished portrait artist and the house was filled with her paintings, which she proudly showed me. When Miss

Clark was agitated, I encouraged visitors to ask her about the paintings. Inevitably, her hostility diminished as she discussed the portraits.

After a few months of my involvement, Miss Clark stopped driving on her own. Her neighbor reported that Miss Clark often attempted to maneuver her large car out of her little garage unsuccessfully and would storm back into her house in frustration. After a few weeks of this, she stopped trying. Once her meals were delivered and her financial issues were resolved, she became much calmer and enjoyed an additional year in her house, with visits from me approximately twice per month. She remained gruff but often greeted me with a statement such as, "What do you think we should do next?"

I had worked with Miss Clark for more than a year when she developed a serious respiratory infection. She became increasingly afraid in her own home and did not seem comforted by the familiarity of her environment. Although she had been misplacing things since I had known her, she was now becoming lost in her own house. Early on, I had discussed placement options with her niece and nephew and also with Miss Clark. Never willing to discuss thoroughly placement as a possibility, she had stated only that she wanted to be "where her church would go." Financial issues were not a concern, and Miss Clark's family had the choice of several assisted living settings, a choice not available to many families. Assisted living communities were willing to accept Miss Clark, as she had no continence difficulties and although she paced she never attempted to leave a building. After much discussion, her family chose to place her in a nursing facility that had a small dementia wing and a large proportion of African American residents, including a small number who had attended Miss Clark's church. They believed that this would be the most comfortable environment for Miss Clark and would honor her desire to "be where her church would go," although her pastor would have visited her anywhere. I admired how her family considered all aspects of placement, and I supported them in their difficult decision.

I remained involved to assist the family in admissions paperwork and interviewing and also wrote for the nursing facility a detailed summary of Miss Clark's history, personality, and preferences. In this report, I conveyed how important pacing was to Miss Clark's routine, and she was included in a daily walking program at the facility. Furthermore, her mother's beloved paintings were displayed in her room and other locations in the building. I joined her nephew and cousin at her first care conference in the facility and occasionally saw Miss Clark as I visited other clients in the nursing facility. She adjusted well to her relocation and was involved in the life of the facility. Her fearfulness dissipated because she always had reassuring people nearby.

I attempted to have closure contacts with many of Miss Clark's long-standing caregivers. Her close neighbor was in the hospital during Miss Clark's move, and I conveyed word to her about Miss Clark's move to the nursing facility through her daughter. One of the home-delivered meals volunteers had become attached to Miss Clark and appreciated my telephone call informing him of the change and gratefully accepted my compliments on his kindness.

INTERVENTION ANALYSIS

The interventions in Miss Clark's situation were gradual and deliberate. At each visit, I attempted to forge a stronger relationship with her and work myself into her world. At the same time, I was attempting to work closely with her family and with other care providers. This process occurred within the larger reality of the changes in Miss Clark's medical and cognitive function as well as changes in her family situation, specifically her niece's health. Typically, it is necessary that care management plans be modified continually to address changes in the client's situation.

Demonstration of Respect

Respect is the essence of relationship formation with all clients, but it is especially important when cognitive or emotional concerns make trust challenging for clients. The willingness of the care manager to meet clients in their own homes on their own terms begins this process. By allowing Miss Clark to "tour" me through her home, I learned about more than safety concerns; I learned what her home meant to her. I also encouraged Miss Clark to tell me what worked in her own support system and to set her own goals for care. In this case, I showed respect for the family by listening to their perspectives, concerns, and goals. I alerted them to the possibility that I would align myself with Miss Clark and helped them to set reasonable goals to avoid allowing them to feel that I had undermined them. I also kept them informed of my involvement and requested their advice when appropriate.

Use of the Client's Strengths

Miss Clark had a caring family that, despite their frustrations, wanted the best care for her. She was determined to be independent and responded favorably to praise in this area and goals that affirmed this self-view. Comments that affirmed these values were woven through countless conversations and were used to facilitate our relationship and bolster her confidence. She had a trusting relationship with her physician, which was well established in her long-term memory, and she accepted my presence in her home as an extension of his care. She also had good neighbors who cared about her. She had meaningful objects in her home, such as her mother's portraits, which could move with her to her new home, and she had a strong faith and the support of her pastor.

Blurred Boundaries

As with many care management clients, I accepted a higher level of depend-ence in this client. During the middle stage of her dementia, Miss Clark fre-quently called me at home in the evening, because of a day/night reversal in her time orientation. There was also a time during her niece's illness when she called me multiple times during the day to ask the same questions about her niece's treatment. Although this behavior was burdensome, I recognized the value of my availability and accepted her repeated calls. Also, because I recog-nized her calls as a passing symptom, I was more willing to stretch this bound-ary. As can happen with people who are paranoid and anxious, there were episodes of anxiety that might have developed into calls to 911 and unneces-sary hospitalization if a therapeutic avenue of expression had not been avail-able to Miss Clark.

An important boundary to keep intact is the family/nonfamily line. We often find that clients treat us "like the daughter they never had," but it is crit-ical that only family members carry these titles. Care managers support but never replace family, and our efforts must be directed at edifying and enhanc-ing family roles, not allowing even the perception of a family role to be usurped. Miss Clark never placed me in a family role, but her niece and nephew might have seen our relationship as such. The early effort in role clarification was beneficial in averting this possibility.

Changes in the Therapeutic Relationship over Time

Once Miss Clark and I had established a relationship and services were gradu-ally implemented to support her, the most significant change was her worsen-ing cognitive function. No amount of service can offset biological decline, and as is often the case with adults who have memory impairments, when the envi-ronment is no longer familiar, benefits of supported living such as activities and socialization become more valuable than staying in the home. Because of my established relationship with Miss Clark and her family, this transition was planned and participatory, rather than a hurried response to an emergency. I needed to adjust my approach to Miss Clark to her changing level of cognitive ability and did so by increasing the frequency of my contacts.

Benefits and Difficulties of the
Therapeutic Relationship for the Client and the Therapist

Trust and gradual progress toward therapeutic compliance slowly replaced Miss Clark's initial distrust and hostility toward me. She came to a partial acceptance of interdependence, as long as it was expressed to her in terms of independence. Miss Clark became willing to allow me into her home, then transferred her trust in me to other caregivers. She eventually became willing to request assistance from me, first in emotional care, then in instrumental areas of need.

The family welcomed my participation as an intermediary, as much of Miss Clark's paranoia and hostility had previously been directed at them. They were comfortable in maintaining their own limits, as when the nephew was willing to bring meals, but not to assume financial power-of-attorney. When Miss Clark's fearfulness was increasing and her hostility was decreasing, her niece and nephew were able to provide compassionate support to her. Their ability to do so might not have been possible if their relationships had been irreversibly eroded by Miss Clark's paranoia. Instead, they were restored to their primary roles of niece and nephew and were able to make decisions regarding her placement with the certainty that every alternative had been explored.

Initially, my involvement had tangible benefits for Miss Clark: She was able to take her medication properly, obtain necessary home repairs and modifications, improve her nutrition, and remain secure in her finances. In addition, she was able to use me as an unbiased advocate—her fear and isolation diminished, and she was able to process simple decisions with me. She became able to voice her fears, both natural and unfounded, and resolve conflicts with her family that were an outcome of her disordered reasoning.

In the beginning of my intervention with Miss Clark, she was markedly hostile to me. I was able to respond to the personality that had been obscured by cognitive impairment and gain her trust. I was able to guide and support her family, advocate for her with agencies, and represent her physician's care in a tangible way. After several months in the nursing facility, Miss Clark no longer recognized me. She was settled and well cared for, and the only loss was mine, but the loss was genuine.

Words of Wisdom

When care managers are conducting clinical assessments, obtaining services, and implementing care management plans, the client is often lost in the process. Care managers can become committed to giving the services that are available or prematurely establish services that they perceive that the client needs but may not want. This can be particularly problematic when caring for resistant older clients, such as those with early to midstage dementia with symptoms of paranoia, who are noncompliant, or those in dysfunctional family situations. For these clients, issues of independence/dependence and control loom large and must be addressed at the onset of caregiving. Client personality, the disease process, and the intimate nature of entering the home environment further complicate these issues.

The creative approach in care management requires that the care manager operate under the assumption that resisting care is a reasonable attitude for clients to hold. This orientation acknowledges the frail client's tenacious grip on the status quo, however unwise, and the reluctance to accept any change, however necessary. Effectively entering into the world of such clients and successfully bringing about useful change requires time spent in relationship formation.

Care management relationships are of extended duration, and this should be recognized at the onset of intervention. Except for life-threatening situations, it is important to proceed slowly and focus more on the relationship than on solving problems. Few of these situations develop overnight, and all of them require a patient, methodical approach. Knowing and respecting the client are hallmarks of compassionate caregiving and high-quality service delivery. Thorough client-centered assessment, a willingness to listen to client wishes and family perspectives, and an attempt to tailor care and services to an individual situation are reflected in high-quality service delivery. Time spent in relationship formation paves the way for open communication; ongoing modification of the care plan; and, most important, a relationship of trust among client, family, and care manager.

ADDITIONAL RESOURCES

This chapter addresses both the mechanics of entering a client's home for the purposes of assessment and care planning and the complex interactions that create positive relationships in the client's social system. With respect to the former, a handbook created by Emlet, Crabtree, Condon, and Tremel (1996), *In-Home Assessment of Older Adults: An Interdisciplinary Approach*, is helpful. This assessment manual is unique in its format, allowing multidisciplinary teams to conduct jointly and separately in-home assessments of older adults. The writers draw on a common language of assessment measures across several professions and have developed a fine introductory text for those who are new to working in clients' homes.

With respect to the client's experience in care management, Kalish's (1969) seminal article "Of Children and Grandfathers: A Speculative Essay on Dependency" offers a historical perspective. This article is one of the "classic treatises" in social gerontology. Although the reader who is new to the field may find the issues obvious, it is important to consider how revolutionary the consideration of dependence, independence, and interdependence issues were in the early days of social gerontology research. As each successive cohort reaches maturity, it is important to revisit these themes as they are represented in the individual lives of older adults and in the wider social and cultural view.

A similar theme is found in Aronson's (1999) book chapter "Conflicting Images of Older People Receiving Care: Challenges for Reflexive Practice and Research." Aronson identified several narrative "themes" that may unwittingly guide our care management practice: older people being managed, older people managing, and older people making demands. The author challenges the reader to reflect on these views of older adults and the resulting clinical styles that emerge and affect intervention. In the face of increasing emphasis on the management of social and health resources, the author advocated for social workers' focusing on their older clients' perspectives.

No clinician has better addressed the issues of aging and dependency than Lustbader (1994). In her wonderful book *Counting on Kindness: The Dilemmas of Dependency*, she considered the difficulties of giving and receiving care from the various perspectives of family member, dependent older adult, and advocating professional with warmth, sensitivity, and humor. Through anecdotes and narratives, she illuminated the power and helplessness as it is played out in relationships confronted with chronic illness. Lustbader guides helpers toward improving relationships while giving voice to caregivers and care receivers alike.

REFERENCES

Aronson, J. (1999). Conflicting images of older people receiving care: Challenges for reflexive practice and research. In S.M. Neysmith (Ed.), *Critical issues for future social work practice with aging persons* (pp. 47–69). New York: Columbia University Press.

Emlet, C.A., Crabtree, J.L., Condon, V.A., & Tremel, L.A. (1996). *In-home assessment of older adults: An interdisciplinary approach*. Gaithersburg, MD: Aspen Press.

Kalish, R.A. (1969). Of children and grandfathers: A speculative essay on dependency. In R.A. Kalish (Ed.), *The dependencies of old people* (pp. 73–83). Ann Arbor, MI: Institute of Gerontology.

Lustbader, W. (1994). *Counting on kindness: The dilemmas of dependency*. New York: The Free Press/Macmillan.

Maintaining Family Ties— Intervening in Elder Neglect

13

Katherine P. Supiano

CLIENT'S BACKGROUND

MRS. ELLIS, A LONGTIME MEDICAL PATIENT OF THE TURNER GERIATRIC CLINIC, WAS A 90-YEAR-OLD WIDOW who lived in her own home with her single, middle-age daughter, Anne. Mrs. Ellis's husband had been a successful businessman. He died in his early 40s, leaving Mrs. Ellis and her daughter a large estate. Mrs. Ellis's personality had long been characterized by suspicious thinking and distrust. Although Mrs. Ellis and Anne had a trusting regard for their accountant, who had worked with them since Mr. Ellis's death, she had steadfastly refused to sign any legal documents and had never executed advance directives or named a medical advocate. For the same reason, she refused to engage contractors to maintain or paint her home, and the house had fallen into disrepair.

Mrs. Ellis's daughter, Anne, had a persistent mental illness with prevalent paranoid thinking and frequent psychotic episodes. She had never been employed and had become her mother's primary caregiver. Anne was also preoccupied with concerns about money. She was fearful of poverty despite her financial well-being, was reluctant to purchase goods and services, and tended to hoard worthless items. She had no history of psychiatric hospitalization.

Mrs. Ellis had grown increasingly frail and debilitated. She exhibited signs of midstage progressive dementia with increased paranoid thinking, and her behavior included frequent verbal and physical outbursts directed at her daughter. Their relationship historically alternated between devotion and animosity. As Mrs. Ellis's condition worsened, she began to resist her daughter's care, spitting food and striking out. Her mobility declined, and she spent more

197

time in bed. It became difficult for her to get to the toilet in time, and she experienced frequent episodes of bladder and bowel incontinence.

Both Mrs. Ellis and her daughter had trusting relationships with the geriatrician. Despite their difficult behaviors and Mrs. Ellis's long-standing medication noncompliance, the physician demonstrated tolerance of their eccentricities. Because of an unwillingness to execute advance directives, the physician took care to document Mrs. Ellis's stated wishes of minimal intervention and monitored the difficulties in her relationship with her daughter.

As Mrs. Ellis's health declined, the physician ordered home health care. The nurse's assessment revealed an unkempt home and evidence of spoiled food. Mrs. Ellis was sleeping in an old hospital bed that had no mattress. Anne was unwilling to obtain a new hospital bed, considering it "wasteful," but instead had piled blankets and bedding to cover the bedsprings. The home health aide's attempts to implement physical care were met with resistance by Mrs. Ellis. She was combative and verbally berated the aide. The aide reported to her supervisor bruises and reddened areas on Mrs. Ellis's skin, matted feces on her skin and clothing, and evidence of poor nutrition. Meanwhile, Anne frequently called the agency to cancel care, stating that it was not needed. On other occasions, she refused to answer the door when staff arrived. She repeatedly called 911 for assistance in getting her mother to the toilet or off the floor when she had fallen. Because of concerns about Mrs. Ellis's safety, Adult Protective Services was notified by both the home health agency and the geriatric clinic staff.

INTERVENTION SUMMARY

Our initial goal for this situation was to maximize Mrs. Ellis's safety while attempting to honor her previously stated desire to remain in her home with her daughter, with the least possible amount of outside involvement. To this end, we attempted to build on the client's strengths as we saw them: her devoted yet problematic relationship with Anne and her trust in her doctor. As there had been no previous contact with a social worker, it was important that this first contact be as nonthreatening as possible. Mrs. Ellis and Anne allowed me as the geriatric clinic social worker to enter the home because "she was my doctor's own social worker." Similarly, they accepted the involvement of a psychiatric nurse by coordinating her visit with that of their trusted accountant.

In my initial visit, I attempted to establish rapport with Mrs. Ellis and her daughter in their own environment. When I arrived, Anne was attempting to feed Mrs. Ellis, who repeatedly batted away the spoon. Anne was understandably frustrated and stated, "See? She isn't hungry!" Believing that Mrs. Ellis was visually threatened by the oncoming spoon, I asked Anne to sit next to her mother and allow her mother to hold the spoon. Then, holding her mother's hand, Anne could guide the spoon into the food and into her mother's mouth. They were somewhat successful, although Anne was frustrated by the amount of time it took to feed her mother in this manner. This was the pattern; Anne attempted to care for her mother, but any disruption in care resulted in her storming off to another room and leaving her mother alone for extended periods. She had only limited understanding of her mother's cognitive deterioration or lack of ability to summon help.

In separate interviews, the psychiatric nurse and I administered the Folstein Mini-Mental Status Examination and Geriatric Depression Screen instruments to assess Mrs. Ellis's mental state. Mrs. Ellis scored 11 correct responses out of 30 on the Mini-Mental, a score suggesting significant cognitive impairment. Her Geriatric Depression Screen score was 3 positive items out of 15, indicating no obvious clinical depression. The nurse documented the need for 24-hour nursing care and supervision. She was able to assist in obtaining medication compliance by establishing a simple dispensing system. Given the gravity of the situation and the low probability that the course of neglect could be reversed, however, the geriatric clinic staff decided to petition for guardianship and conservatorship of Mrs. Ellis.

In the weeks preceding the court hearing, I addressed the goal of improving the relationship between Mrs. Ellis and Anne. In frequent telephone conversations, I reminded Anne of her unique role as daughter and attempted to reassure her because she felt usurped by the aides' caregiving activities. At the same time, the professionals involved became concerned about who would be most appropriate to serve as guardian and conservator. Given Anne's impulsiveness and frequent changes of opinion regarding care for Mrs. Ellis, we believed that it would be unwise for Anne to assume this role, despite the court's desire to award guardianship to blood relatives. Still, we wanted to preserve Anne's relationship with her mother and prevent her from feeling marginalized. I sought out a private guardian who was known to the clinic, had experience working with challenging situations, and demonstrated qualities of respect for client autonomy. She agreed to serve if appointed.

Simultaneously, Mrs. Ellis was hospitalized for breathing difficulties. Although she initially allowed emergency medical technicians to transport her mother to the hospital, Anne became upset about hospitalization and demanded that her mother be discharged to her home. However, Mrs. Ellis's frail condition convinced the staff to hospitalize her. Anne alternated between demanding nursing facility placement and discharge to her home. During that week, I was in daily contact with Anne, keeping her informed of all aspects of decision making and attempting to support her role.

Mrs. Ellis was transferred to a nursing facility on a guardianship-pending basis. The nursing facility was selected for Anne's convenience, so that she could walk or bike to the facility from her home. Mrs. Ellis's physician provided the nursing facility with an extensive summary of Mrs. Ellis's needs and how to interact with Anne. I met with the nursing facility staff to assist them in dealing with Anne and creating a role for her. I thought that Anne's hostility toward caregiving staff would be reduced if Anne had a role when visiting her mother.

Until the court proceedings, Anne maintained that she should be named guardian and conservator of her mother. She agreed to meet with the recommended guardian on the urging of the physician, and Anne was somewhat mollified by the recommended guardian's willingness to listen to her wishes regarding her mother's care. She accepted my observation that her mother would benefit from an objective person's being involved in decision making but maintained that she knew best what her mother would want. Finally, her accountant took her aside and said, "Anne, you're the only daughter your mother will ever have, and none of this will change that." These words helped her to accept our recommendations for guardianship, thus avoiding the need for the professionals involved to testify publicly as to her unsuitability for the appointment. Throughout these weeks of transition, I was in close contact with Mrs. Ellis's physician. I was able to confer with her accountant by telephone and elicit his support. All of my contacts with others were made to keep these individuals informed and working toward the same goal and to prevent Anne's changes of opinion from derailing the process.

I remained involved in providing support to the nursing facility staff, as Anne initially was highly critical of the aides and frequently berated them in public areas of the facility. In the initial care conference, we developed a routine whereby staff would greet Anne upon her arrival and quickly inform her of her mother's condition. Staff agreed to overlook certain behaviors of Anne's, such as leaving her bicycle in the entryway, and quietly work around them. Mrs. Ellis thrived for many months, her skin healed, and she gained weight. Several months later, she received a diagnosis of having a terminal condition and was transferred to a residential hospice, with both her guardian and her daughter agreeing to this plan. I was able to assist in this transfer, providing support to Anne and information about their relationship to hospice staff.

INTERVENTION ANALYSIS

As is frequently the case in situations of elder neglect, lack of awareness of the older adult's functional or developmental needs is a larger factor than is willful intent to harm. This family's pattern of arguing then angrily distancing themselves from one another prevented the ongoing care and supervision that Mrs. Ellis required. In addition, their consistent pattern of rejecting outside support made it difficult for concerned professionals to enter their world. As Mrs. Ellis cognitively and physically deteriorated, it was difficult for Anne to accommodate her caregiving to the increased demands. Even in situations in which caregiving is straightforward and family caregivers are dedicated and capable, I advise families to keep their primary role a priority (e.g., remaining a daughter to one's mother, with its inherent intimacy and emotional dynamics) and not allow it to be eclipsed by other instrumental tasks.

Demonstration of Respect

In this case, I was committed to preserving the mother–daughter relationship throughout the legal, medical, and residential changes that Mrs. Ellis and Anne would endure. Mrs. Ellis was loyal to her daughter, despite her difficult behaviors and their conflict-filled episodes. Similarly, Anne viewed herself as her mother's caregiver and genuinely attempted to meet her needs. Much of the professional activity in this case addressed reconfiguring Anne's daughter role to her mother's changing needs. This case required listening and tolerance as well as frequent contact. Other cases require active educational interventions in dementing illnesses, behavior management, and self-care techniques.

I honored Anne's role by arranging for her continued involvement in her mother's care. We located a nursing facility that allowed convenience in visitation and helped to establish an appropriate pattern of visitation. Although she did not have legal decision-making authority, Anne was informed of all decisions in her mother's care, and her input was sought and acknowledged.

I attempted to honor the wishes of Mrs. Ellis and her daughter with respect to their autonomy. When Mrs. Ellis was deemed no longer competent by the probate court, I advocated for her previously stated desire of least-restrictive measures of care and sought a guardian who would respect her long-standing personality. In both her nursing facility placement and subsequent hospice placement, I attempted to convey to her caregivers her personality, history, and character.

Use of the Client's Strengths

I appreciated the strengths of both Mrs. Ellis and her daughter. It is tempting in these situations to quickly label personal attributes and behaviors as pathological and problematic. Although the paranoia and noncompliance posed challenges to obtaining necessary care, I chose to regard them as tenacity and dedication and attempted to use Mrs. Ellis's and Anne's independence toward building trust in a strategy of care. I was able to build this trust with Anne in particular by "piggybacking" on the trust that she had in the geriatrician and the family's accountant. Even in situations of significant paranoia, one trusting relationship often remains intact. The clinician who ascertains what those trusting elements are and presents him- or herself to the client in a similar way is less likely to be regarded as an adversary.

As stated previously, I regarded the relationship between Anne and Mrs. Ellis as a strength and, in fact, the most meaningful aspect of their lives. My efforts to preserve and enhance this changing relationship were the most gratifying element of this case, as Anne responded favorably to my stated respect for her role.

In addition, Mrs. Ellis and Anne had considerable financial resources available to them. This initially posed a problem; available assets and an unwillingness to pay bills resulted in withdrawal of services. However, in the long run, their financial resources allowed them to obtain high-quality nursing facility care, once conservatorship- and guardianship-pending status was established. Eventually, the careful management of assets by Mrs. Ellis's conservator/accountant resulted in a trust fund for Anne, securing her financial future and protecting her from potential exploitation.

Blurred Boundaries

My boundaries in this case remained intact with respect to Mrs. Ellis and her daughter. One challenging aspect was presenting myself as an expert in a way that did not convey to Anne that I believed that I knew more about her mother than she did. Another difficult moment was signing the court petition for guardianship and conservatorship, a function that is usually performed by family members. At that moment, I was conscious of potentially usurping Anne's role. To preserve necessary boundaries, I attempted to consider Mrs. Ellis's needs as Anne would have in her moments of highest psychological functioning. Because Anne's emotional problems created barriers to getting help for her mother, I could have been sidetracked into focusing on Anne's needs instead of keeping her mother's needs in the forefront. I was able to remain clear in my objectives by working closely with her physician, accountant, and others who had gained the family's trust toward the goal of providing a safe environment for Mrs. Ellis.

Boundaries are frequently blurred in care management when conferring about and negotiating for the client. By meeting with the people whom the client trusted and by preparing and supporting nursing facility staff in their interactions with Mrs. Ellis and Anne, I was moving out of the immediate circle of my clients into the larger world in which they were living. In this kind of complex interaction in which it was possible to become confused about roles, conferring with my clinical supervisor was also helpful.

Changes in the Therapeutic Relationship over Time

I did not know Mrs. Ellis and her daughter well before the need arose for home health care. My initial home visit was intended to assess Mrs. Ellis and her situation and provide the supports and services that are necessary for safe home living. Over time, my focus shifted to enhancing the roles of long-term caregivers (physician, daughter, and home health agency staff), introducing new caregivers (psychiatric nurse), and facilitating communication among them. Later, as increasing services proved inadequate, my role required seeking legal guardianship protection, finding suitable nursing facility placement, coordinating efforts with hospital and nursing facility staff, and eventually obtaining hospice care.

Although my initial role was instrumental, it quickly changed direction to focus on the emotional mother–daughter relationship in caregiving. As Mrs. Ellis's health declined, she no longer recognized me. My attention shifted from a relationship with Mrs. Ellis to Anne's needs and changing role. Ultimately, I attempted to support the final relationship between mother and daughter, one that would leave Anne with a sense of completion and peace when her mother's life ended. To achieve this goal, it was necessary to remain in contact with Anne; listen carefully to her perceptions; and assist her in presenting herself positively to professional caregivers in her house, the nursing facility, and the hospice.

Benefits and Difficulties of the Therapeutic Relationship for the Client and the Therapist

Mrs. Ellis benefited from this situation by our respectful intervention in a potentially dangerous situation. At the time of her hospitalization, we were confident that she no longer recognized her house as her home, and we believed that we had honored her desire to stay at home for as long as was safely feasible. She was cared for in facilities that fostered her physical and emotional well-being and respected her request for minimal intervention beyond her ability to articulate her wishes. Mrs. Ellis's life ended in a context of compassionate care, and her daughter remained involved until her death.

Because of our work together, Anne enjoyed positive changes in her relationship with her mother. Despite strong resistance to the provision of care for her mother, I believed that Anne would have been traumatized if her mother had died in pain and decrepitude. By allowing her to change gradually her view of herself as caregiver, I was able to help Anne remain an integral part of her mother's life. At the time of her mother's placement in the residential hospice, Anne no longer berated staff or stormed out of the facility in anger.

This case contained many frustrating elements for me. The slow pace of intervention in a potentially dangerous situation was certainly my major worry. Until Mrs. Ellis's hospitalization, I also had to manage frustrated home health workers and emergency response personnel in a way that would keep them involved in the care plan. This required frequent telephone contacts, active listening, and validation and support for their frustrations. My ongoing contacts with Anne were either satisfying or aggravating; it was often like walking a tightrope to offer support to her in a nonthreatening way. The team approach to care was most gratifying, and my effort to elicit the involvement of the physician, health care providers, the guardian, and the family accountant benefited the client, the process, and my own stamina.

Words of Wisdom

This case illustrates the need to exercise patience in a therapeutic relationship. The process of relationship formation is time-consuming and requires ongoing maintenance and commitment to remain involved. It is easy in situations of urgency to overlook the power of relationships. The procedures of guardianship and conservatorship are also lengthy and involved, and it is important that clinicians pace themselves and their clients through this process.

Another important element in this case is tolerance. To join with difficult clients requires a high level of acceptance and a desire to see beyond their problems to their needs and strengths. During Mrs. Ellis's hospitalization, a frustrated health worker strongly advocated that "the best thing for Mrs. Ellis would be to have her daughter as far away from her as possible." Although such "solutions" may be tempting, it is important that clinicians focus their energies for change on existing strengths and use available resources in each situation. It is crucial to recognize the power of history, that these relationships have been developed over a long period, and to search for whatever positive elements or connections can be found.

Team building is the final essential component of this case. It was important that all key individuals in Mrs. Ellis's situation were located, encouraged to provide input, and kept informed of changing developments. No one professional, family member, or friend could have resolved this crisis. It took open communication and the means for every individual to contribute their expertise to bring about the necessary change in the immediate crisis and achieve successful closure. Team building requires considerable energy and time spent in communicating with all parties. This process involves listening to each person's perspective, allowing frustrations to be expressed, and formulating mutual goals that respect the autonomy of the client.

ADDITIONAL RESOURCES

The resources identified in the following fall into three broad categories: those that detail assessment guidelines, those that provide reference for reporting criteria, and those that describe intervention strategies.

With respect to assessment, it is noteworthy that most of the early assessment research is found in the nursing literature. Fulmer's (1989) article in *Nursing Clinics of North America* summarized this content well and presented a history of the changing societal and professional views of elder abuse and neglect. Issues of assessment and diagnosis are elaborated on in Quinn and Tomita's (1997) text *Elder Abuse and Neglect: Causes, Diagnosis and Intervention Strategies* and in Baumhover and Beall's (1996) *Abuse, Neglect, and Exploitation of Older Persons: Strategies for Assessment and Intervention*. The American Medical Association (1993) also developed a set of professional guidelines, *Diagnosis and*

Treatment Guidelines on Elder Abuse and Neglect. Of interest to those who desire more information on the incidence and prevalence of mistreatment of older adults, Goodrich's (1997) survey of State Adult Protective Services Programs is helpful. Information concerning incidence and prevalence studies by the federal government is available on the Administration on Aging website (www.aoa/gov/abuse/report).

In all states, professionals are subject to and guided by mandatory reporting criteria. These guidelines, as well as reporting information, are accessible through a few websites. The National Center on Elder Abuse (1998) completed a report on the incidence of abuse of older adults, and their website (www.gwjapan.com) provides information about reporting, as well as state-by-state links, fact sheets, and publication listings. The Administration on Aging website (www.aoa.dhss.gov/aoa/ webres/abuse.html) also has a link with state reporting criteria.

Intervention strategies are discussed in Breckman and Adelman's (1980) text *Strategies for Helping Victims of Elder Mistreatment* as well as in the Quinn and Tomita (1997) and Baumhover and Beall (1996) texts. An older but useful volume is Steinmetz's (1988) *Duty Bound: Elder Abuse and Family Care*, which places these issues in a family context and illuminates the impact of abuse and neglect across generations.

Less has been written about the important area of prevention of mistreatment of older adults. The American Association of Retired Persons (1987) published a pamphlet, *Domestic Mistreatment of the Elderly: Towards Prevention*, which is targeted at older individuals. This is content that should be made available to families as well. The National Committee for the Prevention of Elder Abuse, located at the University of Massachusetts Institute on Aging, has developed an educational website for older adults, families, and professionals to communicate recent developments in prevention (www.preventelderabuse.com).

REFERENCES

American Association of Retired Persons. (1987). *Domestic mistreatment of the elderly: Towards prevention.* Washington, DC: Author.

American Medical Association. (1993). *Diagnostic and treatment guidelines on elder abuse and neglect.* Chicago, IL: Author.

Baumhover, L., & Beall, S.C. (Eds.). (1996). *Abuse, neglect, and exploitation of older persons: Strategies for assessment and intervention* . Baltimore: Health Professions Press.

Breckman, R.S., & Adelman, R.D. (1980). *Strategies for helping victims of elder mistreatment.* Thousand Oaks, CA: Sage Publications.

Fulmer, T. (1989). Mistreatment of elders: Assessment, diagnosis and treatment. *Nursing Clinics of North America, 24,* 707–711.

Goodrich, C.S. (1997). Results of a national survey of state protective services programs: Assessing risk and defining victim outcomes. *Journal of Elder Abuse and Neglect, 9,* 69–86.

National Center on Elder Abuse, Westat, Inc. (1998, September). The national elder abuse incidence study: Final report. Administration on Aging. Available: http://www.aoa/gov/abuse/report.

Quinn, M.J., & Tomita, S.K. (1997). *Elder abuse and neglect: Causes, diagnoses, and intervention strategies* (2nd ed.). New York: Springer Publishing.

Steinmetz, S.K. (1988). *Duty bound: Elder abuse and family care.* Thousand Oaks, CA: Sage Publications.

Joining Hands to Address Older Adult Substance Abuse

14

Karyn S. Schoem

CLIENT'S BACKGROUND

I FIRST MET MRS. GREEN ON HER INITIAL VISIT TO THE CLINIC. AS A NEW PATIENT AND NEW ENROLLEE IN A MEDICARE HMO, she was entitled to a psychosocial evaluation by a social worker in addition to a physical examination by a health care provider. Mrs. Green was a 77-year-old widow of European American heritage. She lived alone in a local apartment building for older adults. She came to the first appointment alone. Her white hair was stylish, and she wore a necklace with pictures of her three grandchildren set in silver charms. She answered my questions about her health and family history with a smile and without hesitation.

Mrs. Green wore glasses and used a hearing aid, which she said never felt effective. She reported that she had lived in our town throughout her 53 years of marriage and that she had enjoyed going to sporting events, especially hockey games, and dancing with her husband who had died about 2 years earlier. They had been a relatively healthy, social couple, rarely seeing doctors and not used to taking prescription medications. She had come to the clinic to establish primary care as requested by the HMO but reported no acute problems.

Mrs. Green described having good relationships with her adult son and daughter, who lived within an hour's drive. She indicated that they had been supportive in the months after her husband's death and that they had not expressed any concerns about her current functioning. She stated that her financial situation was secure, that she owned and operated a car, and managed her daily affairs without difficulty. She had not prepared advance directives or appointed someone as her power-of-attorney for medical or financial affairs.

Arthritis pain in her joints and frequent difficulty with early morning awakening were two areas about which Mrs. Green had mild complaints. Nevertheless, she felt capable of accomplishing daily tasks, had rarely been unsteady on her feet, and reported that occasional afternoon napping addressed the sleep problems. Mrs. Green stated that she used over-the-counter pain relievers or sleep-inducing products only rarely and as directed. Her appetite had remained stable, she said, as had her weight. She preferred to use microwaveable meals from the freezer.

Mrs. Green reported that she was a pack-a-day smoker and had been since early adulthood. She had been trying to decrease her use but was not interested in quitting. She said that she and her husband were accustomed to a cocktail before dinner and that she had continued that habit, having 1.5–3 ounces of liquor each evening. When asked about family members' alcohol use, she reported that her mother's brother had died of alcoholism and that her sister had a brief period of trouble with alcohol in her 40s but that she had quit drinking on her own without any professional intervention. No one, Mrs. Green said, had ever indicated that she herself had trouble with alcohol. She and her husband were social drinkers and never drank before cocktail hour.

Mrs. Green also denied having any psychiatric history, saying that the hardest period of her life was when her first child, a son, was stillborn. She was devastated but managed to "pull myself out of it" when she became pregnant again. When asked about her impressions of how counseling could be helpful in times of crisis, she expressed the view that personal matters should stay within the family and that one ought to be strong and use the power of one's faith and will to overcome difficulties.

When asked about her memory, Mrs. Green told me that she had a harder time with names than in the past but that she believed that this was a normal part of aging. She reported that she had never gotten disoriented while driving but that to be cautious, she drove only to appointments and the grocery store.

For baseline documentation purposes, I administered the Folstein Mini-Mental Status Examination, a brief assessment of cognitive functioning that documents performance in orientation, registration, attention and calculation, recall, perception, and language. Of 30 possible points, Mrs. Green scored 29, missing one of the delayed recall questions. This score indicated that she did not have obvious cognitive problems at the time of testing. I also administered the Geriatric Depression Scale, a 15-point inventory of symptoms of depression. Mrs. Green scored 2 of 15 on this scale. A score of 5 or above is indicative of possible depression. She answered positively to questions about preferring to stay at home rather than going out to do new things and to feeling bored often. Mrs. Green was examined thoroughly by Lois, the primary care provider, a clinical nurse specialist. She had brought no previous medical records with her and indicated that her former provider, whom she rarely saw, had retired.

INTERVENTION SUMMARY

After the initial psychosocial assessment and physical examination were completed, recommendations were formulated by the health care team and presented to Mrs. Green. Medical recommendations included routine tests and health maintenance measures. Mrs. Green was asked to monitor her blood pressure for the next couple of weeks and to return to the clinic to recheck her pressure because it had been quite high at the time of this visit. She was also scheduled to see the gait specialist on the next visit because of some irregularities in her walking that seemed to impair her balance. We recommended that she quit smoking, and various treatment options were discussed.

Social work recommendations included that she review advance directive material with her children and appoint someone to be her patient advocate. I presented to Mrs. Green educational material that explained normal aging processes, including normal memory changes, safe use of medications (over-the-counter and prescription) and alcohol, and information on smoking cessation.

Upon leaving the clinic, Mrs. Green commented that this evaluation was more thorough than she had anticipated and that there was a lot of information to digest. She said that she remembered why she did not like doctors: "They find things I'd rather not know about." She was hesitant about coming back to the clinic again in just 2 weeks. I reassured her that once the initial evaluation was complete, most likely she would not have to come in frequently, and that knowing her well would help us to determine how to intervene in a way that would preserve her independence, which she had reported was a priority.

Mrs. Green missed her next appointment. When I contacted her by telephone, she said that she had a bridge group that morning and had forgotten about the appointment. I acknowledged how overwhelmed she had been at the first visit and reminded her of our concern about her hypertension. We joked about the unlikely possibility that she would have "the big one," her reference to a major stroke that she hoped would be the way she would eventually die. Instead, I reassured her that treatment was easy and much preferred to the consequences of untreated hypertension. I inquired about whether she had been able to purchase a blood pressure monitor, and she said that it was on order at the pharmacy and that they would deliver it to her the following week with the rest of her standing order. She had talked with her children briefly about the initial appointment—"They like to keep tabs on me, especially during hockey season"—but had not discussed power-of-attorney issues. I suggested that they were welcome to join her at her next appointment if she wanted some help in discussing advance directives.

Later that day, Mrs. Green's son called to ask whether the evaluation had been completed because his mother had told him that, "They say I'm as healthy as a horse." He wondered whether there were any recommendations. I asked him what his concerns were, and he offered that his mother had been keeping more to herself, seemed not to care as much about maintaining her apartment, and sometimes forgot conversations. I advised that he should ask his mother for permission to discuss her care with the clinic staff or accompany her on a future appointment.

When Mrs. Green came in several weeks later, she had on her forehead a laceration that was healing. She reported that she had tripped and fallen in the kitchen the previous week. Her son accompanied her to this visit and reported that he had encouraged her to go to the emergency room the day after the fall. Mrs. Green said that he was making a big deal out of a little thing and that she was feeling completely well. Her son continued, "This is the second time in a month that you've fallen, Mom." She responded, "Well, I don't want to call you or your sister about every little thing. You've got busy lives. I'm doing fine. I can always call JoAnn down the hall if I need something. Really, don't worry so much!"

At this second appointment, we discussed power-of-attorney issues, and Mrs. Green decided that she would like her son to manage her finances and her daughter to manage health care decisions if she were unable to do so. She signed a release of information to allow her son to see "relevant" medical records and asked, "Why would he need to know every little detail?" "Because, Mom, I want to make sure that you stay well and that your blood pressure and your balance and your memory are okay. You'd feel terrible if you couldn't go to Arizona next winter." Mrs. Green was emphatic: "If it ain't broke, don't fix it, Son. I've had a full life and I don't want to spend every last minute fussing over every little ache and pain."

At this visit, the health care provider started Mrs. Green on an antihypertension medication. The risks of smoking and hypertension were again reviewed, and Mrs. Green thought that she might consider nicotine patches to help her quit smoking. She was not interested in any group education or support. I added that she would need to stop drinking while she was taking the new medication as it would interfere with the medication's effectiveness. She also saw the gait specialist, who began to investigate her balance issues. During Mrs. Green's medical evaluation, I suggested that she could make use of a local community organization, Independence for Seniors, that provided free safety evaluations of older adults' homes and could install equipment that may help to prevent falls. Mrs. Green agreed that this would be a good idea, and a referral was made to a resource advocate at this organization.

Collaboration with Independence for Seniors was crucial in providing Mrs. Green with a comprehensive approach to her substance use problems. In the process of providing home safety evaluations, transportation and accompaniment to medical appointments, grocery shopping, and financial help with medications, resource advocates look for typical red flags of substance abuse. These red flags may include poorly organized medication regimens, unpaid bills, inedible food, clients' inability to assess their own safety, poor judgment with relation to others in the household, and stresses such as caregiving.

Independence for Seniors assesses aspects of clients' functioning that are undetectable in an office setting.

With Mrs. Green's permission, George, the resource advocate from Independence for Seniors, reported back to me after installing grab bars in Mrs. Green's bathrooms and removing slippery throw rugs from the kitchen and front hall. George had noticed a half-empty bottle of vodka in Mrs. Green's kitchen and a collection of empty bottles in the far corner of her pantry. He offered to dispose of the empty bottles and also to return, if she liked, in a few weeks to see whether she needed anything else. Mrs. Green agreed. Later she would say that she liked the advocate and his sense of humor and liked the idea of not having to rely completely on her son for home maintenance because she believed that she was often a burden to him.

George visited Mrs. Green 2 weeks after his initial home visit. He and Mrs. Green talked about sports while he rechecked the installations that he had made previously. While in the bathroom, George asked where Mrs. Green stored her medications. She showed him her medicine chest, which contained several half-empty bottles of diphenhydramine hydrochloride, a common allergy medicine. He asked whether she had allergies, and she replied that her previous physician said that it was okay to use the medication to fall back to sleep when she awakened early. He inquired about what amount she found effective, and she thought that she took one dose, "but you know," she said, "I can't be bothered measuring it out when it's 3 A.M. and I'm tossing and turning. I just want to get back to sleep. I usually take a couple of small sips until I fall asleep." Mrs. Green did not think that she took this over-the-counter medication very often, maybe once a week. George began a discussion of safety during the night, including issues of balance and taking medications such as the diphenhydramine hydrochloride. Mrs. Green reported that she had not fallen in many months and changed the subject.

George left by way of the pantry to check on the collection of empty bottles that may have accumulated since his visit 2 weeks before. He again offered to take care of Mrs. Green's empty bottles, scooping the bag up as she hesitantly consented. He said that he would be in touch after the next big hockey game. On the way out, he counted eight pint bottles but did not comment at the moment because Mrs. Green had been defensive about his inquiries. He did offer, however, to get Mrs. Green some housekeeping help because she had commented that she was not as interested in doing routine chores as she used to be. He also took her kitchen clock in for repair. George again reported his findings to me, which I included in my charting for the health care provider. We discussed the issue of smoking safety because Mrs. Green clearly was drinking more than she had reported and was also using diphenhydramine. As well as her risk for falling, her risk of starting a fire was significant.

On his next visit the following week, in addition to having a heated debate about the local hockey team's recent loss, George checked the smoke detectors and asked where Mrs. Green's fire extinguishers were. He asked whether there had ever been any fires in the building as long as she had lived there. She sheepishly reported that she had, in fact, had a small accident in which her couch was burned by a fallen cigarette ash and that the fire department had been called. She said that it was embarrassing and that the management of the building had been rude to her about the incident, which was really nothing after all. Mrs. Green then reported that she would be leaving for Arizona in a month and would need the housekeeping service only twice until she returned in the spring.

George and I strategized about the role that the housekeeper could play. We decided to have her arrange to visit Mrs. Green during different times of the day to help us observe her functioning. The housekeeper, Marge, was also employed by Independence for Seniors and had training in identifying substance abuse. Marge visited Mrs. Green and cleaned her apartment twice, once in the morning and once in the late afternoon. On her morning visit, she took some clothing to the dry cleaners and offered to pick up Mrs. Green's order from the pharmacy. Mrs. Green declined the pharmacy pick-up, indicating that she was friendly with the delivery person and was looking forward to her visit. On her afternoon visit, Marge found Mrs. Green watching a game on the television with a drink in her hand. Mrs. Green invited Marge to join her, but she declined, cleaned the apartment, and left.

Before Mrs. Green left for Arizona, she came in for refills for her antihypertension medication. I chatted with her about what she was looking forward to in Arizona and said that I would see her again when she returned home. Lois, her primary care provider, and I gave her a referral for smoking cessation programs in the area where she was going and once again encouraged her to enroll.

Four months later, I received a telephone call from Mrs. Green's son asking to set up a medical appointment for his mother. He reported that while she was in Arizona, she had fallen and fractured her hip. She had unusual reactions to the anesthesia during and after surgery, and the physicians had thought she likely had experienced a delirium. She returned home with new pain medications and was making progress in her rehabilitation.

I saw Mrs. Green 8 months after her initial visit to our clinic. She was in good spirits, saying that with her new medication the sleep problem had completely resolved and that while she was in the hospital she had been able to cut back her smoking by half a pack per day. She was enjoying the physical therapy and was looking forward to driving again. Mrs. Green's daughter had been staying with her for the first few weeks after her return and accompanied her mother on this visit. When asked how she thought her mother was doing, she gestured that she would like to meet privately with me. I asked Mrs. Green whether I could get acquainted with her daughter while Lois was examining her, and she consented.

Mrs. Green's daughter looked weary. She revealed that she had not come with her mother to previous appointments because she had become frustrated in her attempts to help her mother control her drinking. Her brother, she said, could not make the connection between their mother's physical ailments and behavior changes and her drinking and so she felt alone and hopeless. She reported that she had tried not allowing her mother to purchase alcohol, to which she responded by having the pharmacy deliver it. She had tried pouring the liquor down the drain, but a new supply would soon appear. She had tried threatening her mother with visiting her less often but believed that strategy was cruel to the grandchildren. Soon after their father died, Mrs. Green's daughter realized that her mother had no other social structure to sustain her. Mrs. Green stayed in her home and increased her drinking because she said that she had nobody with whom to go to sporting events or dancing. She saw her mother as a proud woman who did not want to depend on the charity or pity of others.

I discussed the daughter's report with Lois, and together we made recommendations to Mrs. Green. We said that her daughter had expressed concern about her functioning, particularly as it related to drinking. In addition, because her health status and medication regimen had changed while she was away, we suggested that this would be a good time to get an independent assessment of the effect of all of her medications and her consumption of alcohol on her functioning. The factual evidence, we explained, would help us to determine what kind of approach to take with regard to alcohol use. Mrs. Green protested that she was not an alcoholic. Lois explained that the effect of the combination of substances might affect her ability to remain independent.

I asked Mrs. Green what she thought an alcoholic was; she responded that she could stop drinking at any time and that she would know if it were affecting her performance. Her daughter interjected, "Mom, I notice that it's affecting you. You haven't wanted to come over for dinner, and sometimes you seem really foggy on the phone." Mrs. Green shot back, "Well, what do you expect? I've just had a broken hip!" Mrs. Green was referred to Older Adults in Recovery, another local agency that specializes in older adult chemical dependency issues in both inpatient and outpatient settings. Mrs. Green, with the help of her daughter, reluctantly called for an assessment. After asking Mrs. Green for consent to share the findings with our clinic, David, the social worker at Older Adults in Recovery, sent me the recommendations that Mrs. Green had formulated in conjunction with him. They included a series of steps beginning with voluntary abstention (based on Mrs. Green's reports of previous periods of abstinence and a calculation of the risk of home detoxification) up through inpatient treatment.

When Mrs. Green returned to the clinic, Lois and I reviewed the recommendations with Mrs. Green and her son and daughter. She agreed to abstain from alcohol use and agreed that she would follow the steps of progressive intervention if she were not successful. Mrs. Green resumed her housekeeping services and occasional visits from George. These relationships grew strong and served to reinforce the clinic's recommendations. Over the next year and a half,

Mrs. Green's son, daughter, and school-age grandchildren were coached on how to make constructive observations and began attending Al-Anon meetings.

When Mrs. Green fell with a lighted cigarette in her apartment approximately 8 months later, all parties, including Marge, George, David, Lois, the apartment manager, family members, and me, joined for a substance abuse intervention, which took place at the clinic. Each person present confronted Mrs. Green about the consequences that she had endured as a result of her drinking. These consequences included impaired health, jeopardized living situation, threatened close relationships, and inability to take care of the basic activities of daily living consistently. At the end of this collective intervention, Mrs. Green was convinced that she needed a more intensive treatment. She was admitted from the clinic to the Older Adults in Recovery inpatient program and began a 2-week stay. Mrs. Green graduated to intensive outpatient treatment, where she stayed for another month and then was referred back to me for ongoing relapse prevention.

INTERVENTION ANALYSIS

One of my priorities was to facilitate continued feedback among the various service providers on how to build relationships with Mrs. Green, helping her to reach her goals in healthful, constructive ways without supporting the further development of her substance abuse. This approach supported Mrs. Green's independence by allowing her to understand the consequences of her alcohol use from the beginning of our relationships with her.

Demonstration of Respect

The health care team believed that Mrs. Green should be an active participant in her health care, so discussions with her were an important part of developing recommendations for care. Understanding her values in general and her attitudes about health care in particular were important in making successful suggestions. It also meant that we needed to make an effort to give Mrs. Green educational material and resources so that she could make informed decisions. In relation to substance use, we began with an inquiry about what role alcohol and medications had played in her life. We gave her information about the typical changes of aging and how alcohol and medications had an impact on normal aging. We also explained how alcohol could affect the specific issues with which she was coping, such as impaired balance and gait, memory changes, sensory loss, chronic pain, sleep difficulties, hypertension, and grief resolution.

By talking about substance use issues in a neutral and informative way, we hoped to lay the groundwork for frank discussions of this and other traditionally difficult topics. Substance abuse became one of many issues that we could discuss in the context of health care and well-being, which, we hoped, would normalize it and help to counter the stigma of shame and moral frailty that often surrounds this issue. We respected Mrs. Green's wish for continued independence and developed our recommendations to reflect that value. We provided her with information on how each of her physical issues could affect her independence and how she could address these issues in medical, behavioral, and environmental ways.

Mrs. Green was given access to helping services in which she was interested, such as the housekeeping and home safety evaluation. To provide these services, we collaborated with agencies that understood older adult substance use and the importance of continuity of care. Professional enabling (ignoring a client's substance use problem or providing support that allows the client to continue substance abuse unchallenged) was held to a minimum because of the extensive training and collaboration with our partner agencies. We respected Mrs. Green's desire to handle issues in her own way, in her own time, and we also offered her new ways of looking at the issues that connected her drinking with her medical and emotional challenges.

Use of the Client's Strengths

Mrs. Green, a Caucasian, heterosexual woman of sufficient means, probably faced sexism but not the difficulties of racism, homophobia, or poverty that would have complicated her situation. She had sustained a long and good marriage, raised two capable children, and participated actively in her community. She had been and continued to be relatively healthy and was accustomed to relying on herself to solve most problems. Mrs. Green felt good about the life that she had led up to this point and had no major regrets. She was an easygoing and sociable person who made intelligent and interesting conversation about any number of topics. We used these physical, intellectual, and relational strengths to build with her meaningful relationships that we hoped could sustain the difficulties of discussing substance use. This process involved focusing on issues about which she was concerned or in which she was interested in addition to her substance abuse. All of the care providers listened to what Mrs. Green had to say and gave her positive feedback for the gains that she was able to make at the same time that we gave her frank feedback regarding substance use.

Mrs. Green was also practical and liked a good, logical argument, which allowed her to entertain ideas that were emotionally difficult but intellectually solid. For example, even though she had difficulty understanding the role of alcohol in her own life, she agreed, intellectually, that alcohol could have a negative impact on a person's health in many specific ways. Also in relation to substance use, she did not develop a problem with drinking until later in life, which meant that her emotional growth had not been impeded earlier on, giving her a better chance for recovery. We praised Mrs. Green for her thinking abilities, supporting her in fighting the denial that kept her from addressing her substance use. We also acknowledged her courage to return to the clinic to evaluate her health issues in light of the fear that doctors "find things I'd rather not know about."

Through the course of our interactions, we asked Mrs. Green about her daily life and related her ability to handle situations positively to the potential that she had for applying similar strategies to changing her substance use patterns. We discussed the successes that she had experienced in her life and the ways in which she wanted to spend the rest of her years. We used her capacity for insight to explore issues related to her husband's death and connected her feelings to her change in drinking patterns. Mrs. Green's sense of humor was also useful as it provided a lighthearted means by which to bring up difficult topics and to soften the experience of confrontation. Joking about "the big one" led us into discussions concerning the meaning of life and advance directives.

Blurred Boundaries

In this case, there were many opportunities for blurred boundaries with regard to both the client system and the professional system. In fact, the blurring of boundaries was often helpful in producing motivating situations that would move Mrs. Green toward opportunities for better health. Because the service providers represented a spectrum of services that Mrs. Green needed, each of us was able to use our varied interactions with Mrs. Green to reinforce the group's major goals. We saw ourselves as experts in specific areas but at different times also as cheerleaders, errand runners, compassionate listeners, surrogate children, resource advocates, fellow sports fans, or reality reflectors. The skill in being able to convey to Mrs. Green the same basic message from various perspectives allowed us to provide a continuous approach to Mrs. Green's situation.

Understanding one another's expertise and knowing our collaborators well allowed us to anticipate the responses from the other service providers involved, to know how far to go beyond our job descriptions, and to prepare Mrs. Green for what she could expect. As an example, when referring Mrs. Green to Older Adults in Recovery for an assessment, she was concerned about whether the process would be invasive and whether she would be bound to a particular course of action. I was able to describe in detail the people whom she would meet, how long the visit would take, and what she needed to bring and to provide anecdotes about other clients' experiences of the process.

The formal members of our team, funded by a small Department of Community Health grant, included the Turner Geriatric Clinic social worker (myself), the Independence for Seniors resource advocate, and the Older Adults in Recovery social worker. We have primary roles in and allegiances to our own agencies, but we have a special bond with one another. Because of the relatively small amount of funding provided by the grant and because older adult substance abuse has not been a priority in many agencies, we have had great autonomy in the management of the work. We have been able to discover what works by experimenting and making some mistakes along the way. For example, we often have been present at one another's agencies for meetings with clients and/or families even though technically this was not necessary. We learned that being present at such meetings, while time intensive, generated many rewards in terms of client commitment and interagency trust. Training sessions often developed after an interesting or difficult encounter that brought to the fore issues of confidentiality, competence, dual diagnosis, or codependence. We prepared these sessions for all of our staff members and thereby broadened everyone's knowledge and skill. We also included informal partners, such as senior housing management, Adult Protective Services' workers, legal aid lawyers, and our favorite home health nurses and aides. This cooperative crossing of agency boundaries was comforting to Mrs. Green and also impressed upon her that we worked together and would not likely be pitted against one another.

Because of the fluidity of our professional roles, it was sometimes difficult for Mrs. Green to know whom to approach about a particular problem. Often the work was divided by service category, such as concrete need, medical care, or substance abuse assessment/treatment. At other times, the worker who was spending the most time with the client was considered the lead person until the needs changed. Other cases require that the worker who is doing the initial intake, wherever it may be in the system, continue on as the care coordinator. For instance, when Mrs. Green was admitted to the inpatient treatment unit, the onsite social worker took charge of the treatment, family contacts, and future planning. When Mrs. Green was discharged, I became the leader in addressing relapse issues.

Although this arrangement can be confusing for clients, it allows the service providers the greatest amount of flexibility in handling each case effectively. We have found that by communicating regularly through e-mail and voice mail, the confusion is minimal. Confidentiality is always a prime concern. No identifying information is communicated through these electronic devices. We routinely ask clients to sign releases to our partner agencies and other collaborators. Having case conferences that include all interested parties brings many issues out in the open for discussion at an early point in the client–worker relationship. Jointly creating a treatment plan with a client also outlines the expectations, the people involved, and any contingency plans. This methodology was successful with Mrs. Green in helping her to know when further treatment measures were necessary.

Changes in the Therapeutic Relationship over Time

Many times in cases involving substance use, the care providers can set the stage for action but must wait for an external situation that will increase a client's motivation to change. By involving as many members of a client's system in the process as possible, the hope is that a motivational experience that does not permanently impair the client can occur. For Mrs. Green, the service providers began to build a case of useful information from the first visit to the medical clinic. We learned about her values and strengths, family history, and current resources. We educated the family and enlisted them in the process of collecting information that could be motivational.

Mrs. Green's broken hip offered an opportunity to move forward with assessment and a treatment plan as a result of her change in medical needs. It brought her daughter into the picture, which allowed us to confront Mrs. Green with her daughter's discomfort about her drinking. Once we had a treatment plan on paper, we could document in a concrete way Mrs. Green's ability to succeed.

By the time that Mrs. Green fell in her apartment with a lighted cigarette, not only were all of our relationships with her that much stronger but we were also able to enlist the help of her support network. We were able to bring in the apartment manager, who discussed the potential for eviction if her drinking behavior led to a breech of the rental contract, as well as the social worker from Older Adults in Recovery, who facilitated the next step to inpatient and long-term treatment.

Benefits and Difficulties of the Therapeutic Relationship for the Client and the Helping Professionals

Mrs. Green was very likeable. She was a tough and witty woman who could "hold my own with the boys," as she put it. She was a positive person capable of insight, even though her vulnerabilities often had to be approached with humor rather than with straightforward discussion. She refused to feel sorry for herself about the issues that troubled her. After all, she had indicated from the beginning that personal matters belonged within the family, and preferably within the individual who should "tough it out." However, she appreciated people who were straightforward, and often we could confront her directly. Mrs. Green's likeability kept us from feeling the frustrations of the slow pace of the assessment and treatment process as intensely as we might have.

The benefits to all of the care providers involved were feelings of mutual trust, enhanced skill, and substantial effectiveness in addressing the difficult issue of chemical dependency. For us, as for families, even if the outcome of the client's situation is not what we would have hoped for, we gain greater understanding of the limits of our control as well as the power of our collaboration.

Although Mrs. Green was uncomfortable with the attention to her health and habits, through the treatment relationships, she was able to face some of her fears about death, articulate her legacy, and review her life and marriage. She was able to see and receive positive feedback for her strengths and to begin to build a new life for herself as a single person. Her relationships with her children became constructive once again as the children and grandchildren learned new ways to relate to a loved one with a chemical dependency.

Words of Wisdom

Flexible boundaries between the roles of the helping professionals are important to addressing successfully older adult chemical dependency. Cross-training (knowing intimately what your collaborators do) is critical in providing smooth delivery of services. Workers can set the stage for future interventions by knowing what is possible within each system. Appreciating others' expertise and going above and beyond helps to build strong professional bonds. The helping system can then take advantage of the opportunities presented by clients or their environments to move the system toward health. Being able to respond quickly to a situation without becoming preoccupied with bureaucratic issues energizes and challenges workers.

As is true in social work practice in general, the development of relationships is essential to successful work with older adults who have substance abuse issues. Cultivating a treatment system, like a family system, is vital to affecting change in the chemically dependent client/family. In the case of older adults, the "family" system may simply be the professional caregiving system and a collection of interested others, such as volunteer helpers, friends, housing staff, community and religious workers, and mail carriers. A central role can be played by social work in coordinating this informal, changing network so that it functions seamlessly in motivating individuals to enter treatment. A broad range of strategies that include both the client/family system and the professional services system is required for coordination. Examples of strategies that are used to motivate the client/family to address issues of substance use include the following:

- Contacting prospective older adult clients before their first appointment to educate them about the importance of family participation in psychosocial assessment. Preparing the client for the purpose of the session sets the tone for the meeting and helps the worker to use the time most effectively.
- Discussing on the first visit substance use in the context of preserving independence and enhancing quality of life opens the door to formerly taboo subjects and encourages the client to address feelings of shame and guilt.
- Guiding an older adult in articulating his or her views about what is meaningful in life is important in formulating an effective treatment plan as well as enlisting a client as an active participant in health care.
- Attending important family events such as the funeral of a client who was not one of the success stories and meeting extensively with the family that searches for meaning in a suicide demonstrates ongoing commitment to the healing of the entire system, not just the identified patient.

Sample strategies that have encouraged professionals to address substance use issues include the following:

- Obtaining releases of information from the client/family on the first visit will enable the social worker to get needed information about the kinds of services already in place and to understand how substance use issues have been addressed. It also gives the social worker an opportunity to educate respectfully other professionals about effective ways to conceptualize older adult substance use issues and how to approach them from their particular role with the client.

- Taking time to empathize with a harried service provider, offering an explanation for the symptoms that he or she finds so difficult, and supporting his or her good work helps direct care staff to feel effective and builds allies who will refer other clients with similar symptoms.

- Including an insurance representative, particularly from an HMO, in case conferencing can build trust with the insurance representative and may lead to flexibility in the coverage of services. It demonstrates that the social worker's agency will take some fiscal as well as clinical responsibility for the client's treatment success and that the social worker has confidence in the efficacy of the proposed plan.

- Completing time-consuming, nonmedical tasks for a physician so that he or she will listen to your recommendations about assessment builds a mutually beneficial relationship and gives the social worker another opportunity to demonstrate techniques that are appropriate to primary care settings.

- Spending time at other agencies talking to staff, bringing food or flowers, and being a positive force in what many perceive as a hopeless clinical situation builds relationships and encourages helping professionals at all levels of an agency to stretch themselves to provide services for the older client.

ADDITIONAL RESOURCES

It is important to have a basic knowledge of substance abuse screening, assessment, and treatment protocol to begin addressing the special needs of older adults with substance abuse problems. Lichtenberg (1998) devoted a chapter to the detection and treatment of alcohol abuse in his book *Mental Health Practice in Geriatric Health Care Settings*. He presented statistics on the prevalence and nature of the problem and outlines common symptoms. Lichtenberg described the various screening tools that are available and also articulated the many myths that care providers hold about older adults who have substance abuse issues that keep them hidden despite the availability of these tools.

The Hazelden Foundation (Center City, Minnesota; www.hazelden.org or |800| 257-7810) has an extensive education and publishing arm that offers audio and video materials as well as publications for professionals and clients. There are materials specifically about older adults in and after treatment. Another good resource is the American Society on Aging's web-based training on alcohol, drugs, and aging (www.asaging.org). Training options consist of a series of program modules that cover aspects of identification and treatment. At the end of each module are multiple-choice and short-answer quizzes to test knowledge of the material.

The Department of Health and Human Services, Substance Abuse and Mental Health Services Administration/Center for Substance Abuse Treatment (1997, 1998) published the Treatment Improvement Protocol Series, which covers older adult issues, substance abuse services in primary care settings, and coexisting mental illness and substance abuse issues. These are up-to-date and comprehensive. The American Geriatrics Society put together a brochure designed for professionals that provides helpful basic information on screening, classification of clinical findings, and intervention.

Pfeiffer (1998) wrote a succinct and practical chapter on multidisciplinary teams in *Geriatric Interdisciplinary Team Training*. He outlined why teams are particularly useful in providing effective treatment to older adults and gave insight into the stages of team development and the essential needs of healthy, productive teams. This chapter is useful to individuals who are contemplating a team approach or for those who simply wish to understand team dynamics.

REFERENCES

American Geriatrics Society. *Clinical guidelines: Alcohol use disorders in older adults* [Brochure]. New York: Author. (To order, call 212-308-1414.)

American Society on Aging. *Alcohol, drugs and aging: Use, misuse and abuse in later life.* Available: http://www.asaging.org

Lichtenberg, P.A. (1998). Detection and treatment of alcohol abuse. In *Mental health practice in geriatric health care settings* (pp. 133–153). New York: Haworth Press.

Pfeiffer, E. (1998). Why teams? In E.L. Siegler, K. Hyer, T. Fulmer, & M. Mezey (Eds.), *Geriatric interdisciplinary team training* (pp. 13–19). New York: Springer Publishing.

Substance Abuse and Mental Health Services Administration/Center for Substance Abuse Treatment. (1997). *A guide to substance abuse services for primary care clinicians. Treatment Improvement Protocol Series* No. 24. Rockville, MD: Department of Health and Human Services.

Substance Abuse and Mental Health Services Administration/Center for Substance Abuse Treatment. (1998). *Substance abuse among older adults. Treatment Improvement Protocol Series* No. 26. Rockville, MD: Department of Health and Human Services.

The Delicate Balance

15

Ruth Campbell

THE VOICES IN THE PRECEDING CHAPTERS, BOTH AUTHORS' AND CLIENTS', ARE SIMILAR YET DIVERSE. The similarities among the authors are primarily that they all are women older than age 40 and working at the University of Michigan's Turner Geriatric Clinic, often in one crowded room. There is some racial, religious, and ethnic diversity among them—one is African American, one is Japanese; they practice various levels of commitment to Christianity, Judaism, and Buddhism.

The clients reflect both the area of southeastern Michigan in which they live and the over-65 population. Although two of the clients discussed in this book are African American and several are men, most are Caucasian and female. The settings in which the clients are seen vary and include the outpatient clinic, a senior resource center, the client's home, and a nursing facility. We tried to represent various modalities, including individual and group therapy, various supportive and therapeutic groups, and interventions with families and community systems. Several of the clients have had long-standing emotional, physical, and psychosocial problems, but most of them are coping with the process of aging: changes in status, role, income, and relationships; physical and cognitive limitations; and death.

The purpose of this collection was not to present best practices or correct strategies for working with older adults and their families; instead, we believed that glimpses of how real people are involved with real social workers over an extended period of time were needed. We do not expect readers to agree with all of the methods or approaches described here. In fact, the authors often critique their own interventions. Given a chance, they would do some things differently both with their own clients and with other clients presented in this book. We hope that readers, both students and professionals, will use these case studies to explore not only what was done but also what could have been done, encompassing the rich range of options that are available in counseling and care management. The delicate balance that we refer to in the title is illustrated in these chapters as the authors move between autonomy and assistance, past and present, crisis and stability, intimacy and professionalism.

This concluding chapter reviews the six themes analyzed throughout the book: 1) demonstration of respect for the client, 2) use of the client's strengths, 3) blurred boundaries, 4) changes in the therapeutic relationship over time, 5) benefits and difficulties of the therapeutic relationship for the client and the therapist, and 6) words of wisdom. The discussion is based on the preceding chapters but also draws on an authors' retreat in April 2000, during which we examined the relevance of these themes to their work with older clients. The chapter concludes with thoughts about how practice with older adults differs from practice with younger adults and what is unique about the Turner Geriatric Clinic that may differ from other models of care.

DEMONSTRATION OF RESPECT

In many cases, the people we see have strengths that are buried so deeply that the goal of the therapeutic process becomes uncovering and identifying them. As illustrated by the examples presented in the preceding chapters, respect for clients' strengths is demonstrated in a number of ways.

Following the Client's Lead

A prevalent theme in these chapters is "going at the client's pace." With restrictions on their time, an allotted number of sessions approved by managed care, and competing pressures from other clients, helping professionals are apt to rush in and try to "solve" the problems as efficiently as possible. Change is seldom easy, however. Even deciding what change is needed takes time, and building trust with the client, a necessary prelude to change, is an ongoing process that is dependent on the reliability and good faith of the practitioner as the client perceives it. Respecting the pace of each individual often means that the helping professional must slow down his or her own expectations for progress.

In the cognitive therapy group described in Chapter 7, Edwards and Fogler respect Roger's desire to remain guarded and remote even within their time-limited format of 10 sessions. A high achiever for most of his life, Roger after retirement lost faith in his ability to do even rudimentary activities. Because of his doubts about his career and the mistakes that he had made, he became severely depressed. We can imagine how difficult it must have been for him to enter the group, let alone find his place in it. The authors allowed him slowly to discover his role as a problem solver. They departed from the set format when Roger initiated a discussion about computer use and they devised an exercise on activities that group members pursued in retirement to challenge his view that retirement was a dead end. In moving at his pace, they acknowledged his competence and encouraged him to seek volunteer work. Even though he never revealed to the group the depth of his depression or shared his weekly assignments, the authors respected his reticence. Although they felt somewhat intimidated by his career as a professor, it may be that their implicit recognition of his former status restored for him some of the power and self-confidence that he believed he had lost.

In another example of respect for the client's pace, Schoem illustrated in Chapter 14 the long process of helping a client to accept the idea of being an alcoholic. She and her colleagues believed that Mrs. Green should be an active partner in her health care. They gave her educational materials and concrete services, such as help with housekeeping, and respected her wish for continued independence. Although they kept the issue of her alcohol use on the table through subtle interventions, such as the outreach worker's asking whether he could take the empty bottles, they proceeded at her pace until she accepted the treatment process. In this case, as in many others, it took a crisis to accelerate the process, but once it occurred, all of the steps were in place for successful treatment.

Respect for the Client's Interpretation of the Problem

Aside from allowing the client to control the timing of the process, pace is also evident in how the social worker helps to interpret the client's perception of the problem. In Chapter 6, Stern and Ingersoll-Dayton described how the therapist demonstrated respect by accepting Barbara's definition of her problem (that it was her marriage that was causing her such pain) rather than accepting the suggestion of the referring physician to focus on stress reduction. In following Barbara's definition, the therapist agreed to work with the pair rather than individually, giving Barbara the opportunity to air her grievances to Arthur with the therapist as witness. As therapy continued, the treatment eventually moved to individual therapy and then back to couples work with a co-therapist. By giving priority to Barbara's understanding of the problem, Arthur and Barbara were able to move slowly toward reaffirming their relationship's strength.

Respect for the Client's History and Wisdom

Paying attention to the history and wisdom acquired by clients through the years is a significant way of conveying respect. As Miss Clark led Supiano on a tour of her house (in Chapter 12), she illustrated the worth of the structure that Miss Clark had created in her life, which was challenged by her condition. The first in her family to go to college, Miss Clark was viewed as a pioneer in the local African American community. She had cared for her parents until their deaths and had never accepted any help from family members. Supiano made it clear to Miss Clark that she was visiting her at the request of her physician, a person whom she trusted. Although Miss Clark's dementia and suspiciousness created challenges, at each step the social worker affirmed her independence, even assisting her when she got on a ladder to install a smoke detector and staying with her while workers removed her bushes, assuring her repeatedly that they were not stealing them.

The slow transition from independence to interdependence began with a recognition of how threatening change is to someone with declining cognitive ability. Supiano began by respecting Miss Clark's long history of independence, asking her, "You want to stay and think you can stay. What will it take to stay here, and how will you know when it's time to go?" She was also able to listen to her mistaken perceptions (e.g., that workers were stealing her bushes) and respond to the feelings behind the misperceptions. Supiano adeptly balanced between autonomy and the increased need for help by respecting the value that independence played in Miss Clark's life.

Respect for the wisdom acquired with aging is also demonstrated by the kind of programming offered to older adults. Groups such as Exploring the Meaning of Life (Chapter 8) and the Monday writing group (Chapter 9) are an acknowledgment that the participants will have something important to say *because* of their age and their lifetime of experiences. Although many give lip service to the possibility that knowledge is gained through long years of experience, few take the time to sit down and listen to it. In these groups, not only do members and facilitators listen to each other but they also ponder, learn, and come away with a sense of continuing growth and mutual appreciation.

Respect for the Client's Control and Autonomy

The essence of this discussion comes down to respecting the older person's sense of control. When Thomas said in Chapter 4, "I demonstrated my respect by accepting her beliefs about the care of her life and understood her persistence and determination to control her own destiny," she is affirming Mrs. Smith's autonomy despite her significant physical limitations. Observing the stream of helpers who Mrs. Smith managed from her bed, Thomas found ways to shore up this autonomy. She respected her African American history by "not calling her by her first name, not telling her what to do, and never allowing her to feel as if I thought I knew everything." Giving people the option of being seen in their own homes also allows them to be in a setting where they can exercise more control.

This concept of the individual's taking the lead, even though cognitively or physically frail, is one of the core social work values that must prevail whether we are managing people's care or counseling them when they are in need. Rumman's nursing facility group (described in Chapter 10) vividly illustrates this concept when residents and family members chose their own adjectives, positive or negative, to describe themselves. "Moody Mabel" may have been glorifying her bad temper, but she also asserted her right to be difficult and presented herself not as a person with memory deficits but as someone with a unique personality who must be respected.

USE OF THE CLIENT'S STRENGTHS

It is not surprising that the losses and changes of aging assault a person's sense of identity. When one is accustomed to thinking of oneself as an independent person and then is forced by illness to give up most of what constituted that independence, it is easy to lose sight of the strengths that endure. Therapists and care managers can help clients to identify and use their unique strengths and abilities.

Spirituality

Several of the people portrayed in these chapters are physically frail. In Chapter 4, Mrs. Smith ruled her roost from the narrow confines of her bed. Mrs. Smith's strong faith in God was a foundation on which Thomas built a case for helping her.

> She explained how she felt guilty for feeling sad because God had blessed her; after all, she was not in a nursing facility. I asked her whether she believed that God knew her every thought. She said that she did. I then asked her why God did not know that she was already sad, and she started to laugh.

Recognizing her religious belief as a source of strength and incorporating that faith into the therapy was an important way not only to help Mrs. Smith but also to build trust between her and her therapist. It is also interesting to note the change in the therapist as she gradually began to understand what looked like a hopeless situation as a demonstration of Mrs. Smith's management skills and her persistence.

In Chapter 2, Foulk's client, Helen, also believed that it was important to be on good terms with God. She prayed every morning and night and included prayers for her therapist and her therapist's family. Helen had accumulated overwhelming debt because of loans that she had made to her sister but was ashamed of having to declare bankruptcy to settle the debt. Foulk reminded her repeatedly of the Biblical passage in Deuteronomy that states that debts are forgiven in the seventh year. This assurance along with the support and encouragement that Foulk gave Helen helped her through a period of great hopelessness and suicidal ideation.

As in other areas, the line between therapy and religion can be a question of balance. Clients sometimes try to convert helping professionals to their beliefs, and others express outrage at people who have different beliefs than they do. Some believe that prayer alone will help them and that therapy may interfere with this. We have had clients at Turner Clinic with firm new age beliefs who prefer herbal and natural healing to medications and more tradi- tional methods. As authors in this book have demonstrated, discussing reli- gious beliefs, viewing them as strengths, and integrating them into the therapeutic process as much as possible can facilitate progress. Attempting to listen to and understand the client's religious beliefs is preferable to ignoring them.

Coping History

One of the obvious strengths that many older adults have is their history of coping with difficulties. In Chapter 11, Fogler's client, Betty, had experienced a difficult, often unrewarding life that left her feeling hampered by anger and depression. Fogler admired Betty's loyalty to her family, despite the difficulties of having lived with alcoholic parents and an alcoholic husband who had developed Alzheimer's disease. Betty also had painful physical problems and experienced depression and anxiety. Her therapist was able to point out the steadfastness that she brought to her relationships. She was caring for her hus- band and her father and was still concerned about her adult son. Fogler wrote, "Although she had trouble recognizing her own value, she was able to listen and benefit from hearing someone else enumerate her strengths and express admiration for her."

In Chapter 5, Rumman drew on Grace's family support to guide her through her grieving process as she died from amyotrophic lateral sclerosis. Her brother's visit on a weekend was filled with laughter and reminiscence. Her children gave her affection as well as practical support, such as a fax machine to compensate for her difficulty in speaking. Humor often played an important part in the relationship between the therapist and her client, rooting Grace in the funny currents of life and enriching their weekly encounters. Rumman also focused on Grace's creativity, her writing and music, and her fierce independ- ence, which shone even as her physical abilities diminished.

Frequently, the impact of a group in pointing out strengths has great power. In the cognitive therapy group in Chapter 7, Rose's depression and awkwardness in group settings initially made it difficult for group members to identify her strengths. Rose took care of a demanding mother and felt guilty when she left her to socialize with a friend. She became depressed, stayed in bed, and devel- oped psychosomatic symptoms. In the group, her diligence in following assign- ments and her loyalty to her mother were gradually recognized as strengths.

Building on Families' Strengths

Family members can be a potent source of strength for older adults. However, finding a way for the family to provide support can be hampered in institutional settings. Rumman's nursing facility group (described in Chapter 10) treated residents and family members equally, redressing the usual imbalance of the caregiving relationship. Family groups in nursing facilities typically have met separately from the residents and focus on caregiving issues in the nursing facility. Instead, this group's goal was to enrich the parent–adult child relationship through joint participation in reminiscence and other group activities. The group leaders started with the premise that each resident had different strengths and adapted the sessions to showcase these strengths, such as Mabel's musical ability and her wonderful memory for nursery rhymes. Imagine a person with memory loss being celebrated for her memory! Aside from individual strengths, the group interactions strengthened relationships between mothers and their adult children. Many of the adult children mentioned how hard it was to visit their mothers because they had run out of things to say to each other. The group provided enjoyment without the pressure of one-to-one conversation. As group members grew to know one another, the group also strengthened community building among the adult children and their parents. Family members celebrated birthdays with other group members and spent time chatting with other residents when they visited.

One of the important outcomes of using a strengths-based approach is reframing more positively what is first seen as obstructive, difficult behavior. This is apparent in Chapter 13, which describes Supiano's work with Mrs. Ellis and her daughter, Anne. Their relationship could have been viewed (and was by other service providers) as destructive, but Supiano chose to preserve and enhance the relationship, involving Anne in all aspects of her mother's care even as the location and the nature of the care changed. She regarded the relationship between Anne and Mrs. Ellis as a strength and recognized that it was one of the most meaningful aspects of their lives. Although Anne firmly resisted outside care for her mother, Supiano believed that she would be traumatized if her mother died in pain and decrepitude.

The process of listening to Anne and supporting her role while paving the way for help from home health workers was frustrating for Supiano. Her ongoing contacts with Anne were either satisfying or aggravating, and she often felt like she was "walking a tightrope to offer support ... in a nonthreatening way." When Mrs. Ellis entered a nursing facility, Supiano worked to prepare the staff for Anne's needs as well as her mother's, even to the point of persuading the staff to allow Anne to leave her bicycle in the entryway. This not only served to maintain the strength of the mother–daughter relationship but also enhanced the relationship between Anne and the nursing facility staff.

In many of these chapters, the strong ties to and collaborative relationships with physicians, friends, and family members are highlighted. Often, the media portrays social workers as "bulls in a china shop," rushing in to disrupt existing relationships. The reality is more likely to be the opposite. Especially when working with older adults, the strength of their ties to other service providers and loved ones is embraced by the social worker and efforts are made to support them as much as possible. Not all families are loving, and many of these strong ties are not particularly positive, so the social worker must make choices between respecting the family and creating a safe, healthy environment for the client. This is especially true in cases of elder neglect and abuse in which keeping the family together might not be the best alternative. With older clients, the complexity of these issues is heightened by the older person's frailty. Still, the strengths perspective is necessary in weighing what kind of additional supports are needed to keep the bonds as intact as possible.

BLURRED BOUNDARIES

One of the most problematic aspects of working with older adults is deciding where and when to cross established boundaries. This is especially true when working with an isolated, frail person who has a limited social support network. In Chapter 2, Foulk pointed out that she became her client's lifeline over the years because Helen believed that Foulk would always be there when she needed her. How realistic is this approach? Most of the practitioners have worked at the Turner Geriatric Clinic for more than 10 years, and each of us has several long-term clients, some of whom we see routinely and others whom we see sporadically over the years when necessary. But the question remains: Where are the lines drawn? To some extent, crossing or not crossing boundaries depends on the individual client and therapist. Certainly, there are many cases in which the relationship is a traditional 50-minute therapy session or a 1-hour care management home visit. Nevertheless, the issues involved in blurred boundaries still occur.

Transference and Countertransference

These are the familiar issues of therapy—the therapist's identification with the client and the client's identification with the therapist. In Chapter 11, Fogler noticed that the boundaries were slipping when she compared the difficulties of Betty's life with her own less turbulent one. She found that she had to be careful not to overextend herself and increase her client's dependence on her. In a wistful remark that probably resonates with other professionals who work with older adults, Fogler explained how she had to hold herself back from offering Betty a loan when her financial problems seemed overwhelming. Our compassion for our clients often has us thinking that if we took a specific action, we could solve their problems. Sometimes the problems, especially financial ones, seem overwhelming and the resources nonexistent.

   One of the ways in which we tried to address this concern at the clinic was to develop an emergency needs fund with donations contributed by clients and a local foundation. We can pay up to $200 for medications, home health care, or a visit to the hairdresser for a patient recently discharged from psychiatric care who could use a boost in self-esteem. This provision of financial help may be crossing a line of involvement, but it allows us to handle concrete issues, such as not taking medications because a client cannot afford them, in a practical, direct way.

Supiano cautions in Chapter 12 that an important boundary to maintain is the family/nonfamily line. Especially in care management, in which the professional coordinates many of the tasks that family members usually do, it is important to establish that care managers support but do not replace the family. Transference occurs when clients regard the worker as the "daughter I never had." Supiano urges role clarification early in the process but also describes this common dilemma of accessibility. Do you give vulnerable clients your home telephone number, for instance? She reported that Miss Clark called her in the evenings because she reversed night and day and that her relatives called frequently. However, she regarded these calls as a passing symptom, during a particularly intense period, and noted that calls to her might have prevented more complications such as calls to 911 and visits to the emergency room. Usually, it is not our practice to give clients our home telephone numbers, but they are readily available in the telephone book. Most clients do not abuse our accessibility, and it can be comforting for a vulnerable person to have a telephone number as a safety net to get through a difficult period.

Although these strong ties of dependence frequently develop in care management situations, they also occur in a more formal therapeutic relationship. In Chapter 6, Stern and Ingersoll-Dayton described the high regard that Barbara and Arthur had for Stern's efforts as their therapist. Even after seeing another therapist on her recommendation, they requested that she see them again. Their physician also persisted in asking her to help the couple. The author wrote, "Each of these factors contributed to my feeling that I was indispensable to this couple. ... At times, I sensed that the boundary between determining what was helpful and unhelpful had become blurred." The therapist's efforts to cope with this blurring included working with a co-therapist and trying methods such as individual therapy when treatment as a couple seemed unproductive.

Therapy versus Care Management

Another aspect of the blurring of roles is the line between therapy and care management. Often, in these chapters, the authors seem to blend the two modalities. In Chapter 5, Rumman visited Grace at home with the purpose of counseling her for depression but also took her for walks, helped her transfer from her bed, and arranged additional services. Foulk gave a particularly vivid illustration in Chapter 2 of this merging of therapy with care management. Helen was referred to Foulk because she was depressed and indicated suicidal ideation. She came to the clinic for counseling, but as the issues emerged, her anxiety over making the necessary changes led to an extension of the therapy, whereby Foulk accompanied her through a move to another apartment, finding subsidized housing, helping her arrange a move, even providing her own son as a helper. At the same time, Foulk was aware of the lines that she was redrawing. In fact, the blurring of boundaries does give the therapist flexibility, and developing judgment about when and how to set those boundaries is a mark of experience, often built on taking risks and making some judgment errors.

Receiving Gifts

Older people like to give gifts to demonstrate affection and appreciation for services received. In Chapter 3, Dunkle called on peer supervision to help with the delicate—and common—issue of gift giving. Initially, Douglas gave gifts to her in an "effort to have me like him." She was able to link this behavior to his relationship with his children in which he also used gifts to win their affection. However, Dunkle describes how uncomfortable she felt about the gifts and how ungracious it felt to turn them down. She recognized that Douglas wanted to establish a more reciprocal relationship in the beginning, perhaps to become more comfortable with being in therapy, which was a new experience for him. Eventually, she was able to refuse the gifts without jeopardizing the therapeutic relationship.

Rumman also developed a close relationship with her client in Chapter 5 in a more intimate home setting, which toward the end was the client's bedroom. Grace gave her a silver necklace engraved with an initial that they shared. Many people in this older generation are uncomfortable with receiving help, and the opportunity to be a giver is greatly appreciated. When do you accept, and when do you say no? Certainly money is not acceptable, unless it is a reimbursement for specific purchases, but at the clinic, we can suggest that they donate to the clinic emergency needs fund or another worthy cause. Handmade gifts are often a token not only of appreciation but also of pride of craftsmanship. It is often a "play it by ear" situation, but it is important to recognize that gifts are often not used as a way to win the therapist over but as a way of establishing reciprocity, expressing appreciation, and sharing one's pleasures.

Mixed Roles as Individual Therapist and Group Leader

Several of the authors found blurring of roles when, as Edwards and Fogler noted in their cognitive therapy group in Chapter 7, they played two roles with the same client. Seeing a client individually and in a group presents some conflicts because the therapist often knows more about the client than is revealed in the group. In Rose's case, the therapist felt protective of her in the group, knowing her vulnerability and inexperience in social settings. A separation of these two roles is desirable but often difficult to achieve because some of these clients would not participate in the group unless comforted by the presence of someone whom they trusted.

In the Monday writing group that Campbell describes in Chapter 9, Paul clearly felt able to participate because he had developed a relationship with the group leader before entering the group. Meeting during the clinic assessment process, Paul felt that he got to know Campbell and agreed to join the group, although he refused other kinds of intervention. As a newcomer to town, it was not easy for him to join a group of strangers who all knew one another. Campbell suggested the group because during the assessment, Paul told her that he liked to write, but she felt uneasy about bringing him in because of his unstable mental state. She had to be both his strong supporter in the group and his therapist outside it, a balance so delicate that by mutual consent, the therapist role was dropped.

Confidentiality

Finally, as Schoem illustrated in Chapter 14, confidentiality issues surface when working with a team of professionals. Through open communication among team members and cross-training in substance abuse, the team members were able to focus on a common goal and take on various roles at different times. Mrs. Green and her family members participated in joint meetings with team members, and leadership roles changed as her needs changed. Mrs. Green's recognition of her problem and her decision to accept treatment was a long process, but along the way she grew to trust the various team members, and they were united in their goal to treat her alcoholism.

Confidentiality is often an issue in care management and teamwork when the strictures of privacy fade as information is shared. Whenever possible, asking the client to sign a release of information statement is important. Also, including clients as team members, educating them that various disciplines are needed to provide adequate care, and ensuring that they understand that they have the authority to limit or direct the action keep the control in our clients' hands. With substance abuse as well as abuse and neglect cases, the lines often become fuzzy. For example, strict adherence to confidentiality can interfere with necessary treatment at times when a worker in one agency needs information about the client's history from another agency.

Blurring of boundaries is an ongoing theme and issue of discussion among the social workers at the clinic. In part, this is because, unlike other more rigid settings, we are not mandated to do one thing or another. In fact, we are often called on by the physician, family members, or even a neighbor to "do something, anything," to help this person out of a bad situation. Thus, over the years, we have developed a flexible model of service delivery whereby some cases are "strictly therapy" as one would define it for any age group, some are "care management" in situations in which financial eligibility is not the major criterion, and others blend the two. In reality, the distinction between care management and therapy may be an artificial one that has evolved as social work developed as a profession. What we are doing may be closer to the traditional notion of social work as opposed to psychological or sociological definitions. The philosophy that has emerged is to do what the client needs at a given time. What is essential in the process of working this way is, as several authors have noted, questioning your own motives, being aware when boundaries are being blurred and why, and relying on peer supervision and consultation.

CHANGES IN THE
THERAPEUTIC RELATIONSHIP OVER TIME

As mentioned previously, several of our cases are maintained over a substantial amount of time. This is partly the result of selection bias in putting this book together. It was easier to illustrate some of the points we wanted to make when we showed changes over time. However, it is easy to imagine readers' reactions. "That's fine for them, but what do I do if I'm authorized to have only three sessions or if my contact is over a 2-day hospital stay?" The opportunity for long-term therapy is an advantage in our setting where patients see the same physician over time and they are able to carry out a similar relationship with a therapist. Often, therapy is terminated and then as new issues arise, the client returns. Having a stable staff is a benefit to clients who feel secure in knowing that help is available when they need it.

Short-term therapy is also valuable, of course, and in a managed care climate may be all that is offered. Most of our short-term cases can be put into three categories: 1) clients who come with a specific goal about which they want to achieve resolution, 2) clients who come reluctantly, referred to therapy by others (e.g., family members, physicians) who think that they need it and then stay because they like the therapist and do not want to hurt the therapist's feelings but never become really engaged in the process, and 3) those who believe that talking about their problems only touches raw nerves and prefer not to continue.

Change Caused by External Events

Often, changes occur because of events outside the therapy session. In Chapter 14, Schoem remarks that in substance abuse cases, providers sometimes set the stage but then wait for "an external situation that will increase a client's motivation to change." This statement's truth is not limited to substance abuse cases. As seen in Chapter 6, which described therapy with a couple, many interventions were tried, including the marital pair, another therapist outside the system, co-therapists, and both individual and couples therapy—and changes occurred, notably in Arthur's ability to reveal his feelings. Dissatisfaction with the marriage seemed unchanged until Barbara's illness made the couple acutely aware of how much they cared for each other. Without the often-painful therapeutic process, would their sense of oneness as Barbara was dying have been possible? Given the persistence of Barbara's sense of loneliness in the marriage, her ability to accept her husband's nurturing and care at the end of her life may have been compromised without having been through all of their efforts at healing the relationship.

In Chapter 5, Rumman describes how her client's failing health inevitably altered the therapy. Grace needed more assistance in putting on her shoes and socks, walking to the bathroom, and other tasks. Communication became more difficult. When her condition worsened and she moved to a nursing facility, Rumman's relationship with Grace ended. But the nearness of death allowed Grace to review with her therapist the meaning of her life and the legacy that she was leaving behind. The outcome with many older clients, as is true in hospice settings, is not to see them spring up and get better but to help them as their health declines to feel safe, comfortable, supported, and treasured.

Change Caused by Multiple Interventions

Having the luxury of time is important in several of these chapters. Fogler (Chapter 11) describes Betty as entering sessions feeling utterly alone and visibly gaining strength during each session. Crises continually occurred in her life, and as she placed her husband in a nursing facility, arranged for her own move, and acknowledged her substance abuse, the ongoing support of a therapist whom she trusted was crucial to her well-being. It is humbling for a therapist but also comforting to recognize that outside interventions can precipitate a turning point. In Betty's case, the combination of a peer counselor, treatment in a substance abuse facility with follow-up day treatment, and participation in Al-Anon created an environment in which she could finally make significant changes in her life.

In Betty's case, as in others, working closely with community agencies was a key to change. It was the home health aide who discovered stashes of pills in her apartment, which led to a confrontation about substance abuse treatment. The other point not made before is the use of peer volunteers to encourage and support clients as they make difficult changes. Peer volunteers are mentioned in several chapters. In Betty's case, Joan, the peer counselor, brought humor and friendship to Betty, which helped her make the changes that she needed to make in her life.

The peer counselor program (also known as "peer volunteer") was developed at the inception of the Turner Clinic more than 20 years ago to serve as an extension of professional services and to provide input from peers that complements and enhances the work of professional staff. The peer volunteers are part of the team, working as colleagues to bridge the gap between professional therapy and supportive friendship. Joan, both in person and on the telephone, was someone on whom Betty could call and depend as the various relationships in her life shifted and as she confronted ongoing challenges.

Change through Group Interactions

Several of the groups described are short term, limited to 8 or 10 weeks. In the intergenerational nursing facility group, Rumman describes in Chapter 10 the changes that occur on several levels. The residents themselves experienced a heightened sense of their own abilities while they were in the group. Mabel, for example, delighted in being able to play the Autoharp and recall nursery rhymes. These abilities provided her with an affirmation of her individuality—hard to achieve in an institutional environment.

The pleasure of joint participation with their adult children altered the relationship of the family members to the nursing facility, making them part of a community rather than outsiders. Too often, family members find themselves tiptoeing around nursing facility staff, trying to get the best care for their loved ones. In this group, the bonds among resident, family, and staff were strengthened and the parent–child ties were viewed as ongoing and significant regardless of the parent's cognitive and physical status. When a new dimension of Laurie's mother was revealed by her vivid gesture of a tennis serve, the fact that this was witnessed by the group gave Laurie the satisfaction of knowing that her mother was seen as a whole person, not just as a disabled, frail nursing facility resident. The nursing facility group also initiated changes in the system. Family members began to visit group members who were not their relatives, and joint celebrations were held.

The cognitive therapy group, described in Chapter 7, was structured with clear goals and assignments, and within the short period of 10 weeks changes were expected and encouraged. Rose's unexpected visit of an old friend led to an affirming event both within and outside the group. The group encouraged her to leave her mother alone and enjoy her friend's visit. She modified her attitude about her responsibilities toward her mother. Although an outside event precipitated this change, the group's cheering her on reinforced the importance of the progress that she had made.

Changes in one's life often are unpredictable. Sensory loss, sudden pain, or death of a trusted confidant can seriously affect one's sense of identity and purpose. Although long-term therapy is not needed or possible for many people, the availability of help and the knowledge that someone is there and can be called on when needed are significant. Once people with little experience of therapy or assistance with their most intimate affairs understand and benefit from this process, they genuinely welcome it and draw on it. It is important to have in place a system that can accommodate the range of needs and the desire for varying kinds of attachment.

BENEFITS AND DIFFICULTIES OF THE THERAPEUTIC RELATIONSHIP FOR THE CLIENTS AND THE THERAPISTS

The major benefit from therapy for clients is that they are able to make changes, even in small ways, in a long-standing problem or a relationship that has not been satisfying. Time and again, we see people who do not believe that their lives can improve, but, in fact, they do. At the same time, the balance to which we keep referring makes us aware that change is also difficult for our clients. It is slow and frustrating for both the client and the therapist. Sometimes it takes a crisis to make any change at all, yet even the ability to maintain a therapeutic relationship or to attend a group, however passively, is evidence of movement and needs to be recognized as such.

Trust

Many of our clients come to us reluctantly, referred by a physician or a family member, and the first goal is to establish trust, what Supiano calls "growing the relationship." In Chapter 12, she describes how she entered Miss Clark's world knowing that at some point significant changes in the way in which she lived would have to be made. At first, Miss Clark was hostile and distant, but gradually she accepted interdependence with Supiano because it was expressed to her in terms of independence—in other words, in terms she could accept. Once trust was established with the care manager, it could be transferred to other caregivers.

Some people enter therapy with little trust in themselves or others. In Chapter 2, Foulk's client, Helen, had lifelong difficulties with relationships but learned to trust Foulk and eventually trusted a volunteer and other service providers who were introduced by Foulk. Trust in the therapist can develop in many ways, but it cannot be rushed. Often, any implication of criticism or judgment, particularly in the initial stages, can sabotage the therapy. Perhaps the most important gift that the therapist can offer is willingness to listen as clients vent their anger and frustrations. The current generation of older adults grew up with a "stiff upper lip" ideology. It is a loss of face to admit that there are situations that they cannot handle, and it is not safe to reveal anger. For some of our clients, being able to express their feelings in a secure, therapeutic relationship may be a rare experience of being able to sustain a long relationship while freely expressing their feelings.

Resilience

As mentioned in Chapter 1, resilience is a principal ingredient of successful aging and is recognized and strengthened by these interventions. In Chapter 11, Fogler said about her work with Betty, "I learned how resilient the human spirit can be—how even with very little nurturing, an individual can develop strengths to survive difficult situations." The people profiled in these chapters have lived through difficult childhoods, friendless adulthoods, the disruption of war, and loss of family. They falter and stumble, but they keep on going. For all of us who work with older adults, their resilience is one of the most hopeful, rewarding aspects of our work.

Frustrations

Slow progress can be frustrating for both the client and the therapist, as discussed previously. In many of these chapters, the systems involved take time to coalesce, and issues of safety are raised. Both of these factors result in slow progress.

In the Exploring the Meaning of Life group discussed in Chapter 8, Fogler and Stern describe how Andrew, struggling with his own terminal condition, was looking for answers that he could not find within the group. He needed his learning to be directed toward his own personal meaning. Listening and learning from others was not, at this time of his life, what he wanted to do. He did not believe that he got the answers that he needed from the group members or the facilitators. Andrew's participation in the group was frustrating for one of the facilitators who knew his history and current situation well because she was also his therapist. She was forced to accept the way in which he portrayed his life in the group as more satisfying than it really was because of the exploratory, discussion-focused nature of this group, but she was frustrated because she believed that he would have benefited more from the group if he could have been honest about the difficulties in his life.

Another aspect of work with older adults is the barrier of age and status. In Chapter 3, Dunkle found Douglas's manner intimidating and "tiptoed around his anger as I tried to build a more open relationship with him." As the relationship developed, she understood how he used his commanding personality as a cover for his feelings of vulnerability. With his wife's illness, he allowed his compassion and tolerance to show.

Learning and Growth

Learning occurs in various ways. In Chapter 4, Thomas remarks ruefully that she learned to accept her own limits. When she first met Mrs. Smith, Thomas believed that Mrs. Smith's situation was overwhelming and hopeless. As she came to know her client better, Thomas realized that Mrs. Smith had the ability to overcome the odds. She also realized that she was limited by what the client wanted and could not change things that the client did not want to change.

In two groups described in this book, the Exploring the Meaning of Life group (Chapter 8) and the Monday writing group (Chapter 9), both the members and the group leaders collaborate in the learning process. In the Exploring the Meaning of Life group, it is especially poignant to read about Duane, an 84-year-old man with early-stage Alzheimer's disease, who participated in the group, faithfully completing weekly assignments, determined to continue learning and growing as long as possible. In the Monday writing group, the learning occurred on several levels. Members learned about one another. They learned about the unhappiness of Marianne's childhood but also about her great spirit and sense of adventure as she tried different jobs and explored her environment. They learned about how to die by participating in her struggle with cancer, and they learned how life goes on by getting to know her brother and her daughter. They learned history from Richard, science from Paul, and jokes from Laura. And, of course, they learned about themselves through the process of writing and being heard.

Tangible Benefits

Tangible benefits appear throughout these chapters: People are helped to use their medications appropriately; they receive needed assistance in their homes; their financial hardships are alleviated; they move to better, more affordable housing; they become part of a group that expects them and welcomes them each week and acts as a structure that helps to shape meaning in their lives. The most convincing argument for an amalgamation of counseling and care management is the evidence that one complements and facilitates the other. Accepting help is not easy for many of our clients. Through a therapeutic alliance, the ability to trust and accept change emerges and the therapist becomes the appropriate person to introduce new services and supports. Conversely, positive changes in our clients' lives are possible not only through insight, support, or understanding of one's life experiences; having meals delivered can free family members to provide more pleasurable activities, and accepting a home health worker can affect the ability to manage independence.

WORDS OF WISDOM

One of the frequently occurring themes in this book is the assertion that a client was likeable, had a good sense of humor, or was amazingly resilient despite a difficult life. Working with older people is infinitely enjoyable, stimulating, and exhilarating. This spirit seems to be shared, regardless of discipline, by those who enter the field by choice or fall into it by accident and remain, moved by the experience. In this concluding section, two questions are addressed: 1) What is unique about working with older people? 2) What is unique about Turner Clinic's environment and the model of care that has developed there over the years?

Uniqueness of Working with Older Adults

When we discuss differences among the generations, it is important to understand that we are talking about the expectations of this current cohort of older
adults. The reluctance of older adults to enter a therapeutic relationship is
noted in these chapters and elsewhere, but this is clearly a cohort difference;
the older generation has less experience with therapy than do people who are
now in their 30s and 40s. As more people who have seen therapists earlier in
their life grow older, this overall reluctance will decline.

The same is probably true with regard to modes of address. Rules of etiquette and respect will change with succeeding cohorts, but right now, most
older adults prefer to be addressed by their last names in conjunction with a
title such as Mr. or Mrs. During the authors' retreat, one of the participants told
the story of a nursing facility group in which a resident asked everyone, staff
and fellow residents alike, to address her as "Mrs. Collins." In another situation,
one of the authors debated how to address an unmarried client. She assumed
that Ms. was not a term common in this 80-year-old's generation and called her
Mrs. as a compromise. The client was furious and demanded to be called
"Miss," a term that the social worker had completely forgotten about. It is probably safest to ask clients what they would like to be called. As one older woman
said when asked how she would like to be addressed, "It depends on who you
are and how old you are." Both first and last names are used by authors in these
chapters, depending on the nature of the relationships. In the groups presented here, for example, in which one of the goals is to connect people with
one another, the use of first names is the most natural alternative.

Another key difference is the sheer number of years of experience and the
kinds of experiences of most older adults. Aside from the great historical events
such as the two world wars and the Depression, there are the enduring scars of
racism, sexism, and poverty. Differences in attitudes toward material posses-
sions, marriage, child care, work, and other issues of daily life can often subtly
affect the relationship between an older client and a younger therapist. "How
could she have put up with him all these years?" a younger person may ask,
when for the client, "putting up with him" was one of the inherent conditions of
marriage that she was brought up to accept.

Therapeutic styles may be different when working with older adults. One of
the authors commented that when she first came to the clinic after working
with younger adults in psychiatry, she was appalled by the questions that older
clients asked about her personal life. Her younger clients either did not ask
these questions, or, if they did, it was taken as an issue to be addressed in the
therapeutic process, not as a natural, social exchange. We generally agree that
we are more likely to reveal snippets of our personal lives with older people,
and it is seen as a kind of reciprocity, as evidence of their interest in the
younger generation. Younger adults in therapy, although they may be curious
about the therapist's life, usually prefer to use their time to talk about their own

concerns. For many older adults, the embarrassment and ambivalence with which they enter a therapeutic session may be made more comfortable by turning the tables a bit.

Our intervention approaches also tend to be less confrontational with older clients. For example, the cognitive therapy group described by Edwards and Fogler in Chapter 7 is apt to be less confrontational than it would be in a cognitive therapy group with younger adults. There is a sense that the more physically or cognitively impaired clients are, the more respectful group members tend to be about confronting them directly, preferring to be more supportive or protective of their feelings. It may be that we go too far in being protective and that people who work with younger adults go too far in the other direction. But even in a less strictly therapeutic setting like the Monday writing group, described by Campbell in Chapter 9, the members tend to prefer praise to criticism and are hesitant to say anything that might be perceived as negative.

Turner Clinic—A Unique Setting?

In the preface, we provide a brief overview of Turner Geriatric Clinic. After reading the case studies, additional comments need to be made about the climate within which we work. Since the clinic began in 1978, we have developed a proactive stance in service delivery to older people by organizing both a community advisory committee and a volunteer peer counselor program that connect us with the community and their perception of what was needed. The focus from the beginning was to identify what older people in the community wanted and then to find some way to bring it to them. Over the years, through extensive use of social work interns, peer volunteers, and funding from various public and private sources, we have sustained a social work staff and an identity that allow flexibility in meeting the needs of both a medical clinic and a community outreach program. For example, when we recognized that many older people preferred counseling in their own homes (described here in Chapters 4 and 5), we were able to provide this service by successfully soliciting funds from the Area Agency on Aging.

In a medical setting, the key to success is physician support. We have been fortunate in having supportive medical directors. Dr. Ivan Duff was the first medical director of the Turner Clinic and was a proponent of an interdisciplinary approach to helping older adults. Dr. Neal Persky, the current medical director, provides a supportive environment in which to practice. Since 1984, Dr. Jeffrey B. Halter, director of the Geriatrics Center, has incorporated social work funding into larger interdisciplinary grants and provided strong advocacy with hospital administration to increase funding for social work. That social workers are responsible for finding ways to provide the services that are needed has become firmly ingrained. There is freedom to initiate new activities as long as core clinic programs are maintained. Social workers are expected to possess skills in assessment, to combine group and individual modalities, and to work comfortably with an interdisciplinary team.

Supervision largely occurs on a peer basis. The bulk of the staff work part time by choice, and the flexibility of hours and covering for one another underlie the collaborative spirit that has developed. As Foulk notes in Chapter 2, she is secure in knowing that if her client experiences a crisis while she is gone, another social worker will be there to intervene without stepping on anyone's toes. Many of the situations that we deal with are complex, and there is a lot of uncertainty about how to proceed. In addition to weekly staff meetings, there is considerable informal consultation and support. The climate is one in which people are able to take risks and make mistakes and not be castigated for them. Along with that freedom, though, comes a responsibility to be reliable, work independently, and extend oneself when needed.

Is this unique? How replicable are the practices that we discuss in these chapters? We think that they are replicable and that there are many more examples of this kind of collaborative, self-supporting model of social work practice in the community than we recognize. Few of these efforts are written about because practitioners often do not have the time, resources, or interest in publication, but vibrant programs exist throughout the United States and are the hidden jewels of our system. We hope that this book encourages others to describe their models of effective partnerships with older adults.

We believe that the key is to start from what clients, their families, and the community want and need and make this the driving force of our activities. We also believe that what we are doing is valuable and that we define for ourselves as a profession how and what we practice. Finally, creativity is not confined to writing a book or painting a landscape. It should flourish in the places where we work, the colleagues with whom we work, and the clients whose lives we are privileged to enter.

Index

Page references followed by *t* indicate tables.